Gender and Bureaucracy

Edited by Mike Savage and Anne Witz

Blackwell Publishers/The Sociological Review

First published 1992

Blackwell Publishers
108 Cowley Road, Oxford, OX4 1JF, UK.

and
238 Main Street, Suite 501,
Cambridge, MA 02142, USA.

British Library Cataloguing in Publication Data
A CIP catalogue record for this book is available from the British Library.

Library of Congress Cataloging in Publiction Data
Gender and bureaucracy / edited by Mike Savage and Anne Witz.
p.   cm.—(The Sociological review monograph; 39)
ISBN 0–631–85283–2 : $19.95
1. Organizational sociology.   2. Sex role in the work environment.
3. Bureaucracy.   I. Savage, Michael.   II. Witz, Anne, 1952–
III. Series.
HM131.G365   1992   92–29722
305.3—dc20   CIP

Typeset by Hope Services (Abingdon) Ltd.
Printed in Great Britain by T. J. Press Ltd., Padstow, Cornwall.

Contents

Theoretical Introduction

The gender of organizations

Anne Witz and Mike Savage

This book has been put together to show that organizational processes are central to the understanding of gender relations, and concomitantly, that organizations are gendered. In this chapter we lay out the way we think this issue should be conceptualized by developing what we will term a 'gender' paradigm for the study of organizations. We will argue that existing research addressing the connections between gender and bureaucracy has failed to provide a systematic framework of analysis, and has tended to become narrowly focused upon specific, and sometimes diversionary issues (most notably, the now burgeoning interest in 'organizational sexuality'). This introduction is therefore designed to act as a ground–clearing exercise, in which we sketch out the most important issues for the 'gender' paradigm for organizations through a comprehensive analysis of the most important contributions to the study of gender and bureaucracy, and we show how the gender paradigm offers a distinctive way of exploring existing bodies of research in the area. In the course of the introduction we also show how the papers in this volume contribute to developing this approach.

We start by considering the reasons why organization theory and feminist theory have begun to engage in dialogue in recent years, and how new currents in social theory have placed the issue of the relationship between gender and bureaucracy firmly on the agenda. We argue that it is essential to move away from general notions of bureaucratic organization, in order to recognise historically and spatially specific ways of organizing, which can be shown to rest upon particular gendered foundations. The modern Western bureaucracy, as dissected by Weber, is only one way of organizing social relations and it depends upon particular configurations of gender relations.

Having established that bureaucracies are gendered, we turn to consider how this relationship can be conceptualized through detailed analyses of three leading feminist writers: Rosabeth Kanter, Kathy Ferguson, and Rosemary Pringle. We show that these exemplify three different feminist approaches. Kanter attempts to recast Weber for feminist ends, arguing that there are no intrinsic reasons why women need be subordinated within bureaucratic structures. Ferguson adopts a nuanced 'feminist standpoint' position, arguing that bureaucratic structures are inherently patriarchal. Finally Rosemary Pringle adopts a post-structuralist view in which power relations within organizations are conducted within a sexualized framework. We adopt elements from each writer in order to develop our gender paradigm.

In the remainder of the chapter we discuss the theoretical underpinnings of recent scholarship in the two areas where there has been a sustained examination of the relationship between gender and bureaucracy. These are, firstly, feminist theories of the state, where much of the literature ignores the state's bureaucratic character, and secondly organizational sexuality, which we argue embodies a series of highly questionable assumptions. In the final part of the Introduction we pull out some of the implications of the 'gender' paradigm for organizational analysis and briefly introduce the essays in this volume.

1 The agenda established

Until the 1980s there was little dialogue between organizational studies and feminist research. This was partly due to the different research cultures of the two disciplines – the former a well funded and resourced subject largely staffed by male academics servicing male managers and geared to thinking about specific organizational problems; the latter a critical, anti-establishment discipline which appeals specifically to women and helps expose the embedded nature of patriarchal relations throughout the entire social fabric. Yet on top of this lay a major rift in the way the two disciplines were located within social theory: organizational studies being integrated into an instrumental way of thinking; feminism being located within a stratification way of thinking.

Organization theory has for many years been involved in a debate with Max Weber. Weber's famous elaboration of the ideal type of bureaucracy (Albrow, 1970) has been thoroughly discussed, and criticised, since the early years of this century. His stress on the formal rationality of organizations has been subject to incessant critique and it is now widely accepted that organizations can only be understood by considering their implicit, informal ordering, as well as their formal procedures (see amongst others Gouldner, 1956; Crozier, 1964; Giddens, 1982; Morgan, 1986; Crompton; Halford; Ramsey and Parker in this volume). It is by no means clear that Weber would have disagreed with this, his point being the definitional one that bureaucracies can only be differentiated from other organizations through the existence of these formal rules, not that these formal rules are necessarily the crucial means which allow organizations to function. Be this as it may, what has more frequently escaped discussion is the instrumental way of thinking about organizations which Weber helped to establish. For Weber, organizations were the most technically efficient ways of performing any given activity – 'the decisive reason for this advance of bureaucratic organisation has always been its purely *technical* superiority over any other form of organization' (Weber, 1968:973). The critique of Weber has tended to be couched within these terms, not questioning that organizations are the most technically efficient ways of doing things, but rather disputing whether Weber established the reasons why this was the case. As a result, organizational studies became pre-occupied by means rather than ends, rarely engaging with the issues of power and authority, inequality, or social division which were taken up within mainstream social science. The supposed technical efficiency of organizations meant that they themselves did not need explanation.

Whilst organizational studies developed within an instrumental frame of reference, feminist work within sociology developed within, and as a critique of, stratification theory. Stratification theory was primarily preoccupied with analysing social divisions in terms of class, but did so through an analysis of inequality as part of a wider stratification system. This stratification system was seen as based in a macro-level social structure, such as capitalism, or in the structural-functionalist approach, the social system (eg Craib, 1984). Hence stratification tended to be seen as anchored in wide–ranging social structures, such as the division between wage labour and capital, or in the system of norms and values.

Feminists were critical of the gender blindness of much of the early work in this area, and tended to adopt strategies to bring gender inequality into focus. One approach was to locate the specific nature of female subordination in the separation of public from private spheres, and the restriction of women to the 'private' realm of family and household. This perspective was in some ways compatible with more orthodox functionalist and Marxist analyses which also located women's roles specifically within the family, and led to the concentration of attention on familial – ie non bureaucratic – relationships, for instance in the extensive discussions of housework (Oakley, 1974) or in the domestic labour debate (eg Seccombe, 1974). Another approach was to argue that gender was also an axis of stratification (eg Acker, 1973). Delphy and Walby established this by relating gender inequalities to another stratifying system, that of patriarchy (eg Walby, 1986, 1989) or the 'gender order' (Connell, 1986). Much subsequent work has examined how gender inequality relates to other inequalities such as those based around capitalism or racial inequality.

Whatever the strategy adopted, this led to the neglect of organizational structures and practices in reproducing gender inequality. In the first case gender inequality was explored in the 'private' domestic realm, whilst in the latter, the causes of stratification were rooted in the macro structures of society, at a level wider than that of any specific organization. Organizations, such as the state, economic enterprises, or welfare agencies, acted within a larger field and hence did not directly cause inequality themselves. To be sure they drew on, and possibly re-inforced such inequalities, but they were not themselves the crux of the problem. There were some exceptions to this 'organization blindness', but these have not challenged the dominance of this view. Some feminists pointed to the way in which the institutions of the state served to reproduce female subordination. The state was seen as important in preventing women from working in specific areas of the labour market (Walby, 1986; Mark-Lawson and Witz, 1988), in terms of re-inforcing women's subordinate domestic roles through social policy (Land, 1976), or in organizing a military apparatus which legitimizes and underwrites male violence (Enloe, 1983). Yet in all these cases attention was concentrated on the effects of state policy on gender relations, not on the gendered processes internal to the bureaucratic processes of the state.

Another set of organizations which has been the subject of feminist interest have been the voluntary associations, often trade unions, which served to uphold male interests. The best known example of this approach is the powerful demonstration by

Cockburn (1981) and Walby (1986) that trade unions have been extremely important organizational forces excluding women from certain parts of the labour market. In this instance, however, the focus has been on organizations as voluntary associations, pressing particular sectional interests. These are clearly important organizational forms, but there are many others, notably employing organizations, states, welfare bureaucracies, and the like which cannot be seen as voluntary associations of this type.

Generally, notwithstanding these qualifications, the problem of gender inequality tended to be dealt with at the level of a stratification system, not in terms of the conduct of specific organizations. The result was a situation in which organization theorists were not particularly interested in gender, and feminist writers had little interest in organizations, except insofar as they provided examples of a more general set of patriarchal practices.

This position has however been steadily eroded in the past two decades, and is now implausible. A number of developments have been responsible for this. The most significant has been the growing recognition that social structures do not exist in some abstract sense, 'out there', but only insofar as they are instantiated in specific practices. Giddens's critique of structural approaches within sociology is of special importance here. Giddens (1984) argued that structures do not exist except insofar as they are drawn upon by human agents in their social activities. Taken in this sense, structures could best be seen as the 'rules and resources recursively involved in institutions' (Giddens, 1984:24). By taking this step Giddens directly linked structures to specific institutional and organizational practices: in order to examine structures it was necessary to look at institutions, how these drew upon structural resources, and how in turn the institution shaped structures.

Giddens's critique ran parallel, in many ways, to that of Foucault. In the 1970s Foucault argued that power should not be seen as the product of a stratifying system which is located in the macro structures of society. Rather, power should be seen in 'relational' terms, as a set of discourses and strategies operating in particular contexts. Power is not a 'single, all-encompassing strategy' (Foucault, 1984:103), but works through specific institutions. Much of Foucault's work comprised detailed studies of institutional changes and their linked transformation of power relations: in mental asylums (Foucault, 1961), hospitals and clinics (Foucault, 1965), and prisons (Foucault, 1977). In these cases he showed how organizational change was inseperably linked to changing forms of power relations. Whereas in the pre-modern period, institutions excluded and isolated people dangerous to the empowered, in the modern period, power is inclusive, where the population is routinely watched over by institutions with a vast apparatus of surveillance.

Neither Giddens nor Foucault explicitly drew out the implications of their arguments for either organization theory, or feminism. Giddens indeed said relatively little directly about organizations in his statement on structuration theory (Giddens 1984), except to say that in organizations 'the reflexive regulation of the conditions of system reproduction looms large in the continuity of day-to-day practice' (Giddens, 1984:200). It is Stewart Clegg who made the link between power and organizations more explicit. Clegg argues that 'organizations should not be conceptualized as the phenomenal expression of some inner principle such as economic exploitation or rationality' (Clegg, 1989:197). Rather, organizations are 'locales in which negotiation, contestation and struggle between organizationally divided and linked agencies is a routine occurrence' (Clegg, 1989:198). Organizations differ, and they do so due to the struggles waged by diverse social groups to obtain and resist power.

This is not the place to discuss Clegg's idea of 'circuits of power' in depth. The crucial point we wish to establish is that Clegg's account shows that power relations are organizationally grounded and are not simply the conduits for power or stratifying systems which exist outside any specific organization. Hence in order to understand forms of gender inequality it is essential to see how organizational forms structure and are themselves structured by gender.

This having been said, the writers mentioned above play relatively little attention to gender inequality within organizations. Most of these writers are far more comfortable in showing how class relations, rather than gender relations, are imbricated in organizational forms. This is true of Giddens who emphasizes that organizations are typically found in 'class divided' societies, and who ignores gender divisions. Clegg does consider the significance of gender inequality within organizations but only to say that whether organizations reproduce gender divisions is largely a contingent matter. Erik Olin Wright (1985), who has also argued that organizational hierarchies are central to the analysis of class relations with his emphasis on the way in which class relations are based on 'organization assets' as well as property and skill assets, also argues that gender is only contingently related to organizational hierarchies. But this we believe, is far too weak a position. Alongside theoretical work showing the connection between power and organizations there is now a range of work suggesting a close empirical link between the modern organizations found in Western societies and particular forms of gender inequality. We will now briefly consider some of the most salient points of this literature.

2 Gender inequality and modern organisational forms

One of the most important points arising out of the literature discussed above is that bureaucracies differ, and that they differ because of the diverse social values, solidarities and conflicts which go into their making. This apparently obvious point has far-reaching implications for prevailing views of organizations deriving from Weber. It suggests that any common patterns of organizing are due not to any technical, functional imperatives but rather to the common embodiment of particular forms of social and power relations within them.

This insight offers a new way of thinking about the characteristics of the classic Western bureaucracy, as laid out by Weber. He argued that modern bureaucracies were characterized by being distinguished into different areas of jurisdiction, with a hierarchal structure allowing supervision and control of subordinates, the use of written files, specialized training for workers, full time commitment from workers, and the use of 'general rules' (Weber, 1978:956ff). These have often been seen as imperatives for any form of organization in a complex economic and social order, but Clegg (1990) has argued that they can only really be seen as typifying organizations in a specific historical period. Clegg argues that there are many different ways of organizing, and that developments within organizations today testify to the rise of the 'post-modern organization'. Although Clegg may well over-state the significance of these new organizational forms, he is emphatic about their departure from the Weberian model:

> Where modernist organisation was rigid, postmodern
> organisation is flexible . . . where modernist organisation was
> premised on technological determinism, postmodernist

organisation is premised on technical choices made possible through 'de-dedicated' microelectronic equipment. Where modernist organisation and jobs were highly differentiated, demarcated and de-skilled, postmodernist organisation and jobs are highly de-differentiated, de-demarcated and multi-skilled (Cleg, 1990:181).

The implication of Clegg's position is that the classic Weberian bureaucracy has a specific historical location – in the late 19th and early to mid 20th centuries – and that its heyday has now passed. What Clegg does not examine is whether it can be argued that the modernist bureaucracy rests upon a specific configuration of gender relations which were indeed their crucial foundation.

Growing research has indeed begun to throw important light on this question. At one level the very development of the hierarchical structures which Weber saw as typical of the modern bureaucracy took place along gendered lines. In many cases the use of women in subordinate offices took place alongside the reorganization of bureaucracies away from nepotistic, patronage based organizations. The classic case was the reform of the British Civil Service in the mid 19th century, associated with the Northcote-Trevelyan Report, which saw the development of a hierarchical distinction between mechanical and intellectual labour, and almost immediately saw the employment of large numbers of women doing mechanical work (Corrigan and Sayer, 1985; Savage *et al*, 1992; Zimmeck, 1988 and this volume). The British Civil Service was simply a particularly well known case, however, and it can be argued that the development of large organizations around the turn of the 20th century was directly associated with what has been called the 'White Blouse Revolution', the employment of large numbers of women in routine clerical work (Anderson, ed., 1989; Cohn, 1985; Savage, 1992). The modern organization came into being depending on cheap female labour, and in turn helped define women as subordinate workers to men within emergent white collar labour markets.

In this volume Meta Zimmeck develops this theme by examining the introduction of women into the Post Office workforce from the 1870s. She shows how the introduction of women clerks was at first heralded as a major innovation by male managers in the Post Office, allowing the use of a cheaper workforce. But she also shows how once women became established in the Post Office and began to struggle for better conditions and pay this honeymoon period ended, and restrictions on women's employment were reinforced. This is a perfect example of how organizations need to be seen as a site of contest, and how these conflicts shape the organization itself.

In some cases the development of modern bureaucratic forms can be directly linked to the use of women. Savage (1992) has shown, in a case study of employment change in Lloyds Bank between 1880 and 1940, how the introduction of women clerks offered the bank a different way of structuring the chain of command within the bank. Before the large scale introduction of women in the 1920s, the bank relied on age as the main axis of division in an all-male workforce. A high proportion of male clerks could expect to gain promotion to managerial rank after working for the bank for up to thirty years. The introduction of women workers – initially during the First World War but more importantly from the later 1920s – was the direct result of a policy decision made by the bank's directors to allow women to be employed so that the male career could be better systematized. The directors recognized that by employing women in subordinate jobs within the bank, it would be possible to promote 'promising' male clerks more quickly so that they could be moved into positions of authority. This went alongside a new policy of developing the formal training of these male clerks so what they did not learn from experience they could learn by formal means.

This case study is important in suggesting that the historical emergence of the bureaucratic career – a central part of Weber's definition of bureaucracy – was defined in gendered terms, as a male career. As Rosemary Crompton has shown (Crompton, 1986; Crompton and Jones, 1984), the possibility of career progress from junior to senior jobs was premised on the fact that large amounts of routine work were carried out by women who were not eligible for promotion, so allowing the prospects of those men in routine jobs to be enhanced. Most organizations operated a strictly gendered grading system in which women and men were recruited into different grades of employment, with different salary scales and promotion prospects.

Crompton (1986) has also shown that the idea of the male career rests upon another assumption – the existence of a female 'servicer', his wife, who would be expected to carry out a range of duties for her husband, so allowing him to devote more time to the

11

organization's affairs. Many organizations imposed marriage bars on their female work force, forcing them to retire on marriage, and so become fulltime housewives. Male workers, on the other hand, were expected to be able to draw upon fulltime domestic servicers so that they could work long hours, get work done by their wives, and so forth. Modern bureaucratic hierarchies both helped to construct the idea of the dependent housewife and drew upon this for their own advantage.

In their chapter in this volume, Crompton and Le Feuvre take this analysis a stage further by examining whether those women who have successfully pursued careers within banking have done so by becoming 'surrogate' men. They note how few women in both France and Britain have been able to pursue careers within financial organizations. Despite the different labour market characteristics of the two countries, the experience of women is remarkably similar, suggesting that the organizations themselves are the crucial forces shaping women's career paths. Crompton and Le Feuvre go on to show that the few women who have pursued careers have had to do so by adopting male characteristics – especially fulltime commitment to the labour market.

It is however clear that there are major changes taking place in the patterns of men's and women's careers, and that it is possible for more women to gain some sort of career progress within bureaucracies. Savage in this volume takes up this issue and examines whether this means that it is wrong to regard organizations as gendered in the way we have been suggesting. Savage argues that the growing numbers of women in professional and managerial jobs must be related to the major restructuring of organizational hierarchies in the recent period. Although Savage does not invoke Clegg's idea of the 'postmodern organization', he does show that there are now major changes to the older bureaucratic model. Women have entered bureaucratic hierarchies in specific types of jobs, ones which by and large do not allow them to gain significant organizational power. Hence, Savage concludes that the fact that increasing numbers of women are employed in professional and managerial jobs does not mean that organizations are any less patriarchal than they used to be; rather it testifies to the fact that organizations themselves have restructured and that the types of areas into which women have moved are those which tend to be barred from effective organizational power.

We have argued that organizations rest on a gendered base, and that the principles and practices which they embody cannot be understood without reference to their gendering assumptions. We have demonstrated this by showing how the classical bureaucratic type discussed by Weber both constructs gender relations (through the marriage bar, the construction of a subordinate female workforce, and so forth), and draws upon the resulting gender configuration. What is less clear from the foregoing account is whether all ways of organizing depend on gender, or only the type of bureaucracy adumbrated by Weber. In order to address this question we now turn to consider in greater depth the ways in which gender and power can be theorized within bureaucracies. This serves to clarify the relationship between gender and bureaucracy at a conceptual level, and to provide a template to examine and criticise recent feminist theories of the state and organizational sexuality.

3 The feminist interrogation of bureaucracy

This section seeks to clarify the ideas of three of the most important feminist critics of bureaucracy. These are Rosabeth Moss Kanter, whose book, *Men and Women of the Corporation* (1977), represents a pioneering account of the ways in which gender inflects corporate bureaucracies and looks forward to the day when women can inhabit bureaucratic hierarchies as the equals of men; Kathy Ferguson who, in *The Feminist Case Against Bureaucracy* (1984), presents a sustained analysis of bureaucratic structure and discourse as fundamentally alien to, and oppressive of, women and urges women to seek alternative organizational forms rather than their inclusion within male-inflected bureaucratic organizations; and, finally, Rosemary Pringle whose book *Secretaries Talk* (1989) provides the most recent and radical critique of bureaucracy as underpinned by discourses of power and sexuality which mark out gender roles in the bureaucratic workplace. We trace out the similarities and differences between these three major analyses of gender and bureaucracy, pull out the implications of these and other analyses of gendered organizing activities for any strategic response by women to their subordination in workplace and other organizations, and evaluate their strengths and weaknesses. We suggest that each of these writers adopts a different stance in relation to Weber's classic account of bureaucracy and that Kanter offers a liberal feminist revision, Ferguson a radical feminist critique, and Pringle a poststructuralist undermining of Weber.

Rosabeth Moss Kanter's pioneering study, *Men and Women of the Corporation* (1977), looks at the fate of women within the modern bureaucratic organization. Like Weber, she is convinced that bureaucratic organization is here to stay, but, unlike Weber, she is hopeful that the 'tragedy' of bureaucracy – that hierarchies result in self-defeating traps for those who find themselves in subordinate and disadvantaged positions as they struggle for autonomy in the context of constraints – can be balanced by a more hopeful vision in which 'Situations can be modified. The net of rewards and constraints can be rewoven. New tools can be provided. The people who are stuck can be offered challenges. The powerless can be given more discretion, more influence over decisions. Tokens can be provided with allies.' (Kanter, 1977:11) It is particularly the fate of women, who cluster in the powerless and subordinate positions within bureaucracy, that concerns Kanter.

The framework for her analysis of gendered corporate experiences is a thoroughgoing 'socially constructionist' one which focuses attention on the *gender* of organizational participants. As such it must be situated firmly within 1970s feminist sociology and its reaction to an 'oversexualized' and 'overfamilialised' conception of women. She insists that 'the fate of women is inextricably bound up with organizational structure and processes in the same way that men's life-at-work is shaped by them. Differences based on sex retreat into the background as the people-creating, behaviour-shaping properties of organizational locations become clear.' (Kanter, 1977:9) It is the job that makes the person, not gender that makes the job. So, any attempt to read the behaviour of secretaries in terms typical of 'women as a group' is fundamentally misguided, according to Kanter, for what secretaries really display are the orientations of people whose strategies for achieving recognition and control in the workplace are constrained by the social organization of their job.

At the centre of Kanter's analysis of the gendered corporate experience, is the view that power differences, not sex differences, explain the different corporate experiences and fortunes of men and women of the corporation. She denies that there are any intrinsically different, gendered modes of behaviour and orientation within organizations, and insists instead that what look like gender differences are really power differences. The problems facing women in managerial roles are problems of powerlessness, not sex. Women in organizations do not have access to the same opportunities for power and efficacy through activities and alliances as men. So, for example, the greater desire for men as leaders in organizations does not reflect any real sex differences in style and strategy, but the fact that people prefer the powerful as leaders. A preference for male managers and superordinates is, insists Kanter, a preference for power and power is something men possess.

Kanter's discussion of the interstices between gender and power is uncompromising and optimistic because she is suggesting that *power wipes out sex*. In other words, once women have organizational power, their gender pales into insignificance. Nonetheless, the current state of affairs is that male bureaucrats and managers not only possess power, but also strategically exclude women from access to the resources of power and efficacy. Women in organizations are dispossessed of power in a myriad of ways. The two most suggestive analyses of the ways in which women are dispossessed of corporate power are to be found in Kanter's discussions of male homosociability and of the boss-secretary relation.

Male homosociability represents one of the main ways in which management becomes a closed and gendered circle, enabling managers to respond to uncertainty and the constant pressure to communicate that is one of the main characteristics of the managerial role. Kanter highlights the fact that what managers do most of the time is communicate with people, and that much of this communication has to be rapid and accurate. Common language and understanding thus become important, and ease of communication a necessity. 'One way to ensure acceptance and ease of communication was to limit managerial jobs to those who were socially homogeneous. Social certainty, at least, could compensate for the other sources of uncertainty in the tasks of management. It was easier to talk to those of one's kind who had shared experiences – more certain, more accurate, more predictable.' (Kanter, 1977:58) Social homogeneity may be fostered with reference to, amongst other things, social class, educational background, marital status, and gender. Maleness provides managers with a crucial, tacit resource in the quest for sameness. Many male managers said they felt uncomfortable having to communicate with women; they could not 'read them' in quite the same way as they could 'read' their male colleagues. Thus, male homosocialibility is facilitated by what Kanter rather clumsily refers to as homosexuality. This discussion of the male managerial élite and the problems men have in communicating with women leads Kanter to invoke the notion of a 'bureaucratic kinship system' based on homosocial/sexual reproduction whereby men effectively 'clone' themselves in their own image, guarding access to power and privilege to those who fit in, to those of their own kind – in short, to other men.

Kanter's discussion of male homosociability/sexuality describes not only how men possess power in bureaucratic organization but also how they limit access to organizational power to other men. Male homosociability thus represents one way in which women are *excluded* from the corporate resources of power, simply by the fact that they are women and not men. Her discussion of the boss-secretary relation, on the other hand, reveals the terms on which women are *included* within bureaucratic organizations, but how their inclusion is very much shaped by the terms of their subordination to corporate men. The exclusion of women from organizational positions has more to do with their exclusion from the resources of power, whilst their inclusion in the corporate hierarchy has more to do with their subordination within the relational aspects of (male) dominance and (female) subordination. This point is not explicitly recognized or developed by Kanter. Indeed, her invocation of a narrowly defined concept of power as autonomy, as the possession of an 'ability' (to get things done etc.), coupled with her under-appreciation of the essentially relational character of the corporate patriarchy of male dominance and female subordination are precisely what enable her to be so optimistic about gender paling into insignificance once women 'have' power. This caveat aside, her analysis of the gendered dynamic of the boss-secretary relation is insightful and revealing.

Kanter argues that the boss-secretary relation is a relic of patrimony within the bureaucracy. It is a 'bureaucratic anomaly' and the secretarial function is 'a repository of the personal inside the bureaucratic' (Kanter, 1977:101). She invokes the familial metaphor of the 'office wife' to encapsulate the three patrimonial elements of the boss-secretary relationship. These are: first, *status contingency*, where secretaries derive their status not from their formal rank but from the boss they work for; second, *principled arbitrariness*, which describes the absence of limits of managerial discretion in relations with their secretaries, resulting in secretaries being constantly at the beck and call of their bosses and even called upon to perform non-functional tasks (such as collecting their bosses' dry cleaning and reminding him that he's got a dental appointment); and third, *fealty*, which describes the expectation that secretaries display unquestioning personal loyalty to their bosses, who in turn treat their secretaries as part of their personal estate, frequently expecting them to be available as emotional partners and rewarding them with non-material rewards such as 'love' and 'appreciation'. Hence the boss-secretary relation defies analysis within the terms of Weber's classic rendering of modern bureaucratic organizational life, characterized by universalism, legalistic standards, specialization, and routinization of tasks. Instead it displays many of the elements of traditional feudal systems ruled by patrimonial lords:

> When bosses make demands at their own discretion and arbitrarily; choose secretaries on grounds that enhance their own personal status rather than meeting organizational efficiency tests; expect personal service with limits negotiated privately; exact loyalty; and make the secretary a part of their private retinue, moving when they move – then the relationship has elements of patrimony'. (Kanter, 1977:73)

Because Kanter regards the genderized content of the boss-secretary relation as part and parcel of a patrimonial 'relic' which lingers on within a rational, bureaucratic shell, gender discrimination is presented as an irrational impulse within the otherwise rational tenor of bureaucratic organizational life. Thus Kanter quite clearly reads Weber in a 'de-gendered' way and accepts the core truths of Weber's account of the rationality and goal-directedness of bureaucracies. This is precisely why she can treat the genderized boss-secretary relation as a 'parimonial relic' awaiting the modernizing impulse of a rational basis for the organization of secretarial work and the relation of secretaries to their superordinates within organizations. It would appear that, once secretarial work and boss-secretary relations have been set on a more rational footing, they will have been 'de-gendered' in that gender will not taint the form nor the content of the relationship. In this way, Kanter may be seen to be operating within a Weberian discourse of bureaucratic rationality (Pringle, 1989), but without unpacking its gendered subtext. However, as we demonstrated earlier in our historical analysis of the development of modern bureaucratic organization, gender is woven into the very fabric of bureaucratic hierarchies and authority relations.

If the point of understanding the gender relations of bureaucracy is to change these, as Kanter is clearly optimistic about, then another work of considerable importance, both in providing a thorough-going analysis of gender and bureaucracy and in setting out a distinct strategy for change, is that of Kathy Ferguson (1984). However, unlike Kanter, Ferguson does not see bureaucracy simply as a structural shell. She also speaks of a 'bureaucratic discourse' and draws more on Foucault than Weber to produce and original and insightful account of the bureaucratization of society. Ferguson conceptualizes the process of bureaucratization as one whereby the disciplinary technique invades both discursive and institutional practices in the entire realm of human relations, not just the organization or administration of production. Foucault is clearly at the forefront of this analysis, particularly his account of the rise of extensive administrative regulation – what he calls 'the disciplines' – from the 17th and 18th centuries.

Ferguson does retain the insights of Weber in order to instantiate the macro level of analysis, as bureaucratic administrative structures develop alongside advanced capitalism at the level of systemic processes, but utilizes a Foucauldian-derived notion of 'bureaucratic discourse' to establish the connections between macro, institutional and micro, individual levels. The term 'bureaucratic discourse' refers to the speech of the administrative disciplines which both expresses and reflects a particular structure of institutions and practices, and operates as a kind of verbal performance, placing people and objects within a network of social, political and administrative arrangements.

Ferguson provides an analysis of the historical underpinnings of the male-dominated character of bureaucratic organization, linking this to the fact that, historically, men have been included in the public realm and therefore positioned within bureaucratic dis-course. It has been women's historical exclusion from the public realm which means that they have developed a different voice and one which constitutes a submerged discourse. When women do enter the public realm, they find themselves marginal to bureau-cracies and caught between the instrumentality of male-dominated modes of public action and the expressive values of female-dominated modes of action in the private realm. Women's experiences constitute the submerged voice within the overall discourse of bureaucratic capitalism but a feminist discourse promises an alternative to the discursive and institutional practices of bureaucracy.

What is particularly problematic about Ferguson's work is that, in the midst of her broad-ranging analysis of the bureaucratization of the structures and discourses of modern social life, she suddenly introduces a notion of 'male power' which produces women and which she discusses in parallel with a notion of 'bureaucratic technical power' that produces bureaucrats. Ferguson establishes the links between subordination within the discourse and practices of bureaucracy and those of patriarchy by drawing parallels between the characteristics and strategies of subordinates within bureaucracy and of women within patriarchy. So she argues that bureaucratic power creates an organizational arena in which the 'feminization' of subordinates is encouraged. There is a very strong sense, then, in which Ferguson is arguing that the discursive construction of 'femininity' within relations of male dominance and female subordination provides a template for the behavioural attributes of subordinates within bureaucratic hierarchies.

Subordinates within bureaucratic work organizations must, for example, learn to 'please the other', to internalize their superiors' perspectives and anticipate demands. There is a constant vigilance on the part of subordinates. In short, women make 'good', or at least (within a patriarchal discourse) readily positioned, subordinates (within a bureaucratic discourse). There is a notion of 'layers' of discourse, with gendered discourses being superimposed upon bureaucratic discourses. But, as we have already stressed, we would prefer to retain a sense of gender relations and bureaucratic hierarchy as being more intertwined than this.

The real nub of Ferguson's radical, feminist case against bureaucracy is that there are other, more characteristically female, ways of going about getting things done in the modern world. In the long term, she advocates an androgynous revisioning of organizing activities in the public sphere, although she stresses that real androgyny is a possibility that has to be realized through struggle. 'Real androgyny, defined not as simply adding together misshapen halves of male and female, but rather as a complex process of calling out that which is valuable in each gender and carefully disentangling it from that which is riddled with the effects of power, is a *political struggle*' (Ferguson, 1984:70). In the short term, however, Ferguson advocates a separatist solution for women, who need to evolve their own organizational forms rather than become co-opted into existing male bureaucratic structures. The long term aim, then, is the elimination, not the reform, of male-centred bureaucratic modes of organization. Thus Ferguson argues a case against both bureaucracy *per se* and women's participation in bureaucratic organizations. This marks Ferguson's case out as radically different from that of Kanter, who is optimistic about women successfully participating in bureaucratic hierarchies, which are simply distorted, not fundamentally defined, by male power. Ferguson clearly does not believe, as Kanter does, that the integration of women into bureaucratic power structures will alter these structures in any significant way, and neither does she believe that this should be the agenda for feminist action. It is not just the case that women's voices are muted within the bureaucratic discourse, and their modes of acting and relating to others submerged within bureaucratic structures, but also that bureaucratic discourse and structure are masculinist and antithetical to feminist modes of organizing. Ferguson's most distinctive contribution to the debate about gender and bureaucracy is her argument that a feminist project lays the ground for an alternative to the bureaucratic discourse, an alternative which is inflected by women-centred ways of organizing activity.

However, a highly problematic aspect of Ferguson's analysis is that her whole case against bureaucracy is built on an assumption of gender-differentiated modes of social action, for which she never establishes a secure basis. She evokes women's care-taking role in the private sphere as underpinning the radical potential of a feminist discourse and as supplying the grounds for a feminist revisioning of the organizational forms which characterize the public sphere, suggesting that women will inflect organizing activities differently to men. However, she does not want to buy into analyses such as Carol Gilligan's (1982) and Nancy Chodorow's (1978) which assert psychological and moral underpinnings for women's different voice. Instead, she appears to want to ground a distinctive feminist voice within the greater practical (rather than moral or psychological) capacity of women to relate to others, a capacity which she insists is learned through their caretaking role in the private sphere. However, whilst using women's caretaking role as the basis on which to suggest that women will inflect organizing activities differently to men, she nonetheless balks at valorizing any supposed ethic of generosity and care and turning it into a feminine virtue. She recognises that women's experiences are distorted by oppression, they are consequently partial and incomplete, and warns that caretaking is all too easily romanticized, sentimentalized, and sometimes reduced to a terminal cheerfulness or to a masochistic need for self-sacrifice. Indeed, although Ferguson does not go quite as far as saying this, it is implied by her analysis that there may be ways in which men act in the world which, if women could adopt them, might be liberating. In order to avoid the valorization of women's caring activities Ferguson insists that it is friendship rather than caretaking *per se* which provides a model for reciprocity and should inform a feminist anti-bureaucratic vision. Friendship is distinguished by its egalitarian and voluntary quality and is, above all, a reciprocal relation. However, we would argue that Ferguson's attempt to avoid the danger of valorizing women's caretaking role is ultimately unsuccessful because there is nothing particularly gender-specific about the capacity for friendship and because her use of discourse analysis prevents her from locating a notion of female difference within more securely materialist underpinnings of a 'feminist standpoint'.

A crucial element of Ferguson's critique of bureaucratic practice from a feminist point of view is that women have the capacity to go about getting things done in a manner different to that of men. It would appear timely, therefore, to broaden out the discussion beyond the three writers who form the main focus of this section. This theme is a common one in discussions of the modern women's movement, which has been described as evolving a distinctive, contemporary mode of political praxis and organization. Underscoring much of the discussion of the political and voluntary or self-help organizations of the women's movement is the argument or assumption that women's socialization makes them better equipped than men to perform the skills necessary for the creation of democratic, participatory, non-hierarchical organization (Brown, 1992). However, as Brown (1992), in her detailed case study analysis of women organizing a Women's Centre, cautions us, this argument is in danger of being promoted to the status of an alternative determinism and needs to be tempered by a recognition that women who are involved in organizing as women are engaged in an ongoing, creative struggle to achieve the 'collective dream' that characterizes the feminist principle of organizing. The modern women's movement has striven for a non-hierarchical form of organizing and adopted tactics such as the sharing of tasks, skills, information and resources, as well as placing as much emphasis on the content of organizing activities, attending to the internal

21

processes of group activities, as on the accomplishment of tasks. There is a commitment to egalitarian values and an intention to organize without hierarchy and without leaders (Brown, 1992).

Utilizing Weber's distinction between formal and substantive rationality, we can see how a characteristic feature of women organizing is that of the substantive rationality of collectivist-democratic organization (Brown, 1992, Rothschild-Whitt, 1982). Rothschild-Whitt (1982) offers an ideal-type conceptualization of the differences between formal and substantive rationality, seeing feminist values as far more in tune with democratic, substantive modes of organizing the workplace. The ideal type of substantively rational organization has the following dimensions: authority resides in the collective and is delegated, if at all, only temporarily and subject to recall; an ideal of community dictates that relations are holistic and of value in themselves; no hierarchy of position; egalitarian and reward differentials, if any, are limited by the community; and a minimal division of labour where jobs and functions are generalized and expertise is demystified. By contrast, the formal rationality of bureaucracy has the following dimensions: authority resides in individuals by virtue of their incumbency in office and/or their expertise; a hierarchical organization of offices; the ideal of impersonality where relations are strictly de-personalised and role-based, segmented and instrumental; differential rewards by office, where hierarchy provides the rationale for inequality; and a maximal division of labour and splitting of functions.

Rothschild-Whitt's ideal-typification of formal and substantially rational organization is based on descriptions of employing organizations, where the co-operative organization approaches the substantively rational end of the organizational continuum. Other examples of women organizing take the form of organization whose rationale is not economic, but is essentially substantive or value based, such as rape crisis centres, women's aid refuges and self-help health groups, as well as the myriad of lobby groups around single-issue campaigns such as abortion, equal pay, child care etc. Dominelli (1991) suggests that feminist welfare initiatives offer 'pre-figurative forms' for the organization of welfare provision on a basis different to that of the welfare state bureaucracy. The creation of services by women for women, in the form of feminist therapy centres, well-women clinics, refuges for battered women, rape crisis centres and incest survivors groups, have radical potential, not just in the sense of defining new areas of need, but also in devising new organizational bases for provisioning.

Feminist welfare initiatives may act as prefigurative forms for welfare services in capitalist and socialist societies, argues Dominelli, by making these more amenable to people's needs, less hierarchical, and more responsive to consumer control. Within feminist forms of substantively (or value) rational organization, only decisions which follow from the consensus of the group carry the weight of moral authority, which resides in the collective as a whole (Brown, 1992). The guiding organizational principle of substantive rationality is encapsulated in the feminist organizational project of 'structurelessness' and 'leaderless groups'. Formal rationality, the essence of bureaucratic organization, is eschewed and associated with the alienating and hierarchical reality of male dominated modes of bureaucratic organization. Thus feminist organizational principles offer a strong critique of bureaucratic organization – as well as an attempt to evade Michel's 'iron law of oligarchy' where power shifts towards the centre in the form of 'leadership positions' even in avowedly democratic, participatory membership organizations such as trade unions.

Ferguson (1984) further suggests that the very opposition between formal rationality, as directed toward the pursuit of self-interest at the expense of others, and substantive rationality, directed toward altruistic service at the expense of self-interest, becomes untenable within a feminist discourse since it rests on an unfounded separation of self and other. Rather, a feminist perspective on rationality starts from the point of view that rationality – like our very selves – is grounded in social relations and the choices to be made within the context of these relations. Rationality, then, is inescapably relational. A feminist perspective on rationality also explicitly connects reason to emotion.

Another feminist sociologist who takes up the issues of rationality and bureaucratic organization is Dorothy Smith (1987a, 1987b), although her discussion of these issues is embedded within the context of her important contribution to carving out a standpoint for women in relation to the discipline of sociology, rather than within an explicit analysis of gender and bureaucracy. However, Dorothy Smith's contribution takes us more firmly into a 'feminist standpoint' methodology, which grounds a distinctive feminist epistemology and discourse, as ways of knowing and speaking of the social world, firmly within the ways in which women actively engage with the social world *and* within the patriarchal structures within which women engage in daily life. The feminist standpoint emerges out of the contradiction between the systematically differing structure of male and female life activity in Western cultures; it is therefore historically specific as it expresses female experience at a particular point in time and in particular places, located within a particular set of social relations (Hartsock, 1987). The feminist standpoint methodology has a strongly materialist underpinning, and does not valorize or essentialize female qualities or modes of action, as some feminist critics of bureaucracy such as Ferguson (1984) find difficult to avoid completely, but grounds these in women's daily lives within a social world characterized by a sexual division of labour.

Although not centrally concerned with the analysis of gender and bureaucracy, Dorothy Smith locates her critique of the conceptual apparatus of sociology as an academic discipline within a more general account of the 'relations of ruling'; the way in which the governing of modern society is done by concepts and symbols (1987b). She sees the emergence of forms of corporate capitalism as entailing the emergence of an abstracted conceptual mode of organization of society – or rational administrative practices:

> They constitute a generalized and generalizing practice of organization occupying an increasingly abstracted conceptual space, detached from the local and particular as the locus and center of the organizational processes. . . . Social relations, organizations, and so on become conceptualized as discrete and self-conscious processes quite separable as such from the particular individuals who performed and brought them into being as concrete social activities. (Smith 1987a:75, 76)

The emergence of academic disciplines such as sociology was part of this general historical move towards the transformation of actualities into the forms in which they could be thought of in an abstracted conceptual mode of ruling. But this historical push towards rational administrative organization with its transformation of the concrete actuality of social action into an abstracted, conceptual organizing frame was a gendered process, as women were pushed outside the relations of ruling and, instead located in more immediate work practices which sustain it and are essential to its existence.

Dorothy Smith offers us a brilliant analysis of gendered 'modes of knowing and experiencing and doing, one located in the body and in the space which it occupies and moves into, the other that passes beyond it' (1987b:89) – into the conceptual mode:

> If men are to participate fully in the abstract, conceptual mode of action, they must be liberated from having to attend to their needs in the concrete and particular. Organizing the society in an abstracted conceptual order, mediated symbolically, must be articulated to the concrete and local actualities in which it is necessarily and ineluctably located. . . . The place of women, then, in relation to this mode of action is where the work is done to facilitate men's occupation of the conceptual mode of action. . . . At almost every point women mediate for men the relation between the conceptual mode of action and the actual concrete forms in which it is and must be realized, and the actual material conditions upon which it depends'. (Smith 1987a:83; 1987b:90)

Dorothy Smith's revealing analysis of gendered ways of acting, experiencing and knowing the social world enables us to understand the gendering of activities in both the private and the public spheres, and to see how potentially powerful and nuanced Kanter's use of the term 'office wife' *actually* is. For it is women both outside *and* inside bureaucracies who are engaged in similarly gendered modes of acting, ones which order the materiality of the everyday world, be this a kitchen or an office. They are facilitating, cleaning, tidying, bolstering, soothing, smoothing over, sustaining etc. Women's housekeeping and caring activities are fundamentally geared towards relieving men of having to bother with the messy, untidy, unpredictable bodily mode of existence, but equally women are concerned with the concrete underbelly of conceptual activities when these are located within bureaucratic administrative organizations, by doing the clerical work and 'tidying' the information flowing through the office, taking short-hand and doing typing to render the thoughts of the boss in material form. We argue that this leads us forward in a different and more productive way than, say, Ferguson's, when considering women's strategic response to bureaucratic, male-dominated forms of organization. The issue becomes less one of counterposing gendered modes of acting in the world, and then evaluating one above the other, than of recognizing their fundamentally *relational* quality. A vital element of a radical strategy becomes forcing men to see how their entry into the conceptual, authoritative, organizing mode is a *privileged* activity which they engage in at the expense of, but only because of, women. The whole concept of 'dependency' within the context of gender relations acquires an interesting new twist, for it is men who are dependent upon the concretizing activities of women in order to sustain their involvement in the everyday world of, for example, bureaucratic administration. But men can no longer go on simply organizing the world; they have to take responsibility for tidying it up too.

It is vital to develop a perspective on gender and bureaucracy which foregrounds gender relations as an embedded property of organizations rather than valorizing gender differences as dichotomous sets of attributes or distinctive orientations and modes of action, which are simply 'brought to' organizations. Celia Davies's contribution to this volume is important in this respect, precisely because Davies argues that we must shift from approaches which regard gender as a fixed attribute imported into workplace organizations towards ones which treat gender as a relational quality and gender relations as power relations. Thus the experiential basis of gender-differentiated management styles – such as the 'coping management' style characteristic of nurse management – is to be sought not just in women's experiences outside the workplace, but also in their experiences of 'the gendering of the organization of paid work'. In addition, Davies's careful unpacking of nurses' coping management style demonstrates how gender is embedded not just in organizational *structures*, ie in hierarchies of authority and divisions of labour, but also in organizational *processes*, ie in the accomplishment of work and its management on a day-to-day basis.

To turn now to the third key theorist of gender and bureaucracy, Rosemary Pringle, it is interesting first to observe how Pringle's analysis of the boss-secretary relation in her book *Secretaries Talk* (1988) leads her to adopt a position totally contrary to that of Kanter. Instead of seeing the boss-secretary relation as an exceptional and archaic patrimonial practice, which binds men and women as the incumbents of these work roles into an 'improper' (irrational) authority relation, Pringle insists that the boss-secretary relation is the paradigmatic example of all workplace power relations and, as such, vividly illustrates the workings of modern bureaucracies. Pringle wants to establish that forms of power and control in the bureaucratic organization may be based around the construction of sexuality. In other words, the bureaucratic organization is not 'desexualized', but is saturated with sexuality embodied in its gendered occupants. Pringle effectively re-reads Weber in order to bring out what might be described as an unthematized gender sub-text in his account of rationality:

> It can be argued that while the rational-legal or bureaucratic form presents itself as gender-neutral, it actually constitutes a new kind of patriarchal structure. The apparent neutrality of rules and goals disguises the class and gender interests served by them. Weber's account of 'rationality' can be interpreted as a commentary on the construction of a particular kind of masculinity based on the exclusion of the personal, the sexual and the feminine from any definition of 'rationality' (Pringle 1988:88).

If we see that a series of discourses on sexuality underpin bureaucratic control, then we can also re-read the boss-secretary relation not as a patrimonial authority relation inhabited by gendered organizational participants (as Kanter would have it), but as a mode of bureaucratic control which is crucially under-pinned by a sexualized and familial discourse within which men and women are positioned as subjects and objects. This is indeed what Pringle's analysis of the secretary in the modern bureaucracy does.

Roslyn Bologh's (1990) re-reading of Weber tips us similarly towards unpicking the gendered subtext of his account of modernity, but it is not quite as explicitly geared to interrogating power and authority in the modern bureaucratic organization as Pringle's. Pringle does refer to 'erotic bureaucracies', which suggests that the demise of 'erotic man' and the rise of 'rational man' described by Bologh has involved the sublimation of eroticism, but not its erasure from the modern bureaucratic organization. Indeed, Marcuse (1968) spoke of the ways in which the body (itself an instrument of labour) is allowed to exhibit its sexual features in the everyday work world and of how sex is integrated into work relations. However, the controlled integration of sex into work relations represents the manipulation of pleasure to generate submission, so sexuality in the workplace is not simply a question of power but also of gratification or pleasure. This inextricable linking of pleasure and power is a feature of Foucault's (1980) analysis of sexuality. It has also been incorporated into feminist analyses of gender, sexuality and organization in, we shall suggest, a highly problematic way (cf Pringle 1988, 1989; Cockburn, 1991).

Another key difference between Kanter's and Pringle's analyses of men and women in bureaucratic work organizations is to be found in their concepts of power. Kanter uses the term power in a strictly Weberian sense as referring to the ability to realize one's will or get things done. She sees a fixed amount of power as circulating within the organizations, and the issue addressed by Kanter is the differential access to power between men and women. A notion of power inequalities as in any way built into the very fabric of gender relations themselves is strangely absent from Kanter's analysis. Of course, remaining within a strict Weberian notion of a distinction between power and domination, a recognition of power as a property of gender relations themselves would be taking us into a consideration of dominance. Curiously, Kanter is not really concerned with relations of dominance; she declares her focus is on power – and of course, as we saw above, believes that 'power wipes out sex' and that men and women can gain equal access to organizational power. For Kanter, then, it is not men as men that dominate women in organizations; it is men as incumbents of powerful official positions that have more power than women.

Pringle, on the other hand, adopts a Foucauldian view of power as not something that is possessed, nor something of which there is a fixed amount somehow circulating through an organizational structure. Rather, power *is* a relation – although not in the Weberian sense of a relation of dominance and subordination, nor a social relation, but a discursive relation. As Pringle insists, power relations cannot simply be read off from structural inequalities nor do they merely reflect these. Rather, power refers to a complex strategic situation, always in flux. The vital element present in Foucault's definition of power is that power continually creates the possibility of resistance. Thus Pringle insists "Male power" is not simply and unilaterally imposed on women – gender relations are a process involving strategies and counter-strategies of power.' (Pringle 1989a:92). So in Pringle's account of the boss-secretary relation, it is not simply the case that bosses 'have' power and secretaries do not. The secretary has her own 'quiet means of resistance' (Pringle 1989a:47).

One of Pringle's 'strong' claims is that discourses around sexuality position men and women in subject and object positions within organizations but that sexuality is about pleasure as well as power. Control through pleasure may indeed be more effective than control through coercion, because it is less likely to meet with resistance. Here, she departs quite sharply from radical feminist analyses of sexual harassment in the workplace, where it is claimed that sex and power are inseparable and that harassment is merely one manifestation of a series of 'controlling' elements of heterosexuality. So, in fact, Pringle ends up disagreeing both with Kanter's view, that power and sex are independent dimensions of organizational life, and with radical feminist views that the two are inseparable and both are coercive.

Instead, Pringle's distinctive contribution to the debate about men and women within bureaucratic workplace organization is to point to the positive side of heterosexuality – that it is also about pleasure and that this is its radical moment for women in organizations as 'sexual pleasure might be used to disrupt male rationality and to empower women' (Pringle 1989a:166). Cockburn (1991) in her analysis of men's responses to women's struggle for workplace equality also urges that 'What needs to change is not the sexiness of women but the vulnerability of women. The long agenda for the women's movement in organizations must be to strengthen women's position and confidence in many different ways so that we can re-introduce our bodies, our sexuality and our emotions on our own terms' (Cockburn 1991:159). Cockburn distinguishes this long agenda from a short agenda of women's equality policy, which has been to effectively ban sexuality from the workplace. However, what both Pringle and Cockburn lose sight of is that, if power is discursive, and if discourses about sexuality set the parameters of pleasure as they simultaneously constitute and regulate sexuality, then how is the pleasure of sexuality any *less* problematic than the power of sexuality?

Lisa Adkins's chapter in this collection identifies this aspect of both Pringle's and Cockburn's work as problematic, and her critique suggests that the limitations of such a strategic response to the sexuality of organization arise out of a fundamentally flawed and partial conceptualization of sexuality itself. Adkins is critical of both Pringle and Cockburn for distinguishing between 'coercive' sexuality, such as sexual harassment of women by men, and 'non-coercive' sexuality, which they understand in terms of desires and pleasure and as not necessarily constituted by or through male power. Adkins makes the extremely important point that both Pringle and Cockburn neglect the ways in which heterosexuality is made compulsory for women and insists that both coercive *and* non-coercive heterosexual interactions are structured by male dominance and both are clearly exploitative for women.

By teasing out some of the differences between Kanter's and Pringle's analyses, it is possible to discern the fairly radical shift in perspective from a 'gender' one to a 'sexuality' one. In Kanter's gender paradigm, power is analytically distinct from 'sex' (although here Kanter is really talking about gender, referring to socially and situationally constructed sets of behaviours, dispositions and attitudes). Power is a structural property of bureaucracy and *can* be acquired by women. In Pringle's sexuality paradigm, gender is used loosely to refer to collective identities and behaviours of men and women as 'classes' of persons, but the real nub of organizational inequalities between interacting men and women situated within gender relations is the power of sexuality. 'Power' and 'sexuality' cannot be prized apart quite so easily in Pringle's account of bureaucracy, and the site of resistance for women is not to acquire more power (and hence to wipe out sex) but to acquire more sexuality and empower themselves on their own terms.

If we re-read Weber's account of rationality in such a way as to recognise its masculine, masculinist and patriarchal undertones (Bologh, 1990) and claim that the rationality of bureaucratic organization is premised upon the construction of a particular kind of masculinity (Pringle, 1989c), then a further question emerges of what is to be done about this sexuality now that it has been 'outed'. It is not just specifically gendered male-female workplace relations that become 'sexualised', but organization *itself*. Is it possible to simply sweep organizational sexuality back under the carpet, once we have identified and named its overtly damaging elements – such as naming certain sexualized workplace activities as 'harassment'? Is a de-sexualized workplace possible or even desirable? Is it possible to leave one's sexuality behind 'at home' and inhabit the organization as an asexual bureaucrat? Of course, there's an important sense in which men have always claimed the capacity to do precisely this, at least when they can inhabit a homosexual environment devoid of the distractions of women who are, in the eyes of men, irredeemably 'their sex'. Kanter describes the insecurities about their corporate husbands' sexuality expressed by some wives, who feared that sustained interaction and close contact with women managers would excite male sexuality in a supposedly 'de-sexualized' sphere of activity. However, as we have seen, Pringle's message is quite different from Kanter's because she does not see organization as de-sexualized, but describes how sexuality structures the boss-secretary relation. So there exist quite different views on the embeddedness or otherwise of sexuality within organizations, and unresolved issues emerge from the foregrounding of sexuality over and above gender in the analysis of male power in bureaucracies. We will in due course return to what we describe as the 'turn to sexuality' generally within recent analyses of men, women and organizations. But first let us pull together the insights provided by Kanter, Ferguson and Pringle and, then, in the next section, turn to another set of writings which address the relation between gender and the bureaucratic administrative structures of the modern state.

Kanter, Ferguson and Pringle each adopt a different approach to their subject matter, in terms of their orientation to the Weberian paradigm of bureaucracy, their analytical framework for the analysis of gender in organizations and their strategic response to current gender inequalities in organizations. Rosabeth Moss Kanter presents us with a feminist revision of Max Weber's classic account of bureaucracy, operating within and broadly accepting a Weberian account of bureaucracy, whilst treating the subordination of women within corporate hierarchies as either an 'irrational' relic persisting within a modern, rational organizational shell (as in the case of secretaries) or a problem that has to do with their exclusion from the resources of power (as in the case of female bureaucrats). Her analysis of gender is uncompromisingly 'socially construction-ist', with its focus on gender roles as essentially situated and learned behaviours, whilst her prognosis for women in bureau-cracy is an optimistic one which looks forward to the equal participation of women within corporate bureaucracies. We have indicated that her conceptualization of the relation between gender and organizational power is flawed, largely because she does not recognize the gendering of organizational power itself. But these are not separate dynamics of bureaucratic organization; they are intertwined. Gender is embedded in the power relations of bureaucracy, just as power is embedded in gender relations in the form of male dominance and female subordination.

Kathy Ferguson moves us into a more radical, feminist critique of the gendering of bureaucracy, presenting us with a blend of Weberian and Foucauldian insights into modern organizational life as consisting of both bureaucratic structures *and* discourses. Her analytical framework leans towards a more relational account of gender relations as ones of male dominance and female subordination, whilst her strategic response to the problem of female subordination within bureaucratic structures and discourse is a separatist one, advocating that women develop parallel, independent organizational shells which reflect women's preferred ways of acting in the world. We have suggested, however, that Ferguson never satisfactorily resolves the tension between a social constructionist and an essentialist rendering of the underpinnings of patriarchy. It is, nonetheless, a more thoroughgoing critique of male-dominated bureaucratic structures than Kanter's, but still one that leaves the insights of Weber intact, albeit adding discourse analysis.

Rosemary Pringle's recent work poses the most fundamental challenge to Weber's analytical framework and represents a poststructuralist undermining of Weber, neither accepting the Weberian paradigm of bureaucratic rationality, as Kanter does, nor using discourse analysis to complement Weber's analysis, as Ferguson does. Instead, Pringle substantially questions the un-thematized gender sub-text of Weber's model of bureaucratic rationality and dislocates power from any structural underpinnings in order to locate it instead in discourses. One major difference between Pringle's analysis and those of both Kanter and Pringle may be found in her paradigm shift away from a social construc-tionist 'gender' paradigm and towards an equally socially con-structionist 'sexuality' paradigm. We have suggested, however, that Pringle's prognosis for women in bureaucracies is highly problematic, due to her insistence that discourses of sexuality are sites of both women's subordination *and* resistance.

4 Gender and the state bureaucracy

There is today a lively debate about feminism and the state. However, very few of the contributors consider the state as a bureaucracy, despite the fact that Weber sees the modern state as 'absolutely dependent upon a bureaucratic basis' (1974). It is therefore highly appropriate here to consider the relation between gender and the modern bureaucratic state along with that of the relation between gender and bureaucratic workplace organizations. Some similar trajectories of analysis, as well as some parallel concerns, emerge in the literature that deals with each of these substantive areas.

One trajectory in feminist theorizing about the bureaucratic form of both the state and workplace organizations is the increasing use of Foucauldian analysis alongside or instead of a Weberian view of bureaucratization. This is particularly evident in the work of Australian feminists, most notably Rosemary Pringle and Sophie Watson (1990, 1992), who use Foucault to effectively deconcretize or deconstruct the state into a 'site of a number of discursive formations'. Foucault has also provided feminist critics of bureaucratization with a means of treating bureaucracy less as a structure and more as a set of discursive practices about organizing activities (cf Ferguson, 1984), as well as with a means of opening up the possibility that the public sphere of bureaucratized activities and power relations are not de-sexualized and dispassionate spheres of social action, but are grounded in discourses of sexuality (Pringle, 1989a, 1989b).

Similar questions are posed by feminist critics of bureaucratization at both the level of the state administration and the administration of production. Some of these concern strategies for action that follow on from feminist critiques of bureaucracy. Will the insertion of women at the higher echelons of bureaucratic administrative organization, whether of production or politics, fundamentally transform these structures? This raises the issue of whether bureaucracies are inherently masculine, as suggested by Ferguson (1984), or whether women can be admitted, as maintained by Kanter (1977). Indeed, should the goal of women be to enter and participate in the 'relations of ruling', as Dorothy Smith (1987a) would call them, or will women's distinctive modes of acting in the world be quashed and distorted within these masculinist institutions? Once women 'have' power, can they ensure that they use it in such a way as to minimize the disempowerment of others who are subordinates – as Kanter (1977) believes, at least in the context of corporate bureaucracies? Can female bureaucrats further the collective interests of women by reforming male-dominated ways of behaving once they participate in these? Do women *want* to participate in masculinist organizational structures, or would they be better advised to concentrate on evolving more women-friendly modes of organizing activities independently of existing male-dominated structures? These are just some of the issues that inform feminist discussions of bureaucratic administration at the level both of the state and of the organization of production and services.

There are important differences between feminists concerning the importance of the state for feminism and particularly whether women's interests are best pursued through, in or in spite of the state. There are different feminist *theories* of the state and different feminist *strategies* in relation to the state. We will look at different stances towards the state before focussing on one of the most thoroughgoing attempts in recent years to recruit women into the state bureaucracy and thereby further the interests of women: the Australian femocrat strategy.

There is no feminist theory of the state as such, although a number of feminist perspectives on the state can be discerned. However, a number of these have tended towards an overly functionalist rendering of the state-society relation. Both Susan Halford and Sophie Watson, in their respective contributions on the local and national state bureaucracies in this collection, adopt a similarly critical stance towards the incipient functionalism of much feminist theorizing of the state, and their analyses go some considerable way in moving us beyond this. This incipient functionalism may be seen to derive from the use of a generic Marxist view of the state (a point which is argued by Sophie Watson in this collection). Broadly, three state-gender paradigms have dominated discussions of the state and gender relations in the 1980s, and these we might usefully term Marxist-feminist, dual systems and radical feminist. Differences between these paradigms turn on, amongst other things, whether the state is either a capitalist or a patriarchal state or both. In addition, a fourth paradigm of the state-gender relation has emerged recently. This a post-structuralist one, which seeks to move beyond an overly functionalist reading of the state and declares the state to be 'fraternal' rather than 'patriarchal'.

The first, the Marxist-feminist paradigm, finds its fullest expression in the works of Mary McIntosh (1978) and Michelle Barrett (1987). Both writers examine how the state sustains women's oppression and subordination within capitalism, but contend that the state only indirectly oppresses women because it is capitalist rather than patriarchal. Although capitalist society is one in which men as men dominate women, it is not this but class domination which is fundamental in shaping social, economic and political relations. Athough the dominant class is composed of men, it is not as men but as capitalists that they are dominant (McIntosh 1978). The second, dual systems paradigm, holds that the state is patriarchal as well as capitalist. Zillah Eisenstein has argued that male dominance is formalized by the modern state, which maintains and reproduces patriarchy (1981). Eisenstein refers to a 'capitalist patriarchal' state and uses the 'relative autonomy' framework developed by some Marxists, which sees the state as constrained by its capitalist underpinnings, but as neither completely independent of these nor completely determined by them. Eisenstein suggests that the state may be seen as relatively autonomous not only of the economic class structure, but also of the sexual class structure (1981:227). The relative autonomy of the state in relation to patriarchy occurs in terms of the choices made within the bourgeoisie on patriarchy, so patriarchal interests are represented by men of the capitalist class, who enforce the sexual class relations of patriarchy via the machinery of the state (Eisenstein, 1984:92).

So, in complete contrast to the Marxist-feminist paradigm, which contends that it is as capitalists not as men that the ruling class rules, Eisenstein insists that ruling class men *are* dominant as men as well as capitalists. An even stronger claim made by Eisenstein (1984) is that, because the bourgeoisie is male, the state is therefore more 'relative' than 'autonomous' along its patriarchal dimensions. Here, Eisenstein argues that gender interests are less differentiated from the state than class interests, because these are literally 'embodied' in male state actors. Another writer who uses the dual systems paradigm and sees the state as patriarchal as well as capitalist is Sylvia Walby (1984, 1990). Nonetheless, there are some important differences between them. Eisenstein emphasizes the mutual accommodation of patriarchal and capitalist interests by means of, for example, state welfare policies, whereas Walby emphasizes the frequently conflicting interests of patriarchy and capitalism played out at the level of the state. Walby also draws attention to sets of patriarchal interests other than those of the dominant class, notably those of working class men, who have used their political organizations to influence state policy in ways which benefit them at the expense of working class women. The major difference between these two dual systems formulations of the state-gender relation lies in Walby's insistence that the state is more autonomous than relative in relation to patriarchy. The state is not monolithic but is continually engaging with gendered political forces, so its actions are the outcome of competing political pressures. Because Walby regards first-wave feminism in the late 19th and early 20th centuries as an historically important articulation of the political interests of gender, she emphasizes the discontinuities and the major changes in how the state represents men's interests, rather than its relatively unchanging patriarchal underpinnings, as Eisenstein is apt to do.

The third paradigm which has characterized feminist theories of the state is the radical feminist one, represented by the work of Catherine MacKinnon (1983, 1987). MacKinnon's premise is that feminism has no theory of the state as such, although it has a theory of male power. The question posed by Catherine Mac-Kinnon is 'what is this state, from women's point of view?' Her answer is deceptively simple: the state is male. So how does she manage to argue this? Catherine MacKinnon deploys what she calls a post-Marxist, feminist method – which is to all intents and purposes a 'feminist standpoint' epistemology devoid of materialist underpinnings – and claims that the state is male because it adopts the standpoint of men, or the male view of the world, which it then calls objectivity. In this way, the male point of view masquerades as 'point-of-viewlessness'. MacKinnon treats the 'state' and the 'law' as virtually synonymous, and she is thus able to argue that the state is male because the law sees and treats women the way in which men see and treat women.Thus, the nub of her whole analysis of the male state is her critique of liberal jurisprudence or law, and by unpacking the patriarchal underpinnings of liberal legalism we find the mechanism whereby male dominance is at one and the same time legitimated and rendered invisible. In Catherine MacKinnon's analysis, then, there is a strong sense in which the state institutionalizes male power over women through law. Looking at the legal definition of rape, she claims that 'Rape is a sex crime that is not a crime when it looks like sex' and declares that surely this is someone else's definition imposed upon women's experience. She goes on to say that 'Women who charge rape say they were raped twice, the second time in court. If the state is male, then this is more than a figure of speech'. One of the vital questions raised by MacKinnon's analysis, although not by MacKinnon herself, is that, if this is what the state looks like from women's point of view, then is masculinity inherent in the state form itself or is it possible to imagine another form of state that is not an embodiment of masculinity? The irony of MacKinnon's position is that she appears to be ruling out any possible role for law and the state in furthering women's interests, and yet, along with Andrea Dworkin, has taken a leading role in initiating law reform as the means of protecting women from pornography (Eisenstein 1991).

There are some important similarities and differences between writers who wish to theorize the state as patriarchal. Catherine MacKinnon argues that the state literally 'embodies' men's interests, whereas Sylvia Walby grants it considerable autonomy, arguing that the state does not necessarily represent men's interests, although it usually does. But it is possible to move beyond piecemeal comparisons and, following Drude Dahlerup's (1986) lead, to disentangle two elements of a definition of the state as 'patriarchal'. One is a purely *nominal* definition of the state as 'manned' or staffed predominantly by men; the other is a more *substantive* definition of a state as systematically representing the collective interests of men. Catherine MacKinnon (1983, 1987) in fact conflates these two elements – it is male in both the nominal and the substantive sense and, indeed, the state does not so much 'represent' as 'present' the interests of men. Zillah Eisenstein (1981, 1984) argues that the state is substantively patriarchal because it is nominally patriarchal, ie it represents the interests of men because the ruling class is male. Sylvia Walby (1990), however, refers to a patriarchal state in the substantive sense only – it invariably, although not necessarily, represents the interests of men. We see it as vital to use a substantive definition of a patriarchal state, for it is not the gender of state actors which renders the state patriarchal, but the ways in which the competing political interests of gender are displaced onto or 'distilled' through the state. A nominally patriarchal state is not necessarily a substantively patriarchal one, although it is clear that, if the legislative, administrative and policy making arenas are largely in male hands (ie nominally patriarchal), then the more likely it is that the state will be substantively patriarchal. It is nevertheless analytically useful to keep these two elements of a definition in mind, although naive to presume that the two are unrelated in the operation of real states.

Feminist discussion of the state has recently taken a new turn away from the notion of a 'patriarchal state' as a coherent structure systematically representing men's interests and a post-structuralist paradigm of the state-gender relation has emerged. This turn owes much to the work of Foucault and his deconstruction of 'the state' into a 'site' rather than a 'structure'. It seeks to avoid the reification of 'the state' which creeps into much feminist discussion of the state and gender relations. This new turn in feminist theorizing also emerges out of the specific experiences of Australian feminism in the 1970s and 1980s and is represented in this collection by Sophie Watson, who engages in a comparative analysis of women's engagement with and in the state in Britain and Australia in order to flesh out a Foucauldian inspired framework of the relation between the modern state and gender.

Indeed, Sophie Watson suggests that post-structuralist developments in feminist theorising about the state have been made
possible by the strategic form of women's engagement with the
Australian state – the 'femocrat' strategy – so that strategy feeds
back into theory, just as theory informs strategy. Rosemary
Pringle and Sophie Watson (1989) eschew both nominal and
substantive definitions of the state as 'patriarchal'. They conceptualize the state not as a structure or an institution, nor as an actor or
an object, but as 'a site of a number of discursive formations'
(1989:237). The state is not coherent, nor even contradictory, but
erratic and disconnected. They acknowledge the specificity of the
state, but insist that it is the site of competing discourses, practices
and struggles:

> The discourses that construct the state assume a masculine
> subject rather than self-consciously defending or creating 'men's
> interests'. . . . What feminists are confronted with is not a state
> that represents 'men's interests' as against women's, but
> government conducted as if men's interests are the only ones
> that exist (1989:234).

But interests are not pre-given. Instead, they have to be
continually constructed and reproduced, and this applies in the
case of both men's and women's interests. Here the notion of a
'discursive strategy' becomes central to any analysis of the state,
for it is through discursive strategies, that is, through creating a
framework of meanings, that interests come to be constructed and
represented. Thus, feminists are *necessarily* involved in struggles
both in and through the state in all its aspects. Judith Allen (1989)
takes the line of reasoning underpinning the feminist post-
structuralist paradigm one stage further to argue that, because of
the fundamentally problematic nature of the term 'the state' which
feminists have, after all, inherited from other theoretical agendas,
feminism does not even need a theory of the state.

Turning now to the question of feminist strategies in relation to
the state, it is clear that the liberal democratic state has been
important to feminism, because women have sought to represent
their interests both through and in the state. The long tradition of
equal rights or liberal feminism in, for example, Britain and the
United States, has continually lobbied the state, its legislature and
policy-making bodies in order to advance the position of women in
modern society (cf Banks, 1984; Eisenstein, 1981; Walby, 1990;

Bacchi, 1991). In this way, feminism has sought to use state power on behalf of women, taking the rhetoric of liberal democratic state at its word and stretching it to cover women as bourgeois individuals (Eisenstein, 1991). Walby (1990) has similarly argued that equal rights strategies are a manifestation of the political interests of gender, and that women's collective struggles have had the important effect of opening up the public sphere to women, albeit largely on men's terms. Zillah Eisenstein (1981) has argued a case for the radical potential of liberal feminism, on the grounds that, by stretching the political tradition of liberalism to include women, equal rights feminism unmasks the patriarchal under-pinnings of the liberal democratic state. Feminism is then pushed towards its more radical stage as women realize that they can only make limited gains as 'individuals' because they are members of a sex-class.

But women have not just advanced their political interests by working *through* the state. They have also sought to alter fundamentally the character of the state itself by working *in* the state administration, particularly in Australia, where the 'femocrat strategy' has emerged out of a political alliance between the Labour Party and the feminist movement. 'Femocrats' are feminists working in the state bureaucracy on women's issues and their credentials as feminists are used as criteria for appointment to a position in the state bureaucracy. Their brief is to talk about and prepare policy proposals concerning women's interests. Their appointments are often linked to affirmative action or equal employment opportunity programmes, developing, implementing and monitoring these programmes. What is significant about the femocrat phenomenon is that it provides an historic instance of women working *as feminists* within male dominated bureaucratic structures. There are two categories of feminist intervention in bureaucracy identified by Hester Eisenstein (1989, 1991). One is a 'bureaucratic-individual' intervention where women enter the bureaucracy of state or national government at a policy-making level as self-identified feminists; the other is a 'bureaucratic-structural' one, where women create new structures within government or university administrations specifically designed to benefit women (such as women's policy units, women's studies programmes, or ministries for women's affairs). Other forms of feminist political intervention are 'legal reform' through legislative change, 'political participation in a leadership role', but in non-feminist political parties or trade unions as a self-proclaimed feminist and, finally, 'alternative structures', where feminists create independent organization outside of existing political and administrative structures (cf Eisenstein 1989, 1991).

We may classify these various interventions as feminists working *in* the state (bureaucratic-individual, bureaucratic-structural), *through* the state (legal reform and political participation), or *in spite of* the state (alternative structures). Which of these strategies is pursued will depend on the character of national politics in any one country, the national character of the women's movement which is shaped by a country's political structures, and the particular mix of feminist theory and practice that has emerged historically in each country (Eisenstein 1991).

What are the lessons to be learned from the femocrat phenomenon in Australia for a deeper understanding of feminism and/in the state or women and/in bureaucracy? As Hester Eisenstein (1991), herself an erstwhile femocrat, observes, the femocrat recruited into the state bureaucratic machinery in order to effect change on behalf of women is constrained to work within the parameters of a masculinist administrative culture, whilst simultaneously contesting the masculinist character of the state. Of course, critics of the femocrat phenomenon would argue that femocrats invariably become co-opted by masculinist modes of acting, and lose touch with the constituency of women whose interests they are there to represent. However, Eisenstein argues that femocrats do make a difference. Their very presence results in an infusion of ideas about women, power and sexuality into the state bureaucracy and changes the terms of debate. This positive evaluation of Australian femocratic feminism is shared by Sophie Watson in this volume who argues that femocrats have not only made a difference for women generally, through policy reforms, legislative change, and welfare services for women, but they have also made changes in the state bureaucracy itself. Watson emphasizes, however, that negotiating the path of contradictions, conflicts and dilemmas through bureaucratic state institutions is particularly difficult for femocrats – and that, indeed, there is no one single type of femocrat, so different problems have been encountered and a variety of different strategies devised by femocrats in negotiating their way through masculinist state bureaucracies. In addition, femocrats have met with hostile reactions from feminists outside the state, whom Watson sees as adopting some of what she calls the 'purist' anti-state tendencies of British feminist theory of the late 1970s in their negative evaluation of femocratic feminism – that femocrats have 'sold out', conformed through, for example, 'dressing for success', and rejected or lost touch with the grass roots women's movement. However, such a negative stance towards femocratic feminism forecloses important opportunities to learn from these experiences and build on them in the future.

There are important lessons to be drawn from the attempts by women to advance the interests of women from within the state bureaucracy. The experiences of femocrats as they continually confront the problem of negotiating their way through male networks of power on both an individual and collective basis reveal much about the gendering of bureaucracy itself, as indeed Susan Halford's chapter in this collection, examining the experiences of women's committees in the local state bureaucracy in Britain rather than the federal state bureaucracy in Australia, demonstrates. It is clear from Halford's analysis that the development and implementation of equality policy by and for women in local state bureaucracies meets with considerable resistance from men at both an individual and a collective level – although, paradoxically, she also found that supporting gender equality policy may actually provide men in organizations with the opportunity to enhance their own, individual bureaucratic careers! Similar observations have been made of the femocrat strategy in federal state bureaucracies in Australia, where male bureaucrats may find it 'politically expedient' and thereby advantageous to their careers as civil servants to sponsor women's policies.

There are also issues about language and style which femocrats – and indeed all women in bureaucracies, whether recruited for their feminist credentials or not – have to face. Femocrats regularly get into trouble for behaviour that is perceived by men as too 'womanly' – ie extravagant, emotional – and so end up deliberately monitoring their language and gestures, but at the same time as they are self-consciously introducing new modes of behaving into bureaucracies. Faced with networks of powerful, experienced and knowledgeable men, women also need to form alliances with sympathetic progressive male bureaucrats as well as to construct their own networks. Men still occupy the key decision-making posts within bureaucracies, and women are continually engaged in lobbying influential male decision makers. This raises the issue of styles of interaction, which in turn raises a further issue as to the different strategies adopted by heterosexual and lesbian women. Eisenstein recalls how, in the course of her own experience as a femocrat:

> It ran through my mind that each male bureaucrat, whatever his style or his location in the hierarchy, had a tradition of ten thousand years of bureaucratic power behind him, stretching back to Babylon. The senior women groped for an appropriate style, eschewing a nurturing role for fear of being treated as a mother, but unable really to use the male style . . . of exerting authority through rage, as this evoked a particularly deadly form of rage in return (1989:101).

Women in state bureaucracies are strangers in a male world. Most interestingly, we find echoes of Kanter's analysis of patriarchal bureaucratic kinship structures in Eisenstein's assessment of the femocrat strategy, as she uses the notion of 'quasi-kinship structures' to describe the ways in which femocrats acculturate themselves into the masculinist state bureaucracy, both in terms of relating to other women and to men. What forms of quasi-kinship relations emerge in this process – father/daughter, mother/daughter, sister/sister, brother/sister? Athough Eisenstein herself does not develop this insight, it would seem an interesting issue to place on the research agenda.

We have seen how earlier pioneering work on women in organizations, such as Kanter's, focussed on the problems women experience in attempting to play a game in which men had made the rules *and* judged the players. This problematic also underscores Hester Eisenstein's evaluation of the femocrat phenomenon in Australia, where women similarly seek to operate within a fundamentally masculinist state bureaucratic administration. Other work (cf Cockburn 1984, 1990, Walby 1986) has focussed on the ways and means of male power in workplace organizations, uncovering the exclusionary and segregationary devices employed by men and attempting to render the tacit rules of the game explicit and, it should not be forgotten, amenable to feminist action within organizations. Underscoring this tradition of feminist analysis lies an instrumental approach to male power – men dominate organizational structures and are in positions of power which enable them to pursue strategies in their own interests and at the expense of women. In other words, organizations are patriarchal in a nominal sense, of being literally 'manned' and in the substantive sense of routinely representing men's interests over and above women's. The 'femocrat' strategy in Australia may be seen as one possible response to a nominally and substantively patriarchal state bureaucracy, for this operates on the assumption that if women are appointed to powerful positions with a brief to represent the interests of women, then organizational bureaucracies will be rendered less substantively patriarchal as they become less nominally patriarchal. But the important lesson to be learned from the femocrat strategy is the recognition that there is no necessary correspondence between the gender of state bureaucrats and the sets of interests that they represent in the daily course of administrative decision-making. That is, a nominally patriarchal bureaucracy is not necessarily a substantively patriarchal one, just as a less nominally patriarchal structure is not necessarily a less substantially patriarchal one. Simply recruiting women to the higher echelons of bureaucratic organizations does not necessarily mean that the character of the organization will become less masculinist and more feminized or woman-friendly – as Kanter tends to assume. On the contrary, individual women in senior bureaucratic positions may perforce have to learn to act like men in order to function effectively at these levels. The key element of the femocrat strategy is the recognition that the collective interests of women in bureaucracies have to be actively forged and explicitly articulated. This applies equally to the collective interests of men in bureaucracies, whether in the workplace or the state, and this is something which the feminist post-structuralist revisioning of the state-gender relation places firmly on the agenda (cf Watson and Pringle, 1989, 1992; Watson in this volume).

The search for a radical alternative to the femocrat strategy emerges from the argument that there are fundamentally different male and female modes of social action and that bureaucracies institutionalize typically male forms of action, as indeed Kathy Ferguson has argued. So where does all this talk of women operating within masculinist, bureaucratic state administration leave the notion of specifically female modes of organizing activities? Hester Eisenstein (1984) has expressed scepticism about radical feminist visions of creating a utopia of woman-centred values, and yet admits that the expression of 'maternal' values (by, for example, women of Greenham common) constitute a powerful if ephemeral symbolic statement. The problem for feminism, however, is how we move from symbolic statements to the effective integration of 'woman-centred values' into contemporary public life. Eisenstein displays an ambivalence here. At one point she concludes that:

Feminism seemed to promise a world of nurturance and

acceptance, a redress of the hurts suffered by women at each others' hands in an era when female solidarity was impossible culturally. The entry of women into positions of significant power, even when this is accompanied by a feminist programme and personal commitment, has meant that relations among women of this kind cannot, structurally speaking, partake of the quality of nurturance and mutual acceptance that was part of the feminist utopia. (1989:102)

Here, Eisenstein would seem to be suggesting that (dubious) blueprints of female organizing activity cannot be successfully transposed into existing, masculinist bureaucratic organization. However, in a later publication, she appears to move closer to an appreciation, if not a·wholesale acceptance, of specifically women-centred organizing activities. Drawing on Sara Ruddick's (1989) analysis of 'maternal thinking', Hester Eisenstein suggests that modes of maternal thinking and acting should be seen and valued as learned, social categories, but that we need to accept that not everything that we have learned as women in the past is useful for us in the future, nor is everything symbolised by women's culture in the past necessarily progressive. This echoes Kathy Ferguson's concern when, in making out her feminist case against bureaucracy, she warns that in seeking alternative organization forms, women should not valorize the relational qualities of 'caring' but of 'friendship'. In other words, the message of Hester Eisenstein and of Kathy Ferguson is that women need to pick and choose as they move forward. Being aware of these issues and striving to move forward on the basis of these, uncertainties notwithstanding, means that being a femocrat *is* different to being a woman bureaucrat, concludes Hester Eisenstein (1991).

There are, then, a number of different feminist perspectives on the state as well as a variety of strategic responses by feminists. A number of the points raised in this section are picked up and developed further in the chapters by Susan Halford and Sophie Watson in this volume. Both look at the state bureaucracy and gender. Susan Halford evaluates the experiences of Women's Committees as initiatives taken at the level of the local state bureaucracy in Britain, whilst Sophie Watson engages in a comparative analysis of feminist theory and strategy vis-a-vis the state in Britain and Australia. A central tenet of the argument to emerge from Sophie Watson's evaluation of the different form and extent of feminist interventions in the state arena in Britain and

Australia is that feminist theory of the state has both influenced and developed from these interventions. Watson argues that in Australia the weakness of Marxist-feminist perspectives and a more diverse academic feminism combined with a more open state and political culture conducive to creating space for feminist interventions, have all combined to produce 'Australian state feminist and party politics agendas, assessing the achievements of intervention in the state than in Britain. Watson charts the course of Australian feminist interventions into the political and bureaucratic arenas from the early 1970s, tracing the links between feminist and political party agendas, assessing the achievements of femocratic feminism positively, and suggesting that the experiences of femocrats has productively fuelled debates about the tensions between the politics of gender 'equality' and those of gender 'difference', and that these issues are beginning to inform a pragmatic feminism and enter into policy discussion in the political arena. The links between feminist practice in the state and feminist theory of the state are emphasized by Watson, whose own analysis of femocratic feminism both informs and is informed by a new feminist post-structuralist theory of the state.

Although Sophie Watson observes how feminists have not attempted to work within state arenas to the same extent in Britain as they have in Australia, nonetheless she does note important shifts in feminist involvement with the bureaucratic and political institutions of the state after the election of the Thatcher government in 1979. This occurred primarily at the level of the local state bureaucracy and was largely the outcome of feminists influencing the Labour Party. The strategic intervention of feminists in the local state bureaucracy has been the setting up of women's committees. Susan Halford's work (1989, 1991, 1992 this volume) takes stock of this feminist strategy and her case studies of a number of local authorities not only provide valuable insights into the processes whereby gender relations become embedded in bureaucratic organizations generally, but also add further grist to the mill to recent feminist challenges to existing, overly functionalist theorisations of the relation between the state and gender. Halford stresses the problematic nature of the state for feminists, for the state is implicated in gender inequality at the same time as it provides a vehicle for meeting feminist goals. It is the recognition of this latter quality that led feminists aligned to socialist politics to press for change in local government. Halford believes that local state institutions may in principle bring about some positive changes for women, but that the gendered dynamics of local government structures and cultures generate powerful and pervasive resistance to positive policies for women. Halford's chapter is important precisely because it does focus on the bureaucratic institutions of the local state, thus drawing out the implications of experiences of women's initiatives in local government for a broader understanding of both gender and the local state, as well as of women's experiences of bureaucratic organization *per se*. Halford concludes on both an optimistic and a pessimistic note, pointing to the measure of success achieved by women's initiatives in creating feminist modes of organizing activity within male-dominated local authority bureaucracies, but also noting how women have met with rather less success in challenging broader male-dominated bureaucratic structures, which continue to operate according to male discourses of rationality and to be underpinned by gendered organizational culture and hierarchies of status and power.

The realization by feminists that an understanding of the nature and operation of the state bureaucracy is a vital, and yet neglected, aspect of feminist theory of the state and gender is not necessarily leading feminists along the same trajectory of theorization. We have seen how a feminist post-structuralist trajectory of theorizing the relation between the state and gender has led writers such as Watson, Pringle and Allen to deconstruct the state into a 'site' rather than a 'structure' and to stress the incohate and fragile nature of sets of power interests forged in state arenas. But another recent trajectory of theorizing has been to strengthen a Weberian analysis of the state as an 'institutional ensemble', and to stress the importance of the linkages between the bureaucratic institutions of the modern state and those of civil society (cf Franzway, Court and Connell, 1989; Witz, 1992). Like Susan Halford in this volume, writers incorporating insights from a Weberian perspective insist that the state has a double-edged character in that the state institutionalizes the interests of men (although in different ways and to varying extents) and yet at the same time has been a vehicle for advances in the position of women. The state is thus seen 'as a realm of practice whose core is an institutionalization of power relations' (Franzway *et al*, 1989:35) and it is recognized that 'bureaucracy, the form of institutionalization central to the modern state, is marked both by a strong sexual division of labour (. . .) and by a cultural masculinisation of authority' (Franzway *et al*, 1989: 46). Reconceptualizing the state as an institutional ensemble, recognizing the centrality of bureau-cratic organization to the ways in which modern states act, and acknowledging that patriarchal interests have to be continuously represented through state institutions along with other competing sets of interests, provides an alternative to feminist theories of the state to that which deconstructs and dissolve it into simply another set of discursive strategies of power.

5 The Sexuality of Organization

As we indicated above, some recent writing has shifted the focus from gender and organizations to sexuality in organizations. We will show how there is a certain tension between writers who focus on 'gender' and those who focus on 'sexuality', particularly as the turn towards sexuality has been effected within a Foucauldian or post-structuralist framework of organizational analysis. This tension relates to the underlying conceptualization of power and gender within organizations. Tensions, however, may be productive. One way of expressing this tension is as follows. Do bureaucratic organizational structures formalize masculine modes of social action to the extent that we can talk of these as patriarchal structures, in both the nominal and substantive sense of being staffed by men and representing men's interests in organizing the world? Or are organizational power relations more fluid and diffuse than this, embedded not in 'structures', but in discourses?

The turn to sexuality which we are currently witnessing in radical organization theory raises a whole host of issues which go somewhat deeper than the question of whether men and women behave differently in the world. The sexuality paradigm sees gender as underpinned by the more complex embeddedness of sexuality, of our bodily existences in organizations, and assumes that by analysing sexuality you also analyse gender. Whilst the turn to sexuality has been welcomed by some, it has been regarded by others with deep suspicion. There is a danger that sexuality becomes valorized, and there is a tendency in much of the literature on organizational sexuality to slip over the fuzzy edges between 'sexuality' and 'gender'. This is largely because both gender *and* sexuality are seen as socially and historically constructed, but it is the Foucauldian 'technology of sex' which is displacing or obscuring from view 'technologies of gender'. Foucault provides a crucial underpinning for the sexuality and organization paradigm, particularly his view that 'the body is . . . directly involved in a political field; power relations have an immediate hold upon it; they invest it, mark it, train it, force it to carry out tasks, to perform ceremonies, to emit signs' (1977:27). Thus sexuality assumes central importance in the utilization of power; it becomes subject to control through a proliferation of discourses concerned with sexuality, referred to by Foucault as a 'discursive ferment that gathered momentum from the 18th century onwards' (1979:18). The analysis, stocktaking, classification and specification of sexuality derives from the growth of rationality and becomes a matter for administration and management.

Since Foucault a proliferation of academic discourses on sexuality in bureaucratic organizations has emerged. Gibson Burrell (1984), one of the initiators of this academic discourse on organizational sexuality, is aware of the seeming paradox that, given Foucault's thesis about the proliferation of discourse on sexuality, it has been strangely absent from organization theory. Gibson Burrell also admits the irony of the fact that the prospect of an eroticized sociology of organization has been opened by male academics, and that its relation to feminist scholarship remains a considerable problem. This is not to say that feminist scholars are not participating in this turn towards a sexuality paradigm, but that the emerging dialogue between feminist and organizational theories, to which we drew attention earlier, is proceeding on terms and within agendas initiated by male theorists, not the least of whom is Foucault.

In their pioneering and important publication, *'Sex' at 'Work'*, Jeff Hearn and Wendy Parkin refer to the 'booming silence' about sexuality in the mountainous literature on organizations which, one might be led to conclude, are inhabited by a breed of strange, asexual figures. Similarly, Mills (1989) criticises organization and management theorists for presenting a picture of corporate reality which excludes gender from the dynamics of organizational experience and from the construction of organizational culture. Gibson Burrell (1984) declares that the issue of sex is one which organizational analysis has avoided for too long. And yet, for those of us with more finely tuned sexual antennae, it is claimed that:

> Enter most organisations and you enter a world of sexuality.
> . . . This can include a mass of sexual displays, feelings,
> fantasies, and innuendoes, as part of everyday organizational

life, right through to sexual relationships, open or secret,
occasional sexual acts, and sexual violations, including rape.
(Hearn and Parkin 1987:3)

As we discussed earlier, Weber still sets the terms of the
dominant discourse on power and organizations and, although
organization theory is very much bent on demonstrating the
limitations of Weber's model, his fundamental premises are not
disputed. We saw how Weber has been criticised by organization
theorists for what he did not see, such as the informal as distinct
from the formal modes of organizational activities. In one sense,
the growing literature on sexuality and organizations represents a
continuation of this tradition. But the recent literature on sexuality
in organizations, as distinct from mainstream organization theory,
is particularly interesting because it also suggests a rather more
thoroughgoing critique of bureaucracy.

Whilst writers like Burrell (1984) adopt a starting point which
declares that the historical process of desexualization parallels
those of rationalization and capitalism, others (Hearn and Parkin
1987, Pringle 1989b) want to establish that sexuality is very much
at work within organizational settings themselves. Thus, we see
two ways in which current writers key their analyses of sexuality
and organizations into Weber's classic account of bureaucracy:
one which 'adds on' a historical dimension neglected by Weber
–the process of desexualization; the other which 'adds in'
sexualization as a fundamental, but neglected, structuring principle
of bureaucracy.

Gibson Burrell's early work (1984) in this area represents the
'add on' approach in the sense that he calls attention to an
historical process of the desexualization of labour, which involved
the repulsion and expulsion of many human feelings out of the
organization. The process of organizational desexualization has
historical roots in the civilizing process, the development of
religious morality, the development of calculative rationality and
the development of control over time and the body. In the course
of the civilizing process since the Middle Ages (Elias, 1978)
sexuality is subject to ever stricter control through social constraint
and individual restraint. Another process from the later medieval
period onward was the transformation of the Catholic Church into
a centralized bureaucratic hierarchy and the creation of a set of
sexual taboos to eradicate sexuality as far as possible from the
medieval Catholic Church. Linked to the civilizing process and

bureaucratization was the development of purposive rationality and its concrete expression in legal rational bureaucracies. Sexuality becomes further sublimated in the interests of calculative rationality, and a political economy of sexuality emerges in the capitalist labour process through the introduction of time discipline and body discipline. There become times and spaces for work, and times and spaces for non-work activities, within which sexual activity becomes subsumed. A neglected aspect of Weber's thesis concerning the causal links between the protestant ethic and the spirit of capitalism is how 'Puritan accountancy, which emphasized savings and discourages consumption, thus found itself reflected in the balance sheet of the body' (Burrell, 1984:108), as too much expenditure of sexual energy is said to sap energy that could be put to more productive use in the workplace.

In Burrell's analysis, then, organizational desexualization becomes a dimension of the development of modern administrative forms neglected by Weber. However, although Burrell wants to suggest that sexuality still pervades organizations, for '. . . one suspects that much activity of a sexual nature takes place', he is forced to see sexuality as an 'underlife' of the organization rather than as itself a pervasive structuring principle. This approach contrasts with other writers who see sexuality as more embedded within organizations, and who therefore 'add in' sexuality to our conceptualization of organizational realities.

These writers effectively pose a fundamental challenge to Weber's account of bureaucracy precisely because they 'add in' sexuality into the bureaucratic phenomenon, rather than tacitly accept organizational life as purposively rational and hence desexualized. Hearn and Parkin (1987) represent the 'add in' tradition for they claim that 'Sexuality although often subjugated to the demands and powers of organizations has a power and a *potential power* of its own' (Hearn and Parkin 1987:61). So they argue that work organizations both construct sexuality *and* are constructed by and through sexuality; that they are, in themselves, arenas of sexual practices. Sexuality is not banished from the bureaucratic arena. Neither are sexual practices illicit organizational activities as Gibson Burrell suggests. However, as Adkins points out in this collection, Hearn and Parkin, although they appear to be foregounding sexuality in organization, ultimately reduce instances of sexuality, such as sexual harassment and displays of pornography, to a by-product of capitalist processes. In addition, Adkins claims, they simultaneously essentialize and naturalize heterosexual relations, which simply become 'acted out' under capitalist work relations. But why, asks Adkins, should capitalist hierarchies call into being a sexuality in which women are sexually exploited by men? These are pertinent criticisms of Hearn and Parkin's work.

Another representative of the 'add in' tradition is Rosemary Pringle (1989a, 1989b). The argument that sexuality provides a tacit resource in the very construction of the male bureaucrat and his modes of being and acting is fleshed out considerably in Pringle's (1989a) book *Secretaries Talk*, in which she demonstrates how the relative positioning of men and women within bureaucratic workplace organizations draws heavily on discourses of sexuality. It is through the sexual positioning of women vis-a-vis men within organizations that the relations of power and authority within bureaucracies are gendered. Pringle adds in sexuality to organization by reading an unthematized gender sub-text *into* Weber's account of the shifting basis of social action and the emergence of the bureaucratic organization form. The unthematized gender sub-text in Weber's account of 'rationality' is specified by Pringle (1989b). She argues that Weber essentially provides a commentary on the construction of a particular kind of masculinity based on the exclusion of the personal, the sexual and the feminine from any definition of 'rationality'; this is the gender sub-text. So, whilst the rational-legal, bureaucratic form presents itself in Weber's analysis as gender neutral, it in fact constitutes a new kind of patriarchal structure where 'The apparent neutrality of rules and goals disguises the class and gender interests served by men' (Pringle 1989b:161).

Perhaps the most comprehensive 'state of the art' collection on sexuality in organizations is that edited by Jeff Hearn, Deborah Sheppard, Peta Tancred-Sheriff and Gibson Burrell, *The Sexuality of Organization* (1989). Contributors to Hearn *et al* (1989) provide important insights into gender, sexuality and organizational structure. A number of compelling paradoxes emerge. It is men who use or deploy their sexuality at work far more than women, and yet it is women's workplace identity that is frequently saturated with sexuality (Gutek 1989). But of course this becomes less paradoxical once it is clearly established that the real nub of the matter is that it is *heterosexuality* which structures organizations, and within which men establish both their difference from women – as they simultaneously forge a male homosociability – *and* their power over them. Catherine MacKinnon is correct to urge us not to analytically separate sexual difference from dominance. These are not separate moments; they are mutually forged.

Adrien Rich (1983) has spoken of 'compulsory heterosexuality' and it is this which pervades organizational structures and daily interactions. This is vividly demonstrated by Marny Hall's (1989) analysis of the lesbian corporate experience, where she argues that lesbian women are liable to experience double jeopardy because of their gender as women and their lesbianism as sexual orientation. Most of the lesbians Marny Hall interviewed did not disclose their lesbianism, not even (or especially?) to other women in the organization. This leads to inevitable schisms between lesbians' 'private' and organizational existences and, for some, constant anxiety about discovery. However, in Marny Hall's discussion of lesbians in organizations we do begin to see how 'gender' and 'sexuality' are dislocated within our own experiences of organizations. Several women expressed the view that their lesbianism, because of its 'invisibility', was less of a hindrance than their gender, which they could not disguise.

The latent theme of 'compulsory heterosexuality' underscores how women's organizational experiences are defined and controlled by men, for whom sexuality becomes a resource in creating and affirming the gender order at work (cf Gutek, 1989). David and Margaret Collinson (1989) demonstrate how it is men's (hetero)-sexuality which is dominant in the workplace. Their case studies of three organizations reveal how male sexuality is privileged and embedded within organizational practices, but particularly how, paradoxically, the apparent desexualization of organizational life masks the fact that male (hetero)sexuality saturates and sets the tacitly agreed parameters of organizational practices. Thus, management in the three organizations studied tended to be either blind to, tolerate or even accept traditional forms of male sexuality. Male 'sexual drive' discourse on the shop floor and amongst white collar executives serve to exclude women from sexualized male spaces and maintain their dominant executive positions, and the use (or abuse) of hierarchical power by superordinate men to facilitate sexual relationships with subordinate women leads David and Margaret Collinson to argue that men's sexuality and organizational power are inextricably linked.

The embeddedness of male sexuality within organizations means that (hetero)sexuality is at one and the same time a tacit structuring principle and a resource to be drawn upon. There is an important sense in which men are 'already there' in bureaucratic workplace organizations and organizational women are intruders in a male domain. Consequently, women who attempt to position themselves in organizational spaces or offices where men 'already are' have to devise elaborate strategies for managing their sexuality. The hidden agenda here is that women have to pre-empt the possibility of their sexualization by men. At the same time, they must behave like men but not *be* men and behave unlike women and yet be women. This is the paradox of women's organizational experiences. And yet it appears that men find it extraordinarily difficult to desexualize women.

Deborah Sheppard (1989) reveals how organizational women have to be constantly vigilant not to 'call up' their own sexualization by men. Modes of dress have to be gendered (skirts) and yet not sexualized (skirts not too short). One women manager interviewed by Deborah Sheppard relates how, after a successful completion of an arduous department auditing procedure, the male vice-president with whom she had been working commented 'You know you're a real sexy broad'. She immediately looked to the fact that she had been wearing a red dress as evoking that response. The strategies deployed by women to manage the personal boundaries related to sexuality and gender ranged from 'blending in' by being 'feminine enough' (in appearance and self-presentation) at the same time as 'businesslike' (in behaviour) to a 'rightful place' one, which asserts or raises gender (as femaleness) to a level of awareness that is challenging or threatening to the male status quo. Interestingly, both strategies involve being 'not sexy', whilst they vary along the dimension of 'behaving or being like a woman'. Sheppard provides an explicit and unambiguous definition of sexuality in terms of *eroticism*. In effect, the management of femaleness and maleness entails both the management of behaviour and the presentation of the body on view in a public space, with a view to the reaction the particular mode of presenting the body calls up in the other. But within organizational settings, men simultaneously de-eroticise their own bodily presentation (the grey suit) and constantly eroticise women's bodily presentation. If it is through our bodies that we present our selves, then we can begin to unwrap this central paradox of organizational life: which is that the desexualization of the male bureaucrat is paralleled by the sexualization of women subordinates.

Tellingly, in the editorial postscript to *The Sexuality of Organisation* (Hearn *et al* 1989), an issue that is far from resolved and indeed identified as an 'emerging theme of the book' is that of the precise nature of the relationship between sexuality, gender and organizational structures. However, the editors' real point here is that issues relating to gender and sexuality have been neglected within organization theory, when, in our view, it is the nature of the relation between gender and sexuality *within* the context of organization theory which emerges as an unproblematized theme in this collection. When is a mode of acting or of being 'genderised' and when is it 'sexualized'? Where does sexuality end or begin in relation to gender? Isn't an important political point being elided in much of the literature on sexuality and organization, which is the *choice* of terminology in workplace studies. Why do we choose to refer to gender or to sexuality? Ironically, contributors' choice of the term 'sexuality' is sometimes arbitrary – it is not, for example, necessarily linked into a Foucauldian framework which dissolves gender as a structuring principle into strategic discourses on sexuality. But the whole point of 'gendering' sociological discourse itself has been to establish how male dominance and male power is embedded in and sustained by *social* practices, not premissed on biological imperatives. This was the political reason for the choice of terminology by feminist workplace theorists in the 1970s: to escape the tyranny of 'biologizing' women. The current state of play is that, whereas the use of the term 'gender' usefully counteracted a 'oversexualized' version of womanhood, the use of the term 'sexuality' ambiguously counteracts an 'overgenderized' version of womanhood. In neither version has the question of the nature of the relation *between* sexuality and gender been adequately resolved. There is a considerable amount of worrying slippage between the two terms, gender and sexuality, as well as a hint of tautology.

All this new talk about 'sexuality' in organization alerts us to previously neglected, and indeed 'censored', aspects of organizational life. Whilst we applaud the new agendas for discussion that are being created, we nevertheless wish to emphasize our qualms about the over-hasty displacement of the 'gender paradigm' and the over-eager substitution or slippage into the 'sexuality paradigm'. We think that issues relating to causality, particularly the interrelation between gender and sexuality, remain vital issues, and yet these are getting lost. Even if these issues are addressed, which they frequently are (cf Burrell & Hearn, 1989), they are simply never satisfactorily resolved. We would argue that this is because the turn to sexuality is accompanying the turn to post-modernism in the study of organization, and that this is why questions of the relation between gender and sexuality, and particularly issues of causality, can never be satisfactorily resolved. Instead, we are left with seamless webs. 'Organizations are seen as scenes of power, both gendered and sexual', '. . . sexuality and organization suffuse each other', '. . . organization is incorporated into sexuality', 'the production and reproduction of organization are part of the social organization of sexuality' (Burrell & Hearn, 1989:26, 19, 18). Ultimately, sexuality is seen as an all-pervasive 'politics of the body' rather than a separable, discrete set of practices (Burrell & Hearn, 1989). There is constant reference in the literature to the fact that the relationships of sexuality and sex, and gender and sex are 'problematic' (cf. Burrell & Hearn, 1989) and yet the question of their precise relationship remains elusive. We suggest that, in short, this is because this question cannot be addressed with organizational sexuality paradigms that rely so heavily on Foucault, but can only remain obscure within such a framework – and, indeed, that theorists of sexuality and organization are incautiously throwing out 'gender' with 'modernism', regarding the former category of analysis with its structural underpinnings as tainted by the latter.

A number of contributors to this volume are similarly sceptical about recent post-modernist trends in organizational theory and about the 'turn to sexuality'. Rosemary Crompton and Nicola Le Feuvre, whilst accepting that some aspects of the post-modernist paradigm of organization are valid, nonetheless warn against jettisoning a formal bureaucratic model of organizations. Their detailed empirical case study of women's career strategies in banking in France and Britain demonstrates that the notion of a 'bureaucratic career' still has considerable explanatory mileage, so they urge feminist writers not to reject completely established strategies of 'mainstream' organizational analysis in favour of post-modernist approaches. Indeed, they show how insights from the two approaches may be fruitfully combined. Celia Davies's analysis of nurses' management style reveals how we have barely begun to understand the complex processes underpinning the gendering of work as an ongoing, daily accomplishment – and her analysis suggests that feminist labour market theorists have perhaps focussed too much on structures and not enough on processes. Lisa Adkins's contribution throws down the gauntlet to those working within both the 'gender' and the 'sexuality' paradigm. She argues that feminist labour market theorists have paid insufficient attention to the ways in which sexuality structures workplace relations thus neglecting, for example, the ways in which the sexual commodification of women's labour provides a vital underpinning of occupational segregation. Equally, theorists who do consider sexuality and organizations focus on the sexuality, but neglect the gendering, of organization, particularly the ways in which sexuality structures gender relations and how male dominance structures both coercive and non-coercive heterosexual interactions between men and women. The concept of 'sexual work' is developed by Adkins to capture the double-edged nature of women's workplace activities, in that they engage simultaneously in economic production and sexual servicing of men, who in their capacity as either workers or customers, appropriate women's sexual servicing work. In short, women have literally to work heterosexually in ways defined and controlled by men.

6 Conclusions

We have suggested that the most debated areas in the study of gender and bureaucracy tended to move us away from the crucial issues laid down by Kanter, Pringle, and Ferguson. Although feminist work on the state proliferates, very little of this addresses the crucial issues of how the state is a bureaucratic institution, and examines how this affects its patriarchal nature. And, despite the enormous growth of interest in organizational sexuality, there are good grounds for being suspicious of research in this area. All too often, it appears the examination of sexuality removes the focus from the wider field of gender relations. This is not to say that there is not a series of valuable insights from these two areas of inquiry, but rather to say that these two debates should not be confused with a wider debate about the gendering of organizations.

It is our belief, therefore, that the research agenda on gender and bureaucracy should return to the gender paradigm which we have identified in this essay. The centrepiece of this perspective is the relationship between gender and power within organizational settings. We have argued that this involves moving away from formalist analyses of bureaucracies towards a recognition of both how they are shaped by specific struggles and how they in turn lead to specific types of gender configurations. We have argued that it is necessary to investigate how gender is embedded within different power relations, but that it is essential not to let this emphasis slide into the more specific issue of sexuality.

This essay has served as a ground clearing exercise, which has allowed us to indicate how a gender paradigm of organizations might be built up, and the types of issues it would address. Yet clearly there is a lot to do, and we are aware that a number of issues remain to be resolved. We have indicated at various points how individual articles in this collection might contribute towards this perspective, and we conclude by explaining how they have been placed in the volume for this purpose.

One of our central arguments concerns the historical specificity of organizational forms and the fact that they are inevitably shaped by a wide variety of social forces, gender notably amongst them. Organizations are the embodiment of different forms of patriarchal power relations, which themselves set the stage for further conflicts, so that organizations are constantly changing in a fluid way. This is not to say that in certain periods a certain organizational type may gain a certain fixity – we have suggested as much for the 'classic' modern bureaucracy. But these cannot be regarded as a permanent settlement.

The first set of papers take up these questions of the *histories* of organizations. Meta Zimmeck considers the employment of women in the Post Office between 1870 and 1920. This was one of the first large employers of women clerical workers and Zimmeck shows how women were initially welcomed into the workforce as cheap and pliable labour. As soon as women began to organize and demand better pay and conditions, the attitude of male superiors changed and after 1900 steps were taken to ensure women were fixed firmly into subordinate roles. Zimmeck is able to show that women's condition of entry into organizational employment is that they are subordinate and that any attempt to challenge this is met with firm male resistance.

Rosemary Crompton and Nicola Le Feuvre also consider a similar issue, the influx of women employed in managerial jobs in banking in Britain and France. As in the case described by Zimmeck, the introduction of women in senior positions was heralded by some as a major breakthrough and an indication that there were no real barriers to women earning promotion to senior posts. Crompton, however, shows that women in both France and Britain faced similar problems in developing their careers, and that the bureaucratic, organizational career designed by and for men cannot easily accommodate women.

Mike Savage takes up the same point in a different way. He shows that although women have moved into professional and managerial employment in Britain in the past twenty years there is little evidence that they have moved into positions of real organizational authority. Rather, they are channelled into positions demanding high levels of expertise but generally little real power. Using a case study of banking, Savage shows how the increasing numbers of women managers is linked to a widespread restructuring of the bank organization, involving the concentration of power and authority at senior levels of the bank, and that there are remarkably few cases of women who reach these levels.

The three papers in the *Histories* section all show that the entry of women into organizational employment, or their entry into new types of jobs within bureaucracies does not mean that women gain access to significant power. Rather, women tend to enter specialized subordinate positions. The nature of these positions obviously changes over time, and there are large differences between Zimmeck's women clerks and Crompton's and Savage's women managers, but they are all similar in being excluded from the channels of power.

The second section examines the success of feminist *strategies* for changing the patriarchal nature of bureaucracies. Susan Halford begins by examining the fate of feminist initiatives in British local government. These feminist initiatives, which achieved a high profile in the early and mid 1980s as many local authorities set up Women's Initiatives to tackle gender discrimination, have actually had limited access. Halford shows how this is largely due to the strategies used by male bureaucrats within local government to undermine these new developments, and she shows how this can be seen as a typical element of male bureaucracy.

Sophie Watson's paper examines the femocrat strategy in Australia, and compares this with feminism in Britain, which remains more rooted in a politics of social class. She shows how Australian feminism has developed an interest in 'feminisms of difference' related to post-structuralist currents, and discusses the emergence of the 'femocrat', and the issues this raises for theories of the state.

The final section *Theories*, develops particular theoretical issues which we have identified as being crucial to the gender paradigm. Lisa Adkins examines one specific area of interest, that in organizations and sexuality, and subjects Pringle's and Cockburn's analysis to serious criticism. She shows that these writers do not examine the heterosexual male construction of sexuality at work, and do not recognize the co-ercive nature of sexuality as experienced by women. This argument is backed up by detailed research of employment relations in tourism.

Celia Davies analyses the nature of 'gender talk' in nursing. Nursing is an interesting case since it has historically emerged as a female occupation, and hence lacked the characteristic gendered hierarchy found in other organizations. Davies examines whether, in this case, a gender analysis becomes irrelevant, and shows that even in a largely female occupation, gender issues pervade many aspects of the job, especially issues of management style.

Finally, Karen Ramsey and Martin Parker discuss the gendered nature of organizational culture. Engaging in a debate with Weber, they argue that the structure of bureaucratic rationality should be seen as a crucial ingredient behind the gendering of organizational cultures. They argue that gendered assumptions are built into superficially innocent areas of organizational life, and in a way reminiscent of Ferguson, suggest that feminism needs to find other, non-bureaucratic ways of organizing.

References

Acker, J., (1973), 'Women and Social Stratification: a case of intellectual sexism', in J. Huber (ed.), *Changing Women in Changing Society*, Chicago: University of Chicago Press.

Albrow, M., (1970), *Bureaucracy*, London: Pall Mall.

Allen, J., (1990), 'Does feminism need a theory of the state', in Watson S. (ed.), *Playing the State*, London: Verso.

Anderson, G., (ed.) (1989), *The White Blouse Revolution*, Manchester: Manchester University Press.

Bacchi, C.L., (1990), *Same Difference?: Feminism and Sexual Difference*, Sydney: Allen and Unwin.

Barrett, M., (1980), *Women's Oppression Today*, London: Verso.

Banks, O., (1981), *Faces of Feminism*, Oxford: Martin Robertson.

Bologh, R.W., (1990), *Love or Greatness. Max Weber and Masculine Thinking; a feminist inquiry*, London: Unwin Hyman.

Brown, H., (1992), *Women Organising*, London and New York: Routledge.

Burrell, G., (1984), 'Sex and Organisational Analysis', *Organization Studies*, 5, 2, pp. 97–110.

Burrell, G. and Hearn, J., (1989), 'The Sexuality of Organisation', in J. Hearn *et al* (eds), *The Sexuality of Organization*, London: Sage.

Chodorow, N., (1978), *The Reproduction of Mothering*, Berkeley: University of California Press.

Clegg, S., (1989), *Frameworks of Power*, London: Sage.

Clegg, S., (1990), *Modern Organisations*, London: Sage.

Cockburn, C., (1981), *Brothers: Male Dominance and Technical Change*, London: Pluto.

Cockburn, C., (1991), *In the Way of Women: Men's Resistance to Sex Equality in Organizations*, Basingstoke: MacMillan.

Cohn, S., (1985), *The Process of Occupational Sex Typing: the feminisation of clerical labour in Great Britain*, Philadelphia: Philadelphia University Press.

Collinson, D.L. and Collinson, M.C., (1989), 'Sexuality in the Workplace: the domination of men's sexuality', in J. Hearn *et al* (eds), *The Sexuality of Organisation*, London: Sage.

Connell, R.W., (1986), *Gender and Power*, Oxford: Blackwells.

Corrigan, P. and Sayer, D., (1985), *The Great Arch*, Oxford: Blackwells.

Craib, I., (1984), *Modern Social Theory*, Brighton: Wheatsheaf.

Crompton, R., (1986), 'Women and the Service Class', in R. Crompton and M. Mann (eds), *Gender and Stratification*, Cambridge, Polity.

Crompton, R. and Jones, G., (1984), *A White Collar Proletariat? Deskilling and Gender in Clerical Work*, Basingstoke: Macmillan.

Crozier, M., (1964), *The Bureaucratic Phenomenon*, London: Tavistock.

Eisenstein, H., (1990), 'Femocrats, Official feminism and the uses of power', in S. Watson (ed.), *Playing the State*, London: Verso.

Eisenstein, H., (1991), *Gender Shock: Practising Feminism on Two Continents*, Sydney: Allen and Unwin.

Eisenstein, Z.R., (1981), *The Radical Future of Liberal Feminism*, New York: Longman.

Eisenstein, Z.R., (1984), *Feminism and Sexual Equality*, New York: Monthly Review Press.

Elias, N., (1978), *The Civilising Process*, Oxford: Blackwells.

Enloe, C., (1983), *Khaki Becomes You*, London: Pluto.

Franzway, S. Court, D. and Connell, R.W., (1989), *Staking a Claim: Feminism, Bureaucracy and the State*, Cambridge: Polity.

Freeman, J., (1975), *The Politics of Women's Liberation*, London: Longman.

Ferguson, K.E. (1984), *The Feminist Case Against Bureaucracy*, Philadelphia: Temple University Press.

Foucault, M., (1961), *Madness and Civilisation*, London: Tavistock.

Foucault, M., (1965), *The Birth of the Clinic*, London: Tavistock.

Foucault, M., (1977), *Discipline and Punish*, London: Allen Lane.

Foucault, M., (1979), *The History of Sexuality*, (vol 1), London: Allen Lane.

Foucault, M., (1984), *A History of Sexuality*, London: Peregrine.

Giddens, A., (1984), *The Constitution of Society*, Oxford: Polity.

Giddens, A., (1982), in A. Giddens and G. MacKenzie, *Social Class and the Division of Labour*, Cambridge: Cambridge University Press.

Gilligan, C., (1982), *In a Different Voice*, Cambridge Mass: Harvard University Press.

Gouldner, A., (1954), *Patterns of Industrial Bureaucracy*, New York: Free Press.

Gutek, B.A., (1989), 'Sexuality in the workplace: key issues in social research and organisational practice', in J. Hearn *et al* (eds), *The Sexuality of Organisation*, London: Sage.

Hall, M., (1989), 'Private Experiences in the public domain: lesbians in organisations', in J. Hearn *et al* (eds), *The Sexuality of Organization*, London: Sage.

Hartsock, N., (1987), 'The feminist standpoint: developing the ground for a specifically feminist historical materialism', in S. Harding (ed.), *Feminism and Methodology*, Milton Keynes: Open University Press.

Hearn, J. and Parkin, W., (1987), *'Sex' at 'Work' the power and paradox of organisation sexuality*, Brighton: Wheatsheaf.

Hearn, J., Sheppard, D.L., Tancred-Sheriff, P. and Burrell, G., (1989), *The Sexuality of Organisation*, London: Sage.

Kanter, R.M., (1977), *Men and Women of the Corporation*, New York: Basic.

Land, H., (1976), 'Women; Supporters or Supported', in S. Allen and D.L. Barker, *Sexual Divisions in Society*, Basingstoke: MacMillan.

Mackintosh, M., (1978), 'The state and the oppression of women', in A.M. Wolpe and A. Kuhn (eds), *Feminism and Materialism*, London: Routledge.

MacKinnon, C., (1982), 'Feminism, Marxism, method and the state: an agenda for theory', in N.O. Keohane, M.Z. Rosaldo, B.C. Gelpi (eds), *Feminist Theory: A Critique of Ideology*, Brighton: Harvester.

MacKinnon, C., (1987), *Towards a Feminist Theory of the State*, Cambridge, Mass: Harvard University Press.

Mark-Lawson, J. and Witz, A., (1986), 'From "Family Labour" to "Family Wage"? The case of women's labour in 19th century coal-mining', *Social History*, 13, 2 pp. 151–174.

Mills, A., (1989), 'Gender, Sexuality and Organization Theory', in J. Hearn *et al, The Sexuality of Organization*, London: Sage.

Morgan, G., (1986), *Images of Organisation*, London: Sage.

Oakley, A., (1974), *Housewife*, London: Allen Lane.

Pringle, R., (1989a), *Secretaries Talk: Sexuality, Power and Work*, London and New York: Verso.

Pringle, R., (1989b), 'Bureaucracies, Rationality and Sexuality: the case of secretaries', in J. Hearn *et al* (eds), *The Sexuality of Organization*, London: Sage.

Pringle, R. and Watson, S., (1990), 'Fathers, Brothers, Mates: the Fraternal State in Australia', in S. Watson (ed.), *Playing the State*, London: Verso.

Pringle, R. and Watson, S., (1992), ' "Women's interests" and the post-structuralist state', in M. Barrett and A. Phillipps (eds), *Destabilizing Theory: Contemporary Feminist Debates*, Cambridge: Polity.

Rich, A., (1983), *Compulsory Heterosexuality and Lesbian Existence*, London: Onlywomen Press.

Rothschild-Witt, J., (1982), 'The Collectivist Organization: an alternative to bureaucratic models', in F. Lidenfield and J. Rothschild-Whitt (eds), *Workplace Bureaucracy and Social Change*, Boston: Porter Sargent.

Savage, M., (1992), 'Gender and Career Mobility in Banking 1880–1940', in A. Miles and D. Vincent (eds), *Building European Society*, Manchester: Manchester University Press.

Savage, M., Barlow, J., Dickens, P. and Fielding, A.J., (1992), *Property, Bureaucracy and Culture: Middle Class Formation in Contemporary Britain*, London: Routledge.

Seccombe, W., (1974), 'The Housewife and her labour under capitalism', *New Left Review*, 83, 3–24.

Smith, D.E., (1987a), *The Everyday World as Problematic*, Milton Keynes: Open University.

Smith, D.E., (1987b), 'Women's perspectives as a radical critique of sociology', in S. Harding (ed.), *Feminism and Methodology*, Milton Keynes: Open University Press.

Walby, S., (1986), *Patriarchy at work*, Cambridge: Polity.

Walby, S., (1990), *Theorising Patriarchy*, Oxford: Basil Blackwell.

Weber, M., (1968), *Economy and Society*, University of California.

Witz, A., (1992), *Patriarchy and Professions*, London: Routledge.

Zimmeck, M., (1988), 'The New Women and the Machinery of Government: a spanner in the works', in R. McLeod (ed.), *Government and Expertise: Specialists, Administrators and Professionals 1860–1919*, Cambridge: Cambridge University Press.

Histories

Marry in haste, repent at leisure: women, bureaucracy and the post office, 1870-1920

Meta Zimmeck

Between these two extremes [of caring for children and manual labour] there lies what may be called a neutral or debatable ground of labour requiring the exercise of qualities which are the exclusive property of neither sex. It is in this neutral field . . . [that] the activities of women are confined to those departments of the labour market into which men do not care, or actively object, to enter. Thus, if there were no question of economic competition, it seems to me that the invasion by woman of these departments . . . formerly monopolized by men would be bound to awaken a certain amount of opposition; since her consequent desertion of the dull, unpleasant, and monotonous tasks assigned to her, might mean that these tasks would have to be performed by those who had hitherto escaped the necessity by shifting it on to her shoulders. Hence a natural and comprehensible resentment.[1]

One of the most useful interpretive tools for understanding the structure, processes and culture of bureaucracy has been provided by Kanter who, basing her work on the principle of 'proportion as a significant insight of social life,' has explored the internal dynamics of groups. She outlines four types of groups: (1) uniform, with exclusively one kind of member; (2) skewed, with a large preponderance of one sub-group, dominants, over another, tokens, in a ratio of, say, 85:15; (3) tilted, with more balance between a majority and a minority in a ratio of, say, 65:35; and (4) balanced, with sub-groups participating on terms of equality in a ratio of, say, 60:40 or 50:50. Kanter's mode of analysis is remarkably open and flexible. Although each type has characteristic processes of interaction, the content of the interaction is determined by the group's specific circumstances. Kanter recognizes, indeed

© *The Sociological Review* 1992. Published by Blackwell Publishers.

welcomes, class (although in a somewhat muted way), gender, race, ethnicity, religion, sexuality, physical impairment or disability, and age as factors which may define sub-groups in interaction. In this way she transcends the tug of war between capitalism and patriarchy, class and gender which has dominated the debate about labour market segmentation and the tortuous rethinking which is advocated when an additional factor is sought to be added to the causal menu.[2] Moreover, although Kanter's analysis is presented in terms of dyads (women/men, black people/white people, old people/young people, etc.), it naturally leads to a pluralistic analysis – taking into account simultaneously all factors which are required adequately to describe specific circumstances. And, although Kanter's analysis, on the whole, is discontinuous (concentrated on skewed groups), it nevertheless posits 'tipping points' at which one type of group is transformed into another. It thus lends itself to historical analysis.[3]

The Civil Service in the years 1870 to 1920 provides a case study, albeit a partial one, of Kanter's typology as historical process. Other than the statistically pyrotechnical Cohn (who, however, fails to provide basic longitudinal data) there has been no explicitly quantitative analysis of the employment of women in the Civil Service. Given the unavailability and/or unsuitability of the data, studies have taken a predominantly narrative approach based on qualitative materials.[4] Before 1870 the non-manipulative Civil Service was male.[5] However, by 1914 women comprised 21 per cent of total staff. The First World War stimulated a great influx of women temporary workers to provide replacements for men serving in the Forces and to fill posts created by the expanded role of the state. At the Armistice women were in the majority, 56 per cent of the total. These gains proved ephemeral and were decimated by the Treasury's 'reconstruction' programme, which gave unprecedented priority to ex-servicemen and corralled women into the lower reaches of the grading structure. By 1923 women constituted 25 per cent and by 1938 27 per cent of total staff – that is, a gain of only 6 per cent since 1914.[6] Thus the Civil Service prior to 1870 was a uniform organization (all men), but by 1914 it had developed into a skewed organization with men as dominants and women as tokens. The transition from a skewed organization to a tilted organization and onwards, which the First World War had foreshadowed, failed to take place until well after the Second World War.[7] Thus, it would seem, between 1870 and 1920 there were two tipping points, or more accurately, one tipping point around 1870 and another, more diffuse, of *inversus interruptus*.

These tipping points demarcated two phases in the employment of women civil servants. The first was a honeymoon which began in 1870, when the Post Office inadvertently acquired women telegraphists in its nationalization of telegraph companies. With the exception of some diehard misogynists, mandarins viewed as 'highly beneficial'[8] the engagement of women on certain types of work, and, once women had demonstrated competence, provided additional opportunities. Senior men expected that the employment of women would generate real advantages to the Civil Service and to themselves as managers – increased efficiency, reduced costs, a stick to beat non-élite male trade unionists. Thus they encouraged the employment of women for purely instrumental reasons with only the most cursory interest in women *qua* women. The élite's agenda notwithstanding, women flocked to one of the few genteel and reasonably well-paid occupations open to them. For a time they were too timid and disorganized to rock the boat. However, from the late 1890s onwards, with the second tipping point on the horizon, there was a phase of estrangement and discord. Energized by the suffrage campaign and by the realization that self-help was required to improve their position, women organized themselves into trade unions, seized the initiative and, for the most part having abandoned special pleading based on their 'femininity', began to demand 'a fair field and no favour' – the same means of recruitment, allocation, promotion, conditions of service and pay as men. The implications of this programme for Civil Service structures, procedures, culture and, most importantly, their own status was not lost on senior men. In consequence they sought to limit the damage by blocking moves by women (and non-élite men) for reform by any and all means available to them.

This paper will examine the employment of women in the Civil Service, particularly women clerks, as historical process. In so doing it will attempt to follow Kanter's exhortation to investigate exact tipping points,[9] although it is clear that the conclusions reached will be less precise as to quantification and more complex as to causality than Kanter anticipated. This paper has three parts. In the first it will describe the organizational structure of the Civil Service and the way in which women were added to a 'uniform' organization. In the second it will describe the honeymoon period in which élite male civil servants used women as a means to an end, and women adopted the classic low profile defensive stance of tokens. In the third it will describe how this honeymoon came to an end as women, in the majority within their own sections, offices, and branches if not overall, rejected the whole panoply of tokenism and took an active role in demanding equal treatment, while male civil servants, both élite and non-élite, engaged in damage limitation.

Marriage lines: the introduction of women

In the late 19th and early 20th centuries, the position of women in the Civil Service was structurally anomalous. As newcomers to an all-male organization women were not so much integrated as bolted on. The Civil Service which they joined had been remodelled, beginning with the Northcote-Trevelyan Report of 1854, to echo mid-Victorian administrative reformers' view of the proper organization of society, and women were simply put in their 'place'. First and foremost the Civil Service was bureaucratically hierarchical: the grading structure was based on a complicated division of labour and ranking of its value and importance. The main distinction lay between 'intellectual' work, which was assigned to a small minority of university-educated men in the First Division (and foremost among these were the men of the Treasury, who controlled staff or establishment matters in the Civil Service), and 'mechanical' work, which was the lot of the rest. Each grade was designed to be watertight: various promotion levels, 'efficiency bars' and long incremental salary scales gave an illusion of upward mobility, but movements between grades or even departments were comparatively rare. Secondly, the Civil Service was socially hierarchical: recruitment to grades was designed to translate outside hierarchies into inside hierarchies. Each grade was purpose-built for a particular social class with a particular level of education and 'culture'. Thus in the Treasury (service-wide) grades before 1920 the First Division was reserved for middle- or upper-middle-class men with a university education, preferably at Oxford or Cambridge; the intermediate grade, for middle-class men educated at public schools (this was the top grade in 'non-intellectual' departments such as the Inland Revenue); the Second Division, for lower-middle-class men educated at grammar schools); the assistant clerk grade, for working class men educated at state primary and secondary schools.

Senior men's decision to employ women did not precipitate any re-examination of the bureaucratic principles underlying Civil Service organization and it did not stimulate anything but the most patronising and platitudinous consideration of women's place in employment. It was unthinkable to treat women like men (or men like women), and so the male élite did not incorporate women into the existing men's grades. Rather it herded them into a separate women's grading structure, which was organized on the same bureaucratic and class lines as the men's. Thus, in the women's departmental grades in the Post Office (which, given the uneven distribution of women amongst the various departments of the Civil Service and the distortions caused by restricting their opportunities, had the most fully articulated hierarchy) there were miscellaneous senior posts including that of medical officer for middle-class women educated at university; women and girl clerk posts for middle-class women educated at girls grammar schools or public schools; telephonist posts for working-class or lower-middle-class women educated at state primary and secondary schools but with 'cultured' voices; telegraphist posts for the same group but with specialized technical training; and sorter posts for the same group but without any specialized training or 'nice' manner.

This similarity was deceptive. Men's and women's grading structures were not separate *but* equal. They were separate *and* unequal. Although women were supervised on a day-to-day basis by senior women like Miss Smith of the Post Office Savings Bank, they were still ultimately subordinate to men, be they the heads of branches, departments or the Treasury. During the interwar period a small number of women entered the administrative grade (formerly the First Division). There were only forty-three of these by 1939, only two of whom were in the Post Office.[10] Until then few, if any, women exercised authority over men because men's objection to working 'under' women operated powerfully to limit the scope even of these exeptional women.[11] When men's and women's grades were 'assimilated' into a mixed-sex grading structure in 1920, the constructed inferiority of women's work was maintained by the 'almost universal downgrading'[12] of the women's grades vis-à-vis the men's. Assimilation, instead of validating the alignment of hierarchies as recognized by custom and practice, shifted women's grades down a notch. Thus women clerks were assimilated to the clerical grade and not, as were the male Second Division clerks to whom they were comparable, to the executive grade, and women assistant clerks/writing assistants were shoved right off the bottom of the scale into an anomalous women-only grade.

Just as the Civil Service had gendered grading structures, so too did it have gendered work. In principle work was distributed on the assumption that men and women were 'naturally' different with different mental abilities and physical capabilities which fitted them for different types of work. Men were equipped for decision-making, problem-solving and command, and women, with their 'gentleness, patience and natural resisting power to the dulling effect of monotony on the sharpness of attention'[13], for execution. These assumed proclivities justified the creation of a primary sphere of work for men and a secondary sphere for women, which included the less complex, interesting and responsible (and more 'mechanical' and 'manipulative' in Northcote-Trevelyan parlance) work in lower status departments with lower pay, fewer opportunities for advancement, and women-only conditions such as a marriage bar and restrictions on mobility and mores both inside and outside the Civil Service. Even when Treasury mandarins were orchestrating 'assimilation' after the First World War, they merely replaced the language of spheres, in which women were separate and unequal, with the language of pyramids, in which they were incorporated and unequal. That is, they were determined that, come what may, women's subordination would remain constant, if not in a separate sphere, then in the lower levels of a pyramid with themselves at its apex: 'women up to a point and men above'.[14] Male managers achieved this by hampering women's ability to climb within the mixed grading structure and by reserving certain types of work, grades, branches or even departments (for example, the Foreign Office, Colonial Office, Admiralty and War Office to men) to each sex.[15]

However complicated the process of gendering and however tortuous its logic, the result was the same – the better work went to those on the sunny side of the so-called 'scientific frontier' between men's and women's work.[16] For example, when the introduction of typewriting was mooted in 1877, departmental officials should have found the decisions on whether to adopt it and who to employ to do it fairly straightforward: one typist could do the work of two or perhaps more hand copyists, and women (at 17–23s per week) were cheaper to employ than men (30–35s and occasionally more) or boys (20–30s). However, there was a certain amount of havering, as senior men pondered the implications of employing women in close proximity to themselves.[17] For a time the Treasury and the Civil Service Commission, 'anxious to encourage the use of any appliance which can be shown to economize labour', strenuously promoted the employment of less than economical boys as being both cheap and comfortable.[18] In the end senior men achieved a compromise between productivity and propriety. They employed men (and boys) as copyists or typists in small offices where work relationships were face-to-face, where there was a certain amount of to-ing and fro-ing by other civil servants or members of the public, and where 'the copying is of a nature that must be left to men'[19]. Some departments even retained the services of hand copyists or put them on typewriters without reducing their wages.[20] They employed women in large offices where suitable accommodation could be provided, where work was 'mechanical', impersonal and unlikely to cause a blush, and where they could be 'protected'. Thus the 'scientific frontier' was on occasions curvaceous in order to keep the 'best of the worst' for men and boys.

The boundaries between the spheres of women's and men's work were fairly flexible. Particular tasks and 'skills' moved from men to women and, less frequently, from women to men. In addition tasks and 'skills' also moved down and, less frequently, up the grading scale. Indeed the only tasks and 'skills' exempt from the basilisk eye of senior civil servants were their own, to which they gave a more than generous valuation.[21] The reasons for senior men's policy of downgrading work and moving it across the gender frontier were complex. They were responding to economic pressures (or perceived economic pressures) in revenue-generating departments like the Post Office to make a profit and in the Civil Service as a whole to slow the growth of the wages bill in a period of expansion of services and staff. As Cohn has shown in his comparison of the Great Western Railway and the Post Office, feminization took place more rapidly and completely where work was labour-intensive rather than capital-intensive – ie, where the employment of women produced a significantly lower wages bill (say, 50 per cent) without any loss of efficiency.[22] However, senior men were not only responding to labour market economics, from which the Civil Service was to some extent insulated by its special status and its exposure to parliamentary interest (not to say meddling), but they were also responding to its bureaucratic, class and gender politics: external lobbies v. government/Civil Service, Treasury v. other departments or one department v. another, male civil servants v. women civil servants, one group of male civil servants v. another, one group of women civil servants v. another.

The honeymoon: the integration of women

In 1871 the Post Office introduced the grade of woman clerk in the Clearing House Branch of the Receiver and Accountant General's Department and allotted to it work which involved sampling and checking (in effect, quality assurance work) telegraph traffic and preparing accounts for messages sent by newspapers and by railway companies on behalf of the Post Office. From there it spread to the Department's Dublin and Edinburgh offices, to other parts of the Post Office, including the Returned Letter Office, the Savings Bank Department, the Money Order Department and the London Telephone Service, and to a few other departments. After 1911 it was used to staff the new welfare services under the National Insurance Commissions and the Board of Trade, and women clerks from the Post Office were transferred to provide the nucleus of this new clerical force. From an initial complement of forty-five in 1871 the women clerk grade grew to about 2700 in the Post Office and an additional five hundred or so in other departments by 1914. This first phase of women clerks' employment was comparatively untroubled. Elite male civil servants were able to satisfy their need for employment of a suitable type, which was, in fact, so overwhelmingly pressing that it overrode for a time all other considerations. The joining of these two partners at the point where their very different aims converged was a marriage made in haste from which both partners, as their aims diverged, repented at leisure.

In this honeymoon phase the interactions between men and women conformed to many of those described by Kanter as typical of skewed groups. The grade of woman clerk was one of the first posts created for women, and after 1881 it was the highest post available to women by open competition. Moreover, it grew spectacularly in these early years by taking on new work, created by the provision to the public of new services and the adoption of new technology, and, even more importantly, work transferred from men. Therefore, women clerks had a high profile both inside and outside the Civil Service. Indeed their exploits were given extensive coverage in male civil servants' publications, middle-class women's journals, the popular press, and after 1907 in their own *Association Notes*. As tokens they bore the heavy burden of the conflicting (and stereotypical) expectations placed on them by élite and non-élite male civil servants, who regarded them, in effect, as office drudges, and by women colleagues and supporters, who regarded them as standard-bearers for the cause of women's employment and women's rights. Elite and non-élite men regarded women clerks as 'interlopers' within the masculine world of red tape, to be used and tolerated on the one hand and to be denigrated and fought against on the other, and they took or actively connived at measures for segregation and superintendence which emphasised women's 'difference'.[23] Women clerks' response was somewhat constrained by the experimental nature of their employment, which required them to prove exhaustively their competence on one task before being entrusted with another, their double entrapment within the rigid hierarchies of grade and gender, and their utter powerlessness. It was, perforce, a quietist response, which combined over-achievement with modest self-effacement.

Although there were a few powerful supporters genuinely committed to the welfare of women clerks, such as Henry Fawcett, postmaster from 1880 to 1884 and husband of the suffragist, Millicent Garrett Fawcett, most senior male civil servants approached their employment in a genially instrumental frame of mind. The leading lights of the First Division viewed 'an abundant supply out of doors of poor gentlewomen with a sufficient amount of education for almost any work required of us'[24] as a means to managerial ends. That is, their aim was to exploit the weaker market position of middle-class women in order to obtain efficient, cheap and compliant workers.[25] In the first place they wished to maintain, if not increase, efficiency. This was only possible, they believed, if they employed women clerks under carefully controlled conditions. Women clerks should be employed, they asserted, on the right sort of work, 'monotonous day-to-day work',[26] which employed substantial numbers and required low levels of supervision. Women clerks should be segregated as much as possible from men in order to avoid 'undesirable' social contacts and direct comparisons of output. To this end women were confined to their own suites of rooms (generally on the top floors) – work rooms, cloak rooms, dining rooms and kitchens – with access via their own entrances and staircases – even at lunchtime until they were liberated by the Liberal Government in 1912. Managers occasionally went to absurd lengths literally to heighten boundaries:

> 'On one occasion allowance had not been made for an extremely tall youth who found himself looking over the partition every time he stood up to pull out a ledger. He was immediately christened "Giraffe" and either removed out of the danger zone or the partition was raised.'[27]

Finally women clerks should be supervised by the right kind of women, 'queen bees' such as Miss Smith of the Savings Bank Department. Within these parameters male managers found that women clerks were an undoubted success: 'They have performed the duties excellently; they leave nothing to be desired'.[28]

In the second place, senior men wished to reduce costs. For a start they paid women clerks salaries which were significantly less than those of male clerks on comparable work – between 50 per cent and 92 per cent of male clerks' pay at entry level and between 33 per cent and 44 per cent at the top of the scale.[29] *Ceteris paribus*, these differences in pay alone would have produced significant savings. However, élite men attempted to enhance these savings by other means. They encouraged a high level of turnover through the use of a marriage bar. Their aim was clear:

> 'The institution of a Female Staff of Clerks is conducive to economy inasmuch as the persons forming it are constantly marrying and withdrawing themselves from the Service before they attain to the maximum salaries and before they have the right to claim retiring allowances.'[30]

Indeed they structured the marriage gratuity or 'dowry', which was paid at the rate of one month's salary per year of service with a minimum of six and a maximum of twelve, to provide the greatest inducement to women clerks to resign around the age of thirty, when they were at or near the top of the second class scale.[31] Moreover, male managers limited women clerks' prospects for promotion. They linked promotions from second class to first class and from first class to higher posts to vacancies in the more senior posts and, given the routinized nature of women clerks' works, with its low supervision levels, these were few and far between.[32] From 1895 to 1905 the annual rate of promotion of second class clerks was 1.5 per cent, and it was slowing down – 1.2 per cent in

1903–5. This resulted in large numbers of clerks – 23 per cent of the second class and 75 per cent of the first class in the Savings Bank Department in 1905 – being stuck at the top of the salary scales without an annual increment, sometimes for many years, awaiting 'dead women's shoes' – the retirement, death, marriage or resignation of one of their more senior colleagues. In addition top civil servants tried whenever possible to exact from women clerks the performance of higher duties without promotion or extra pay. In the various Post Office departments employing women clerks in 1905 between 76.9 per cent and 100 per cent of second class clerks at the maximum salary were employed on 'special duties' belonging to the grade above.[33]

Male managers also massaged women clerks' pay scales in order to cut their cost in the early years of service. They initially granted women clerks the meagre starting salary of £40, somewhat obviated by a generous increment, but in 1881, when they introduced open competition (and the grade came in for a great deal of public scrutiny), they increased it to £65. However, in the extraordinarily parsimonious revision of 1897 they reversed the trend and reduced it to £55, and only in the 1908 Hobhouse revision, which was a victory for women clerks' vociferous trade union agitation, did they reluctantly restore it to its pre-1897 level. Managers reduced women clerks' annual increment from £7/10 to £3 for the first six years and £5 thereafter in 1881 and to £2/10 for the first seven years and £5 thereafter in 1897 and only standardized it at £5 in 1908. Moreover, they effected a transition from a six-hour day to a seven-hour day in 1891 by the addition of £20 to the maxima (by lengthening the scale), thereby obtaining a significant increase in productivity at virtually no cost in the early years. The impact of these revisions can be seen by comparing the length of service necessary to attain the salary of £80: initially in the seventh year, then in the sixth year (1881 and 1891 schemes), then in the ninth year (the punitive 1897 scheme), and finally in the fourth year (1908 Hobhouse scheme). The cost savings involved in employment of women clerks rather than male (general, third class or Second Division) clerks is demonstated by their respective pay in the sixth year of service under the various pay schemes: £72/10 (or 60.4 per cent, of male clerks' £120, 1871); £80 (61.5 per cent of £130, 1881); £80 (84.2 per cent of £95, 1891); £67/10 (71.1 per cent of £95, 1897); and £90 (85.3 per cent of £107/10, 1908) – and in the twelfth year – £100 (55.6 per cent of £180, 1871); £110 (57.9 per cent of £190, 1881); £110 (80 per cent of £137/10, 1891);

£95 (69.1 per cent of £137/10, 1897); and £120 (75 per cent of £160, 1908).

In the third place managers hoped to use women clerks as counterweights to male civil servants' trade unionism, particularly that of the agitated and agitating Second Division, who had the temerity to stage a walkout in the Savings Bank Department in 1891. In the eyes of the First Division the Second Division was 'a very serious obstacle in the way of a contented service or of economical administration' with too many officers in too many departments, too great a propensity to look upwards and feel aggrieved at their lack of recognition, and too great an influence on '(in particular) Metropolitan Members' of Parliament.[34] Top men believed that the employment of women served two related purposes. They expected that women would be too ladylike and delicate to engage in the rough and tumble of agitation. So as more and more women were employed, the scope for trade union activity would diminish accordingly – 'a contented woman is better than a discontented man'.[35] In 1871 Frank Scudamore pressed strongly for the more extensive employment of women as telegraphists and as clerks: 'They are also less disposed than men to combine for the purpose of extorting higher wages, and this is by no means an unimportant matter.'[36] They also expected that the threat of replacement by women clerks would keep the Second Division in order. These expectations of the probable conduct and uses of middle-class 'ladies' were on the whole fulfilled in the first thirty years of women clerks' employment. The increased pace of transfers of work to women clerks plus other measures designed to reduce the size and cohesion of the Second Division were a 'decided blow'[37] and effective in checking its power.

In contrast to the mandarins' multifarious reasoning that of women clerks was simple. They wanted work – work which would provide them with economic independence without loss of class status, respectability or femininity. From the middle of the 19th century, growing concern about 'surplus' or 'odd' women, those who could not marry because of a shortage of suitable partners and those who could not be supported by their families because of insufficient means, led to a search for 'fresh modes of activity' for 'ladies in reduced circumstances'[38]. Clerical work in the Civil Service was, perhaps, the most promising outlet for these middle-class women. Unlike make-work occupations such as china-mending, art needlework, and dog-walking, the Civil Service with its special relationship to state and Crown offered real work with high status, possibly *the* highest status.[39] Unlike the professions, it had the potential to absorb significant numbers of women. Unlike teaching and nursing, it provided work in clean and nice surroundings and did not require extended contact with social inferiors. Unlike governessing, companioning, shop work and other occupations requiring living in, it gave women independence and protected them from the unwanted attentions of men. It provided pay sufficient for women to live respectably, a lump sum on marriage, annual leave, sick pay, medical care and a pension in the end – in short, the decent competence and security desired by 'gentlewomen of limited means, daughters of officers in the army and navy, of civil officers of the Crown, of those engaged in the clerical, legal and medical professions, or literary men and artists'.[40] Given these advantages, appointments to the post of woman clerk were highly sought after. Indeed one of the reasons given by senior officials of the Post Office for favouring the introduction of open competition in 1881 was to end the incessant importunings of candidates and their supporters for nominations which carried little hope of success, as the waiting list was already two years long.[41] Open competition did little to discourage the large numbers of candidates for 'the aristocracy of female clerical labour in England'.[42] For example, in 1894 there were 740 candidates for just 40 posts of woman clerk and ten years later, when the Civil Service was beginning to lose its premier status as an employer of clerical labour, there were still 136 candidates for 10 posts.[43]

Once women clerks had entered the Civil Service they were determined to give of their best and to prove their worth. Their approach to work and presentation of self were in large part created by powerful queen bees such as Miss Smith, who was the lady superintendent of the Savings Bank Department from 1876 to 1913. Miss Smith was a firm believer in the separation of the spheres in the Civil Service and in society, but she nevertheless sought to gain every possible advantage for women clerks. Miss Smith believed that 'success could only be achieved by the attainment of an exceptionally high standard', and she applied her 'virility, forcefulness, high enthusiasm and wholesome optimism' to this end.[44] She placed great emphasis on proper training, diligent work and careful supervision, and, having brought her women to a peak of efficiency, she relentlessly pushed for women clerks to be given more and better work in the Savings Bank Department and elsewhere in the Post Office and the Civil

Service, which at the invitation of her superiors she colonized with her 'picked troops'. She also insisted, so far as possible, on the practical supervision of women clerks by their own officers and resisted 'like a tiger'[45] devolving women clerks' work on to sorters, whom she regarded as inferior in background and efficiency.

While thus anxious to demonstrate their achievements, women clerks nevertheless were careful not to thrust themselves forward and not to rock the boat. Indeed the ultimate act of self-effacement was Miss Smith's. 'A very remarkable women, and a wonderful woman and a wonderful "man of business"' in the eyes of her employers, Miss Smith avoided public occasions and did not attend the jubilee of the Savings Bank Department in 1911 so that the men could bask in the limelight.[46] If they had grievances, women clerks either confided them to their women supervisors or petitioned their male chiefs in a ladylike fashion for consideration.[47] They did not engage in public scenes of agitation, and they did not, until sorely provoked, form their own association. According to the Tweedmouth Committee, which reported in 1896, postal women were on the whole contented:

> . . . the evidence given seemed to indicate that no considerable dissatisfaction existed as to their conditions of service, and we are also assured by the Post Office authorities that there is a general absence of complaint from them.[48]

This complacent pronouncement was followed by the draconian salary revision of 1897 which provoked women clerks into open rebellion and the founding of their trade union, the Association of Post Office Women Clerks. The honeymoon was over.

The estrangement: 'amazon cavalry' v. gentlemen bureaucrats

Although male managers' and women clerks' interests for a time ran along the same lines, after 1897 they began quite rapidly to diverge – or rather, élite men's interests as managers and men continued to run along the same lines, whereas women's took a sharp turn. In the early days of women clerks' employment they took what work they were offered, regardless of any reservations they may have had about their pay, conditions of service or status. Thirty years on women clerks' attitude had undergone a sea change from passivity to militancy. In the first place they felt deeply threatened by senior officials' attacks on the prospects and even existence of their grade. They were greatly alarmed by the removal of £10 from their starting pay and 10s from their annual increment in 1897 during a period of rising prices. Top men's efforts to 'skim off' the simpler work from the bottom of the grade and allocate it to new cheaper subordinate grades[49] without increasing women clerks' pay accordingly were, they thought, tantamount to a speed-up. In the second place women clerks were sufficiently emboldened by their successes and by the suffrage movement to formulate their own programme. This went far beyond bare economic survival to demands for equality and justice. Managers' attempts to avoid direct comparability of women clerks and Second Division clerks engaged on the same work in ledger divisions in the Savings Bank Department by effecting a series of mutual transfers backfired and gave women clerks, now totally in charge of ledger work, a sense of strength and confidence. However, women clerks' sudden transformation from busy bees to 'Amazon cavalry'[50] frightened both élite and non-élite men and precipitated strong resistance. Pushed onto the defence, top men relied more and more heavily on the crude exercise of power masked as bureaucratic procedures.

In terms of 'the cost of efficient living' and 'the nature and value of the work performed'[51] women clerks' pay was the 'burning issue'[52] which prompted the formation of the Association in September 1901. Coming, as it did, in a time of inflation (up 16.2 per cent in the years 1885 to 1903[53]), the 1897 reduction of women clerks' initial salary by 15.4 per cent and their annual increment by 16.6 per cent meant a decline in their standard of living, which even the improvement of the scale in 1908 did not ameliorate. Women clerks feared that their social standing would be undermined, since their wages in some instances were lower than those of women telegraphists, who were 'manipulatives'[54]:

> The competitive system under which the Department is recruited results in a specially selected staff, for whom the cheap dwellings of the low working classes with the cheap locomotion provided are quite impossible. In brief, there is scarcely any class upon which the problems of genteel poverty press more heavily. . . .

They feared that in practice opportunities would be closed to women from the provinces (40 per cent of the current force in 1906), particularly Irish and Scottish women, who could not afford to live in lodgings in London in the early years of service and could not afford to go home to Dublin or Edinburgh in the later years of service, since the maximum salaries were lower. They feared that, unable to sustain 'genuine self-support' until after six or seven years' service, they would be forced to take 'assistance from relations or friends'[55], and they also feared that in their later years they would be unable to contribute to the support of aged parents, brothers and sisters, etc.[56] Finally and most poignantly they feared the loss of prestige in the eyes of the outside world. The 1897 salary reduction, the creation of the girl clerk grade as an entry point for the woman clerk grade, and developments in the outside market for clerical labour which rendered the Civil Service less desirable than, say, the London County Council, resulted in a rapid and chilling decline in the number and quality of the candidates for appointment. Indeed in March 1905 for the first time the Post Office appointed candidates who had not reached the qualifying standard.[57] Women clerks, used to being the 'aristocrat[s] of the profession'[58], found themselves so no longer.

In addition to the vexed issue of pay, women clerks were appalled by male managers' insertion under them of two new grades, that of girl clerk in 1897 and assistant woman clerk in 1911, and the allocation of women clerks' duties to the new grades. Women clerks viewed the introduction of the girl clerk grade as a blatant method whereby the Treasury and Post Office obtained 'a cheaper form of labour'[59] without any loss of quality. Male managers, in effect, reduced the cost of women clerks' services in the first two years by the bureaucratic ruse of creating a grade which in every way except pay and age of recruitment was indistinguishable from the one above it. Girl clerks were recruited at a younger age (16–18) than women clerks (18–20) by means of an examination identical to the women clerks', and after a period of satisfactory service (three years reduced to two in 1900) they were appointed as women clerks with any rejects being dispatched to the sorters. They were employed on selected 'simpler duties' done on the men's side by Second Division clerks (the 'simple' nature of which was hotly disputed by women clerks) first of all in the Savings Bank Department and later in the rest of the departments where women clerks were employed. They were paid £35 by £2/10 to £40.[60] for a six-hour day increased in 1908 to £42 by

£4 to £48 for a seven-hour day. Given that the average age of girl clerks on appointment was a few months short of eighteen,[61] fractionally below the minimum for women clerks, and given that the necessity to promote all girl clerks whose record was satisfactory began to reduce the number of posts available to be filled through the women clerks' exams (and resulted in the cancellation of those exams), and given that overall the quality of candidates for appointment as girl clerks was lower than for women clerks, not surprisingly, women clerks gained the firm impression that they had been swindled.

Women clerks suffered an even greater outrage with the creation of the grade of assistant woman clerk and its rather hole-and-corner début. On Friday, 8 December 1911, the Postmaster General announced that the Treasury had authorized the tentative introduction of the new grade, and on the following Monday the first batch of twenty-two sorters specially promoted (not examined) began work in the Money Order Department on 'simpler clerical or quasi-clerical duties' devolved from girl and women clerks. The choice of the Money Order Department, where there was a high proportion of women clerks at their maxima, a considerable number of vacant posts and an indefinite block on promotions pending a review, was of itself provocative, but implicit in this manoeuvre was, women clerks felt, the 'distinct menace'[62] of a hidden agenda. The first issue was the subtle de-skilling of women clerks' duties. Postal officials alleged that the quality of women clerks' duties was declining – ie, that there was relatively more 'simple' work and relatively less 'complex' work so that overall the work was becoming more 'mechanical' or 'quasi-manipulative'. The second issue was the whittling away of women clerks' status by devolving their work onto persons whom they considered to be their social inferiors. Assistant women clerks were, in effect, cloned from the sorters, with the same conditions of service, including an eight-hour day and weekly (and not the more genteel annual) wages on the scale 18s to 34s,[63] which were 4s greater at every point than those of sorters. The third issue was the virtual nullification of the findings of a parliamentary select committee by administrative fiat. The long-anticipated Hobhouse pay scale had been awarded in 1908, and women clerks disputed senior civil servants' powers to alter the settlement. They were also aggrieved by senior officials' attempts to have their cake and eat it, to hold up long-needed promotions in the Money Order Department until the Hobhouse Committee concluded its labours and then to ignore the Committee's recommendations in that very same department: 'If the recommendations of a Parliamentary Committee are to be binding on the staff, they should be equally binding on the Department'[64].

If women clerks were galvanized by the issues of pay and undercutting, they were strengthened and encouraged by their experiences during the exchanges of work between women and men in the Savings Bank Department, 'that unhappy cockpit of the Service'[65], and later in other departments. Sixty-five women clerks joined the Savings Bank Department in 1875, and at that point they comprised 15.4 per cent of clerical staff and, together with a number of housekeepers and charwomen, 2.4 per cent of all staff. 'The experiment [having] been attended with very satisfactory results'[66], more and more women clerks came onto the clerical force – 256 in 1885, 650 in 1895, 1019 in 1905, and 1431 in 1915. Although these increases occurred in the context of the overall expansion of the department, the proportion of women clerks to total clerical staff increased rapidly in the first two decades (to 28.7 per cent in 1885 and 45.2 per cent in 1895, increases of 13.3 per cent and 16.5 per cent, respectively, per decade). Thereafter in the troubled years 1895–1905 the proportion of women clerks decreased by 2.2 per cent to 43.0 per cent. Following the exchanges of men and women staff the proportion of women clerks increased by 12.4 per cent to 55.4 per cent in 1915. The proportions of women staff to total staff followed the same trend, albeit at a slightly lower level (25.3 per cent in 1885, 39.2 per cent in 1895) and then from 1905 at a slightly higher level (46.2 per cent in 1905 and 58.7 per cent in 1915), in consequence of the utilization of other grades, principally women sorters. Thus in terms of gender the Savings Bank Department rang the Kanterian changes – uniform (all men) prior to 1875; skewed in 1875; tilted in 1890; balanced in 1895/1900; and, following the transfers, tilted in reverse, when the department became truly a 'women's department'[67].

As a result of the transfers, women clerks gained not only numerical but moral superiority. In 1906 women clerks made representations for equal pay to the Hobhouse Committee based on the fact that they were doing exactly the same ledger work as Second Division clerks but at half the rate of pay. Male mandarins found arguments for equal pay increasingly difficult to resist, particularly in the cold light of public attention, and as a result they decided to refute women clerks' argument by removing the conditions on which it was based.[68] This they did by effecting 'the completer separation of the work performed by men and women'. Their official line was that movements of the 'scientific frontier' had made it possible to rationalize women's and men's tasks, 'the women to gain in quantity, the men in quality'.[69] But women clerks' response to this obvious piece of manipulation was contempt, liberating contempt, for their erstwhile masters:

> We consider that the manner in which the Department endeavours to maintain a line of demarcation between men's and women's work is both trivial and vexatious, and the so-called 'scientific frontier' proves to be no frontier at all by the ease with which the landmarks are moved to different positions to suit the special end in view.[70]

And women clerks' response to their new duties about which mysteries had been made was contempt tempered by a kind of rough compassion for their rivals in the Second Division:

> I was in the group picked out to make the experiment and duly did the rounds of the men's sections, the Stock Branch where I learned about the day-to-day fluctuations in stock prices and where my teacher instructed in the very important matter of 'Masking the Point', ie seeing that the pin which held papers together was not exposed, in case of injury to unwary fingers. The Deceased Depositors' Branch, the Special Correspondence Branch were other sections which I never could see why they were reserved for men, unless it was that the men could not be trusted with the important work of balancing accounts and making up interests which concerned all depositors in the Bank.[71]

These events were, in a sense, an emotional Rubicon for women clerks: once having taken the plunge they left behind on the far shore self-effacement and self-doubt.

Women clerks were thus determined to gain 'control over [their] own interests'.[72] To achieve this they felt obliged to jettison the whole carapace of stereotyped gender roles forced on them from above and to put in its place a thoroughgoing programme of equal opportunities. In so doing they were conscious of their responsibilities to the women's movement as a whole: 'As we ascend we take the whole women's labour market with us. Many poor women are looking to us to get our standard raised, so that theirs may rise with it.'[73] They made confident (and to male managers unsettling) demands. They sought equality in terms of recruitment and allocation to particular tasks: 'women should compete with men in the entrance examinations; the order of merit, irrespective of sex, should determine appointment'.[74] They wished to take their chances on promotion by merit. The world was their oyster to be opened by their own efforts and they predicted that one day they would find a few pearls:

Q. You contemplate a Lady Secretary to the Post Office?
A. Yes, certainly; and a Lady Postmaster-General eventually. (Laughter).
Q. That really is your claim?
A. Yes, that is our ambition.[75]

They demanded pay based on the value of the work done and not on the sex and presumed marital status and family responsibilities of the worker. In return women clerks offered not 'an innate reverence for procedures, for things as they have been' but rather 'an infusion of imagination, of sympathy, of freshness of vision'.[76] As they took their demands to a seemingly endless chain of committees and commissions, all to no avail, they recognized that real power was located in Parliament and that this belonged to men. Able support for their campaign by sympathetic MPs was not enough. One woman clerk put the matter in a nutshell: '. . . [women] would continue to be bottom dog until they were enfranchised'.[77] And for this reason the Federation of Women Civil Servants, which incorporated and succeeded the Association, adopted 'the removal of the civil and political disabilities of women' as one of its objects in 1913.[78]

Women clerks' change of approach turned the tables on their male colleagues, élite and non-élite. Men who worked in departments with large complements of women found themselves in situations where they were, in fact, in a minority or were made to feel in a minority, and they were greatly disconcerted. When Herbert Samuel, postmaster general from 1910 to 1914 and from 1915 to 1916, attended an 'At Home' given by the Association and found himself alone in a hall full of women, not entirely as a joke he begged the 'keen suffragists . . . some even suffragettes' to treat him, 'an innocent Cabinet Minister, helpless and defenceless', kindly.[79] The same sort of humorous unease was exhibited by a deputy divisional inspector in his address to a dinner meeting of the Association of Women Clerks in the Board of Trade. When he discovered that the Board was going to employ women staff, he and another divisional officer went along to the Post Office in order to discover how to treat these rare creatures: 'Shortly after this incident two timid figures might have been seen peeping around the corner into the room where the ladies were, and hastily retreating when observed'.[80] Not all men acted like shrinking violets in the company of women. In what Kanter has characterized as 'exaggerated displays of aggression and potency'[81] young clerks in the Board of Trade, 'not used to working at all with women on an equal footing' asserted themselves by excessive smoking, rudeness, and 'a somewhat farcical lunch hour lockout.' Older clerks in positions of power in the Treasury and other departments were no less aggressive but rather more suave. They used their considerable wiles to prevent women from achieving their equal opportunities programme not because women's demands were unjust or likely to damage the Civil Service but because they were subversive of the 'sex patronage'[82] which kept élite men in power.

The ties that bind: conclusion

It can be seen from this historical survey of the employment of women clerks in the Civil Service in the half century after 1870 that differences in the proportions of men and women in groups produced different processes of interaction. In the first or honeymoon phase of women clerks' employment male managers were manifestly dominant and women clerks adopted the risk-minimizing stance of tokens – either as worker bees or, in the case of supervising women like Miss Smith, as queen bees. In the second or estrangement phase women clerks, in part driven to respond to policies inimical to their prospects and in part inspired by the 'feeling of comradeship and freemasonry among women'[83], endeavoured to set their own agendas. Women's readiness to assert themselves and their degree of militancy derived to some extent from their increased numbers but most of all from their increased massing in the work force. It is for this reason that the cutting edge of women civil servants' campaign for equal opportunities was not the more numerous sub-postmistresses and telephonists, who were dispersed in small offices in the provinces, but the 'Amazon cavalry' of the Savings Bank Department, who were centralized in one large metropolitan office in which by 1915 they constituted an outright majority of staff. The failure of women civil servants to achieve formal equality before 1961, when equal pay went into effect, and real equality since then was and is due to resistance by male civil servants, both élite and non-élite.

This account of gender segregation in the Civil Service suggests that Kanter's model does not generate a full explanation of the processes which are at work. Kanter's model has proved difficult to apply with precision to a large and complex organization such as the Civil Service where women were (and are) unevenly distributed amongst departments, types of work, types of offices, grades, etc. and where the 'group' may be at one and the same time a ledger branch, the Savings Bank Department, the Post Office or the Civil Service as a whole. More significantly, Kanter's model, an equilibrium model, describes existing groups, but it does not explain transitions between types of groups or predict tipping points – for example, why women were introduced into the Civil Service in the first place and why they failed to make greater headway. Assistance is provided by Witz's formulation of dynamic strategies for 'closure' both within (and between) occupational groups: élite male civil servants pursued an exclusionary strategy 'to secure, maintain or enhance privileged access to rewards and opportunities', whereas women civil servants pursued an inclusionary strategy to attain 'within the structure positions from which [they were] collectively disbarred'.[84] The outcome of these countervailing aims was determined by the respective power of the protagonists, and male civil servants dominated the structures, processes and culture of the bureaucracy as well as the alternative structures, processes and culture of the trade unions. Women were relatively powerless and therefore held in a subordinate position, initially passively and then against their will. As Weber noted in his seminal essay, 'as an instrument for "socializing" relations of power bureaucracy has been and is a power instrument of the first order – for the one who controls the bureaucratic apparatus'.[85] Until women civil servants acquire an equal share of power, they will remain fettered by red tape and will feel 'a natural and comprehensible resentment'.[86]

References

1 Hamilton, C., (1909), *Marriage as a Trade*, London: Chapman and Hall: 115–16.
2 See, as an example of 'one more factorism' F. Anthias and N. Yuval-Davis, 'Contextualising feminism – gender, ethnic and class divisions,' *Feminist Review*, 15, November 1983: 62–75: 'It is not a question therefore of one being more "real" than the others or a question of *which* [gender, ethnic or class divisions] is the more important. However it is clear that the three divisions prioritize different spheres of social relations and will have different effects which it may be possible to specify in concrete analysis. However we suggest that each division exists within the context of the others and that any concrete analysis has to take this into account' (p. 65).
3 Kanter, R.M., 'Some Effects of Proportions on Group Life: Skewed Sex Ratios and Responses to Token Women,' *American Journal of Sociology*, 82, 1977: 965–90; *Men and Women of the Corporation*, New York: Basic Books, 1977; and with B. Stein, *A Tale of 'O': on being different in an organisation*, New York: Harper and Row, 1980. See also two articles confirming the 'Kanter thesis': E. Spangler, M. A. Gordon and R. M. Pipkin, 'Token Women: An Empirical Test of Kanter's Hypothesis,' *American Journal of Sociology*, 84, 1978: 160–70, and J. D. Yoder, P. L. Crumpton and J. F. Zipp, 'The Power of Numbers in Influencing Hiring Decisions,' *Gender and Society*, 3, 1989: 269–76.
4 Cohn, S., (1985), *The Process of Occupational Sex-Typing: The Feminization of Clerical Labour in Great Britain*, Philadelphia: Temple University Press. For the history of women civil servants written by participants see Evans, D., (1934), *Women and the Civil Service: A History of the Employment of Women in the Civil Service, and a Guide to Present Day Opportunities*, London: Pitman and Sons; Martindale, H., (1938), *Women Servants of the State, 1870–1938: A History of Women in the Civil Service*, London: George Allen and Unwin; Brimelow, E., 'Women in the Civil Service,' *Public Administration*, 59, Autumn, 1981: 313–35; and Bagilhole, B., 'Women and Work: A Study of Underachievement in the Civil Service', Ph.D., University of Nottingham, 1984. For accounts using oral sources see Davy, T., '"A Cissy Job for Men; a Nice Job for Girls": Women Shorthand Typists in London, 1900–39', and Sanderson, K., '"A Pension to Look Forward to . . .?": Women Civil Service Clerks in London, 1925–1939', in Davidoff, L. and Westover, B., (eds). (1986), *Our Work, Our Lives, Our Words: Women's History and Women's Work*, Basingstoke, Hants.: Macmillan Education: 124–44 and 145–60, respectively. See also articles by the author: 'Strategies and Stratagems for the Employment of Women in the British Civil Service, 1919–1939,' *Historical Journal*, 27, 1984: 901–24; 'We Are All Professionals Now: Professionalisation, Education and Gender in the Civil Service, 1873–1939,' *Women, Education and the Professions*, History of Education Society, Occasional Publication, No. 8, 1987: 66–83 'The New Woman in the Machinery of Government: A Spanner in the Works?,' in Macleod, R., (ed.), (1988), *Government and Expertise in Britain, 1815–1919: Specialists, Administrators and Professionals*, Cambridge: Cambridge University Press: 185–202; and '"Get Out and Get Under": The Impact of Demobilisation on the Civil Service, 1918–32,' in Anderson, G., (ed.), (1988), *The White-*

blouse Revolution: Female Office Workers since 1870, Manchester: Manchester University Press: 88–120.

5 When information as to the gender of all classes of officers was provided in 1883, there were already 131 postmistresses and 2,658 sub-postmistresses and letter receivers (14.2 per cent and 18.7 per cent, respectively). Given these numbers and anecdotal evidence, it is reasonable to assume that many were in post pre-1870. P[ost] O[ffice] A[rchive], POST92, 29th Report of the Postmaster General on the Post Office, 14 July 1883.

6 The figures for women as a proportion of permanent staff were slightly lower – 23 per cent in 1923 and 26 per cent in 1938. Zimmeck, 'Get Out and Get Under': 103.

7 For the main clerical grades (administrative/executive/clerical) as opposed to the Civil Service overall the tipping point from skewed to tilted did not take place until the 1960s, and it was only in the 1970s that women found themselves in the majority. Women comprised 21.6 per cent of the main clerical grades in 1929, 23.7 per cent in 1939, 29.4 per cent in 1949, 30.0 per cent in 1959, 36.0 per cent in 1969 and 55.9 per cent in 1979. Bagilhole: 134.

8 POST92, 18th Report of the Postmaster General on the Post Office, 29 July 1872: 13.

9 Kanter, 'Some Effects of Proportions': 989.

10 Who comprised 3 per cent of the total. Kelsall, R.K., (1955), *Higher Civil Servants in Britain: From 1870 to the Present Day*, London: Routledge and Kegan Paul,: 175; POA, POST59, List of the Principal Officers in the Post Office, 1 January 1939.

11 For example, Isabel Taylor was promoted to the post of deputy chief inspector of factories in the Home Office in 1933, and in the next fourteen years three less senior men were promoted to the top post over her head. Martindale, H., *(1948), Some Victorian Portraits and Others*, London: George Allen and Unwin, 1948: 59–60.

12 P[ublic] R[ecord] O[ffice], T162/80/E8242, P. Strachey, Joint Committee on Women in the Civil Service, to Hilton Young, Treasury, 11 March 1922.

13 POA, POST30/1815/E4903/1910, [Sir Matthew Nathan, secretary], memo, 18 February 1910.

14 PRO, T1/12265/50322 Pt.1/18, Committee on Recruitment to the Civil Service after the War (Gladstone Committee), minutes, 31st meeting, 13 November 1918, evidence of J.A. Flynn, Ministry of Pensions. Indeed the pyramid still exists. In 1980 women comprised 45.9 per cent of non-industrial civil servants, but they were overrepresented in the lower grades – 99.0 per cent of typists, 80.0 per cent of clerical assistants, 65.9 per cent of clerical officers – and underrepresented in the higher – 39.0 per cent of executive officers, 7.3 per cent of principals, senior principals and assistant secretaries, and 3.8 per cent of undersecretaries and higher. Brimelow: 313 *et passim*.

15 T162/289/E27987, 'Posts reserved to women', [August 1932].

16 'Transfer of Work in the Savings Bank', *Association Notes*, [I], 4, March 1909: 41.

17 The Treasury's top men were a little slow to follow their own advice to others and only began the experiment of employing typists and women in their own office in 1889 after much soul searching. The matter was so emotive that the discussion papers were circulated in a plain (brown?) envelope. After the bugbear of 'structural alteration' was overcome, two women were employed

and quartered in the attic under the beady eye of the head of copying. T1/8371A/18349/88, F.A'C. Bergne, [principal clerk], memo, 25 October 1888; Sir Reginald Welby, [permanent secretary], memo, 12 October 1888.

18 T1/8313A/17893/87, Treasury to War Office, 25 June 1887. The Customs obligingly cooked up some 'scientific' costings to prove that boy typists were the most economical. They did not, however, consider all possible options. Male hand copyists cost 1.5d/folio; boy hand copyists, 0.724d; boy typists, 0.627d; and women typists, 0.892d. T1/8431A/16487/89, R.T. Prowse, [secretary], Customs, to Treasury, 12 February 1889.

19 T1/8752C/12759/93, Treasury minute, 17 March 1894.

20 It was possible to conceal their continued existence or anomalies in their pay and conditions from Treasury surveillance by various ruses such as secondment or payment of wages out of departmental allowances ('hidden under lump sums'). For example, the Admiralty employed a lower division male clerk on the scale £90–250 (1887); the Chief Secretary's Office, Ireland, employed a male 'clerk and typewriter' at 50s per week (1890); and the Exchequer and Audit Department as late as 1903 tried to obtain the Treasury's sanction for higher wages for its male typist: 'The poor fellow has a wife and family and finds it very difficult to struggle along'. T1/9545B/11886/00, John Hennell, [senior clerk], Civil Service Commission, to L.J. Hewby, [second class clerk], Treasury, 22 May 1900; T1/8328B/20227/87, J. Jackson, [supplementary clerk], to Sir Reginald Welby, [permanent secretary], 17 May 1887; T1/8496A/90, Chief Secretary's Office, Ireland, to Treasury, 10 May 1890; T1/8642B/6607/92, J. Harris(?), Exchequer and Audit Department, to Blair(?), Treasury, 5 February 1903.

21 For a dissection of the élite's 'professional expertise', see Zimmeck, 'New Woman'. See also Deacon, D., (1989), *Managing Gender: The State, the New Middle Class, and Women Workers, 1830–1930*, Melbourne: Oxford University Press; and Witz, A., (1992), *Professions and Patriarchy*, London: Routledge and Kegan Paul.

22 Cohn: 52–53 *et passim*.

23 This perception of women as freaks is displayed, trivially if revealingly, in an article on the sub-postmistress of Raitby, Leics., which contained the first photograph of a woman civil servant in *St. Martin's le Grand*, a 'nonpolitical' postal quarterly, which was positively awash with images of bearded and bewhiskered male notables. She was only 3'6" tall but was 'very intelligent and performs her duties to the full satisfaction of her official superiors'. 'St. Martin's Post Bag: Miss Annie Astill', III, 2, July 1893: 200–1.

24 P.P. 1875 c.1113-I xxiii, Civil Service Inquiry Commission (Playfair Commission), Appendix to First Report, Minutes of Evidence, evidence of George Chetwynd, receiver and accountant general, Post Office, 3 November 1874, Q4577.

25 Elite men were, however, in strictly limited circumstances prepared to be kind. For example, in 1891 the General Register Office, Ireland, decided to employ Mary Browning, 'the daughter of poor Browning of the Teachers' Pension Office and a niece of Mr. Balfour's Private Secretary,' as a temporary clerk at a man's rate of pay, 35s per week. In justification the department explained that her father had died of overwork and had left the family in straightened circumstances and that 'his daughter has therefore some claim to the consideration of the Treasury'. The Treasury noted that temporary appointments were within the department's discretion. When the department employed

two more temporary women clerks, disguised in correspondence as 'persons', and moreover, revealed that all members of staff, male and female, would be working together in the same office, the Treasury felt compelled to comment: the permanent employment of a 'biped of the female gender' could take place only if her employment was on 'such clerical duties as [women] are qualified for' and in 'separate accommodation'. When the department applied to convert these three temporary posts into permanent ones, the Treasury demurred – and thus demonstrated the boundaries of avuncular 'consideration'. T1/8606A/6735/91, R.W.A. Holmes, Treasury remembrancer, Paymaster General's Department, Ireland, to F.A'C. Bergne, [principal clerk], Treasury, 26 January 1891; T.W. Grimshaw, [registrar general], General Register Office, Ireland, to Bergne, 23 January 1891; Treasury to Chief Secretary's Office, Ireland, 30 January 1891; Bergne to Grimshaw, 28 October 1891. T1/8632A/2303/92, Treasury to Civil Service Commission, 17 February 1892.

26 POST30/3411/E11913/1915, 'Evidence of Miss M.L. Cale given before the Select Committee of the House of Commons on Post Office Servants [Holt Committee; hereafter Holt evidence], 8 January 1913', Examination of Sir Alexander King, [second secretary]: 29.

27 PRO, LAB2/1800/CEB600, M. Law, memo, 11 November 1918.

28 Playfair Commission, evidence of Chetwynd, Q4520.

29 There were five different scales for women clerks. Original scale, Clearing House Branch and Savings Bank Department, 1871, 1874: £40 by £7/10 to £75 (second class); £80 by £7/10 to £100 (1st class); £110 by £10 to £150 (principal). 1881 scale: £65 by £3 to £80 (second class); £85 by £5 to £110 (first class); £120 by £10 to £170 (principal). 1891 scale: £65 by £3 to £80 by £5 to £100 (second class); £105 by £5 to £130 (first class); £140 by £10 to £190 (principal). 1897 scale: £55 by £2/10 to £70 by £5 to £100 (second class); £105 by £5 to £130 (first class); £140 by £10 to £190 (principal). 1908 scale: £65 by £5 to £110 (second class); £115 by £5 to £140 (first class); £150 by £10 to £200 (principal). The first and second scales were for a six-hour day and those after 1891 were for a seven-hour day. There were at least four different scales for male clerks. Scale in 1871: £80 for two years by £10 to £240 (general body); £260 by £15 to £450 (lower first class); £300 by £15 to £400 (upper first class); £375 by £15 to £450 (principal). 1873 scale: £80 by £10 to £240 (third class); £200 by £10 to £300 (second class); £310 by £15 to £400 (first class); £420 by £15 to £500 (principal). 1890 scale: £70 by £5 to £100 by £7/10 to £190 by £10 to £250 by £10 to £350 (Second Division); £360 by £15 to £430 (first class); £500 by £20 to £550 (principal). 1908 scale: £70 by £7/10 to £130 by £10 to £200 by £10 to £300 (Second Division); £315 by £15 to £450 (first class); £450 by £20 to £550 (principal).

30 T1/7381B/12054/74, Treasury memo, 24 August 1874.

31 Indeed, in the two decades before 1914 the average age of women retiring with a marriage gratuity was twenty-eight and their average length of service was nine to ten years. This was for all established women civil servants and may even have been higher in the clerical grades. POST92, 42nd Report of the Postmaster General on the Post Office, August 1896 *et seq*.

32 Male Second Division clerks, however, had a somewhat easier passage: without reference to vacancies of posts they rose through the scale and were only required to pass 'efficiency bars' at a few critical points where their performance was evaluated and certified.

33 POST30/2243/E8549/1912, 'Association of Post Office Women Clerks, Evidence

Submitted to the Select Committee on Post Office Servants' (Hobhouse Committee; hereafter Hobhouse evidence), August 1906, App.6: 47; App.7: 48.

34 T1/9086B/16557/96, Sir Francis Mowatt, [permanent secretary], memo, 26 June 1896.

35 T1/11334/19291/11, R.F. Wilkins, Treasury, to Bernard Mallet, [registrar general], General Register Office, 6 March 1911.

36 P.P. 1871 c.304 xxxvii 703, Report by Mr. Scudamore on the Reorganization of the Telegraph System of the United Kingdom, January 1871: 78.

37 T1/9086B/16557/96, G.H. Murray, [principal clerk], memo, 19 June 1896.

38 Harkness, M.L., 'Women as Civil Servants', *The Nineteenth Century*, X, 1881: 369.

39 The most senior women clerks of the Clearing House Branch, Receiver and Accountant General's Department, who occupied the 'highest room' with its own balcony at 1 Albion Place, Blackfriars Bridge, dealt with government and royal messages. *Ibid.*: 371.

40 Manners, Lady J., (1882), *Employment of Women in the Public Service*, Edinburgh and London: William Blackwood and Sons: 10.

41 POST30/382/E5664/1880, S.A. Blackwood, [financial secretary], Post Office, to Theodore Walrond, [commissioner], Civil Service Commission, 23 July 1880.

42 K.F., 'At Home and Abroad: A Comparison', *Association Notes*, II, 3, April 1914: 29.

43 Hobhouse evidence, App.2: 41.

44 'Miss Constance Smith, I.S.O.: An Appreciation by a Member of her Staff', *Association Notes*, [I], 20, April 1913: 172–73.

45 T1/11334/19291/11 R.F. Wilkins, [principal clerk], Treasury, to Bernard Mallet, [registrar general], General Register Office, 6 March 1911.

46 T1/11464/18470/12, II.H[iggs, first class clerk], memo, 11 September 1908. Martindale suggests that Miss Smith's motives were both personal and tactical: 'She is said to have disliked the limelight, considering it bad form, and so took care to guard herself from publicity. It was a matter of comment that she made a point of avoiding any public function of a nature which demanded the attendance of the higher officials. This was no doubt sound policy, since her men colleagues were not anxious to advertise the presence of a woman amongst them, and Miss Smith, by absenting herself, was spared the humiliation of finding herself in a less prominent position than was her due in view of her services and the large staff under her control.' *Woman Servants*: 78–79.

47 For example, in 1894 temporary women clerks in the Inland Revenue begged to be placed on the permanent establishment like typists, 'whose services have now deservedly received further recognition'. In 1895, 1898 and 1903 women clerks in the Accountant General's Department in Edinburgh asked the postmaster general to raise their pay maxima to London levels and to institute measures to combat the 'non-existence' of vacancies which blocked promotion. T1/8834A/9975/94, petition of Bessie Hobbs *et al.*, to Inland Revenue, 13 April 1894; Hobhouse evidence: 11.

48 P.P. 1897 c.121 xliv, Inter-Departmental Committee on Post Office Establishments (Tweedmouth Committee), Report, 15 December 1896: 33.

49 For 'creaming off' the better work see Witz, A., (1986), 'Patriarchy and the Labour Market: Occupational Control Strategies and the Medical Division of

Labour', in Knights, D. and Willmott, H., (eds.), *Gender and the Labour Market*, Aldershot, Hants.: Gower: 18.

50 T162/47/E3506/1, W.R. Fraser, [principal], memo, 20 August 1920.

51 Hobhouse evidence: 2.

52 Fawcett Library, FL228, 'Association of Post Office Women Clerks, Letters and Papers, 1908–26' Blanche Miller to Miss Smyth, 27 May 1924.

53 Hobhouse evidence: 6.

54 So strongly did women clerks feel 'their social superiority to sorters that, if a sorter by any chance gets a Clerkship in the Open examination, we transfer her from the office in which she worked as a Sorter, to another Office'. T1/9107A/18708/96, Spencer Walpole, [secretary], Post Office, to G.H. Murray, [principal clerk], Treasury, 11 November 1896.

55 Hobhouse evidence: 16, 2, 4.

56 According to an extensive survey by women clerks in 1913, 25 per cent of all women clerks and 42 per cent of those with ten years' service were contributing to the support of at least one other person, 'responsibilities which it is impossible for [them] to avoid'. Holt evidence: 2, 17, 6.

57 Hobhouse evidence: 5, 4.

58 POST30/2489/E11951/1913, cutting, *The Standard*, 16 August 1906. I am indebted to Martin Daunton for this reference.

59 T1/9107A/18708/96, Post Office to Treasury, 22 August 1896.

60 Postal officials argued, somewhat perversely, that they had trimmed £10 from women clerks' pay scale in 1897 'in order to obviate the excessive increase in salary on promotion from Girl Clerks to Woman Clerks' – that is, from £40 to £65, a difference of £25. Of course, they could have raised girl clerks' scale by £10 and achieved the same effect. POST30/1536/E12171/1908, memo, 14 April 1910. I am indebted to Martin Daunton for this reference.

61 POST30/2489/E11951/1913, F. Wickham, [controller], Money Order Department, 15 May 1906.

62 'New Scheme of Economy', text of postmaster general's announcement, and 'Deputation to Sir Alexander King', *Association Notes*, [I], 15, January 1912: 128–9.

63 The assistant women clerks' scale was 18s by 1s to 20s by 2s to 34s with an efficiency bar at 26s.

64 'Deputation to Sir Alexander King', and M.L. Cale, Association of Post Office Women Clerks, to Sir A.F. King, Post Office, 8 February 1912, *Association Notes*, [I], 15, January 1912: 130 and 137, respectively.

65 *The Civilian*, 23 May 1908, quoted in *Ibid.*: 34.

66 POST92, 22nd Report of the Postmaster General on the Post Office, 28 July 1876: 13.

67 POST59, List of the Principal Officers in the Post Office, 1 January 1875 *et seq*.

68 When Sir Alexander King was giving evidence to the Royal Commission on the Civil Service (Macdonnell Commission) in 1914, he was asked about the purpose of the swap, and the following interchange took place: 'The chairman: What is the advantage? Sir A. King: The advantage is that we can meet criticism like Mr. Snowden's and say that they are not doing the same work. Mr. Snowden: I think I am quite satisfied with the answer as it stands.' 'Branch Reports: Savings Bank Department', *Association Notes*, [I], 20, April 1913: 180.

69 T1/11464/18470/12, Post Office to Treasury, 1 November 1907, Roland Wilkins, Treasury, to Sir A.F. King, [second secretary], Post Office, 14 November 1907.
70 'Deputation to the Postmaster-General,' *Association Notes*, [I], 14, November 1911: 116.
71 Hinchy, F.S., (1971), *So Much in Life*, London and New York: Regency Press: 29.
72 *Association Notes*, [I], 5, October 1909: 44.
73 'The New Policy', *ibid*., [I], 4, March 1909: 40.,
74 'The Civil Service Federation,' *ibid*., II, 4, October 1913, speech of Miss P.B. Mills: 9.
75 Holt evidence: 5. These ambitions have not yet been realized.
76 'Feminism and the State,' *Association Notes*, II, 1, October 1913: 7.
77 'General Post Office', *ibid*: 3.
78 FL228, 'Association of Post Office Women Clerks: Minutes of AGMs', 11th, 20 May 1913.
79 On a later occasion he sent his wife in his stead, and she, 'a constitutional suffragist', gave a speech in support of the Association and the vote ('a subject of which Mr. Samuel and I have agreed to differ'), and was rapturously received. 'The At Home', *Association Notes*, [I], 11, April 1911: 92 and II, 2 January 1914: 19–20.
80 'News from the Board of Trade: The Association Dinner,' *ibid*., [I], 19, January 1913: 168.
81 Kanter, 'Some Effects of Proportions': 976.
82 'News from the Board of Trade,' *Association Notes*, [I], 18, October 1912: 159.
83 'News from the Board of Trade,' *ibid*., [I], 19, January 1913: 167.
84 Witz, *Professions and Patriarchy*: 46, 48.
85 Weber, M., (1965), 'Bureaucracy,' in H.H. Gerth and C. Wright Mills (eds. and trans.), *From Max Weber: Essays in Sociology*, New York: Oxford University Press: 228.
86 Hamilton: 116.

Gender and bureaucracy: women in finance in Britain and France

Rosemary Crompton and Nicola Le Feuvre

Introduction[1]

In this paper, we will briefly discuss first, feminist critiques of a number of key concepts in the social sciences. Second, we will address a longstanding debate within feminism – the question of 'equality' versus 'difference'. These two strands will be brought together in a discussion of recent feminist work on gender and organizations, and its relationship to recent developments in organization theory. We will then report on our empirical work which has compared the organizational careers of women in the finance sector in Britain and France. Our conclusions will re-examine the theoretical issues in the light of our empirical findings.

The feminist critique of 'malestream' sociology, developed from the 1970s onwards, has argued that: (i) the development of sociology as a discipline had focussed on the (masculine) 'public domain' of government and the market place, rather than the 'private domain' of the feminine, and (ii) that sociologists had also taken for granted that the gender order was 'natural', rather than socially *constructed* (Stacey 1981). In respect of the public domain, Pateman (1988; 1989) has developed a feminist critique of a purportedly gender-neutral concept – 'citizenship' – which is of direct relevance to this discussion. Her analysis of the original *fraternal* 'social contract' demonstrates that this was a contract between men-as-brothers which left intact men's (sexual) right to women within marriage. Women were not initially given rights as 'citizens', and the attainment of these rights has, since the 18th century, been the major objective of liberal feminists who have fought for rights in respect of property, education, the franchise, and so on. As the original 'citizen' was male, the development of what Marshall (1951) has described as 'social citizenship' and the welfare state was similarly constructed around the male worker. As Pateman argues: 'Paid employment has become the key to citizenship, and the recognition of an individual as a citizen of equal worth to other citizens is lacking when a worker is unemployed' – or not in paid employment (1989: 184).

Thus 'citizens' – in theory and in practice – were initially defined as male. 'Citizenship' is but one of a range of ostensibly universal or gender neutral concepts within the social sciences which have, increasingly, been shown to rest upon a gender-specific division of labour in the public and private spheres. This has, however, remained implicit until the advent of feminist critiques.

The area of social stratification was amongst the first of the topics to be critically evaluated by second wave sociological feminism. In particular, employment derived occupational 'class' schemes were shown to rest upon classifications in which *male* employment was taken to be the norm (Acker 1973; Allen 1982). The sociological convention whereby employment is used as a measure of 'class' rests upon the assumption that the impact of class processes such as the structuring of relationships of production, and market relationships, may be mapped on to the structure of employment relationships. Scase (1992) has recently provided a clear statement of this assumption: '. . . jobs and occupations are the *outcome* of class relations and they can be directly related to the functions of ownership and of labour. . .different occupational categories are derived from the social relations of production' (pp. 24–5). Braverman's (1974) influential Marxist account of the 'labour process' may be read as a particular account of this mapping. Similarly, Weber's discussion of the nature of bureaucratic authority has been an important element in the identification of an emerging 'service class' in late 20th century capitalism. Weber's character-ization of the ideal-type bureaucrat stresses that such positions are achieved by appointment, rather than election, that specific training and qualifications are required, that the appointment is tenured and that the official receives a salary (in contrast to gifts or other personal inducements) which is commensurate with the positions' ranking within the organization (Weber, 1948: 198–204). In contrast to traditional or charismatic leadership (the other forms of authoritative domination identified by Weber), the selection and status of the bureaucrat rests upon supremely *rational* criteria. Following on from these arguments, Goldthorpe has described service class personnel as owing their positions to 'processes of bureaucratic appointment and achievement' (1982:

170), and Lash and Urry (1987) have also identified the development of a *career* as being central to the identification of the service
class. However, the bureaucratic official has to be free of domestic
labour in order to carry out (his) duties, and service class careers,
which are in practice overwhelmingly male, rest upon the *non*
service class work of women in both the world of work as well as in
the home (Crompton 1986). These examples demonstrate that the
sociological conventions whereby occupations are systematically
related to class processes rest upon a stereotypically 'gendered'
division of labour.

Defenders of class theory and class analysis have argued that as
the focus of their interests was *class*, rather than gender, then the
operationalization of the two concepts should, logically, be kept
separate (Wright, 1989:290–1; see also Crompton, 1989). More
contentiously, Goldthorpe has continued to maintain his 'conventional approach' to the position of women within class analysis,
through the use of arguments such as the fact that wives' social
imagery corresponds more closely to that of their husband's
occupational class than their own, and thus the continuing
conflation of a wife's class with that of the male 'head of
household' is justified (Erikson and Goldthorpe, 1988:548).
However, none of these arguments in defence of specific positions
within 'class analysis' can satisfactorily resolve a basic practical
difficulty associated with occupational or employment-derived
class schemes – ie, that the persistence of occupational segregation
places insuperable difficulties in the way of the development of a
single 'class' scheme for men and women.

The critiques developed by second-wave feminism, therefore,
have drawn attention to the 'gendered' nature of particular social
science concepts. They have also, however, brought to prominence
an issue which has always been present within feminism. As
Cockburn (1991) has argued: 'There has long been heated debate
in the feminist movement as to whether women should be seen as
essentially different from men or essentially similar. The 'difference'
lobby proposes that women's physical sexual difference from men
results in a . . . different psychology and different (and better)
moral values . . . By contrast, the 'sameness' lobby argues that
women and men are more or less a blank slate on which gender
identity is inscribed in the process of a lifetime of learning
experiences' (p. 9). Liberal feminists from the 18th century
onwards have fought for equality and thus 'sameness', but as a
consequence have been faced with what Pateman has described as

'Wollestonecraft's dilemma'. If, as Pateman argues, the social contract is one between men, and if citizenship rights are therefore similarly masculine, then women who seek equal rights with men seek, in essence, to become surrogate men. Similarly, women who seek equal rights with men in the male-dominated world of paid employment have also been constrained to behave as surrogate males.

Recent feminist work on gender and organizations has drawn upon both the feminist critique of mainstream sociology as well as debates within feminism. However, such work has also been informed by contemporary developments within organization theory – in particular, the 'postmodern' critique of orthodox organizational analysis. The intellectual project implied by 'modernity' suggests that there is an inherent progress towards reason and rationality in human societies. This assumption is clearly present in classical models of organizational structure and functioning, as we have seen, for example, in Weber's emphasis on the rationality of the selection criteria for the bureaucratic official. In contrast, postmodernism stresses the indeterminate, uncertain, and chaotic nature of the social world – in this view, organizations are viewed as defensive reactions against inherently destabilizing forces. Thus 'postmodern' organization theorists such as Cooper and Burrell (1988) suggest: '. . . a radical revaluation of the traditional concept of organization as a circumscribed administrative-economic unit . . . Instead we need to see organization as a *process* that occurs within the wider 'body' of society and which is concerned with the construction of objects of theoretical knowledge' (pp. 105–6).

These 'post-modernist' interventions, it may be suggested, may be seen as the most recent developments within a sociological critique of organizational analysis which has, from the 'Human Relations' model onwards, systematically criticised rational, technocratic models of organizational structure and functioning. Gouldner's (1959) identification of 'rational' and 'natural system' models of organizational structure and functioning, and Mayntz' (1976) critique of 'normatively rational' models of organizational decision making may be cited as examples. However, our objective in this paper is not to develop a critique of these recent 'postmodernist' contributions, but rather, to illustrate the linkage between these ideas and recent feminist work.

It is a relatively straightforward matter to demonstrate that bureaucratic organizations rest upon a gendered division of labour. Bureaucratic careers rest upon full-time, continuous employment – that is, the male norm. The gender/grade structures of bureaucratic hierarchies demonstrate that it is overwhelmingly men who are at the apex of such hierarchies, and women who are at the base. Recent feminist work, however, has switched in its focus from the demonstration of the barriers faced by women in achieving equality within organizations, to an emphasis upon the way in which gender differences are *actively* constructed within organizations. The postmodernist emphasis on the significance of *difference* in the construction of organizations and organizational identities has been taken up and developed within such work. 'Difference' is seen as a central mechanism whereby domination may be established over subordinate groups. This approach stresses the significance of the *cultural* underpinnings of organizational structures, and power within organizations.

Thus, for example, Pringle (1988) has recently argued that: 'There is a vast gulf between feminist debates on psychoanalysis, discourse theory, cultural production and semiotics, and the frameworks of political economy and industrial sociology within which most studies of work are situated' (p. ix). In her empirical study of secretaries, therefore, she has organized her material '. . . around discourses of power rather than analyses of the labour process' (ibid p. x).

Recent debates, therefore, have suggested the need to revise theoretical perspectives on the study of gender and organizations. It is against this background that we present our empirical material. As we shall see, at the aggregate level, the employment careers of French women are very similar to those of French men. In Britain, in contrast, womens' employment careers are in aggregate rather different to those of men, being characterized by broken employment patterns, and part-time working. However, at the level of the organization, our data suggests that the experiences of French and British women are very similar. In the concluding section, these findings will be used to evaluate the theoretical arguments discussed above.

The employment patterns of French and British women

At the aggregate level, the employment patterns of French and British women are characterized by both similarities as well as some quite striking differences. In France, the labour force is 41 per cent female, in Britain, 42 per cent. The broad contours of occupational segregation by sex are also very similar – in France as in Britain, women predominate in service industries and clerical work, and are concentrated in lower-level occupations rather than higher. However, in the characteristic employment careers of women there are important differences between the two countries. Fewer French women than British women have taken a 'child-rearing break' in paid employment, that is, leaving the labour force at the birth of their first child, then returning after a few years – usually when the last child is of school age (Martin and Roberts 1984). If French women *do* leave the labour force for domestic reasons (usually childrearing), then this is likely to be long-term. Many women, however, continue to work, even when they have young children. Thus the overall pattern of French women's paid employment is very similar to that of French men – although the *extent*, of course, is lower.

The level of part-time working amongst French women is also much lower than amongst women in Britain. The percentage of British women working part-time is 43, as compared to 23 per cent of French women. Even when French women do work part-time, their hours are likely to be longer than those of British women – for example, 24 per cent of part-time women in Britain are employed for less than ten hours a week, as compared with only 12 per cent of women part-time workers in France (Barrére-Maurisson *et al*, 1989:48).

French women, therefore, tend to work full-time or not at all, and if working, their employment histories are likely to have been continuous (Dex and Walters, 1989). These cross-national variations in women's employment patterns may be explained by a number of factors, demographic and historical. The demographic transition occurred earlier in France, thus married women have been a more significant component of the French labour force since the 19th century. (Tilly and Scott, 1987). Gender-specific exclusionary practices on the part of trade unions have not been as important in France as has been the case in Britain, where the strength of workplace unionism has been an important factor in women's exclusion from employment, particularly in the better-paying jobs (Rubery, 1988; Jenson, 1986). The French state made earlier provisions for maternity leave and associated benefits for French women than did the British government – indeed, much welfare policy concerned with childrens' health in Britain was aimed at excluding mothers from employment (Lewis, 1980). As is well known, state provision for pre-school children is much more extensive in France than in Britain, as are out-of-school care arrangements. A recent report of the European Childcare network placed France, (along with Denmark, Belgium, and Italy), in the group of countries providing the highest level of publicly-funded childcare, whereas Britain was in the lowest group (Phillips and Moss, 1989:14). There are a number of factors, therefore, which taken together provide a plausible explanation for the fact that full-time working and unbroken employment careers are more prevalent amongst French than British women. Indeed, full-time working amongst women, even by the mothers of young children, would seem to be more acceptable as the norm in France than Britain (Procter and Ratcliffe, 1992).

This paper, however, is not mainly concerned with these macro-level differences. Rather, it seeks to explore the consequences at the level of the employing *organization* of the different employment patterns of French and British women. In particular, does the more permanent, and full-time, pattern of working amongst French women mean that they are more likely to achieve success in building bureaucratic careers within organizations?

The use of women's labour in the finance sector

Previous research on the financial sector in Britain has demonstrated that the expansion of women's employment within finance since the Second World War was overwhelmingly concentrated at the lowest grade levels (Blackburn, 1967; Llewellyn, 1981; Heritage, 1983; Crompton and Jones, 1984). Particularly within the banking industry, it was the practice to recruit young women school leavers, (often at lower levels of qualification than young men), who, it was anticipated, would then leave the banks' employ when they had their first child – most usually in their twenties. Young men and women have been recruited into the same grade structure in the banks since the 1960s, since when there has not been any 'official' discrimination. However, whereas the majority of women had usually left full-time employment by the time they were thirty, young men were more likely not only to stay in employment but also to study for the bank's professional examinations, and to be available for geographical mobility. Thus whereas most young men who stayed in banking were able to follow a classic bureaucratic career and achieve promotion to a managerial position, most women never moved beyond the basic clerical level.[2]

By the early 1980s, however, such practices were coming under increasing scrutiny and criticism. The women who entered banking were becoming better qualified; the age at which women had their first child was rising; and the social context was changing. Many women were beginning to question the gender stereotypical division of labour – and promotion opportunities – which prevailed in banking, and bitterly resented being passed over on the promotion ladder by young men. They also complained of the informal exclusionary practices which many male managers practised – for example, discouraging young women from taking the professional examinations (Crompton and Jones, 1984). An equal opportunities referral in 1983 led to Barclays Bank modifying its recruitment policies, and the other clearing banks quickly followed suit (Crompton, 1989).[3] There was a move from a single entry to a multi-portal pattern of recruitment. As a consequence of this change in practice, potential managers were clearly identified at the point of entry. The sex of those recruited at each grade level was monitored. Following these changes, women still make up the majority of lower-level employees, but nevertheless, more than half of the potential managers recruited by Barclays in 1985/6 were women.

These changes, however, have only affected young women. Past discriminatory practices, both formal and informal, continue to have an impact and the grade/gender structure of contemporary British banking (and indeed, the financial sector more generally) indicates that women still predominate massively in the lowest clerical grades, and that few women have reached managerial positions.

It might have been anticipated, however, that the situation in France would be rather different. Aggregate level data demonstrates that the employment patterns of women in the banking sector in France resemble those of French women as a whole; and thus the majority are long-term employees (average years of service for men, 17.5; average years of service for women, 16.0). The overall age structure of female bank employees is very similar to that of male bank employees (the modal age being 35 for both men and women)[4]. There is also evidence that French banks have not formally discriminated against women to the same extent as British banks – for example, there is no history of the marriage bar (ie, the requirement that a woman should resign her employment on marriage) in France, whereas the marriage bar persisted in the British clearing banks until the 1960s (Labourie-Racapé, 1982). Empirical work carried out in the late 1970s suggested that women had indeed advanced considerably further within the finance sector in France than in Britain, and that many more women had achieved non-clerical positions, particularly at the lower levels of management and administration.

Thus a European Commission report published in 1982 stated that in 1974, 44 per cent of junior executives, 14 per cent of senior executives, and 3 per cent of top management in credit institutions in France were women. In comparison, women were only 5 per cent of junior executives in the UK, and entirely absent from the more senior positions. Overall, 28 per cent of French women working in financial institutions were recorded as being in managerial positions, as against only 1 per cent of British women (Povall, 1982, Tables 4;5). The contrast in the figures for the two countries is indeed very striking, but it might be suggested that this comparison is rather misleading because of the very different nature of the finance sector in the two countries, particularly in the 1970s.[5]

The practical difficulties of making cross-national comparisons, particularly in relation to occupations and occupational levels, have been extensively rehearsed (Goldthorpe 1985; Dale and Glover 1989). One strategy for resolving difficulties relating to cross-national comparisons is to match, as closely as possible, the phenomena under investigation in the two (or more) countries, as for example, Maurice *et al* have done in their studies of organizations in a number of different countries (Maurice *et al*, 1980). Thus Labourie-Racapé *et al*'s (1982) investigation into individual banks in four countries (Belgium, France, Britain and the Netherlands) might be expected to provide more reliable comparative information. In fact, this research suggested that the disparities between the grade levels achieved by French and British women are not as great as those suggested by the European Commission report. In the English bank studied, 84 per cent of women were only on basic clerical grades, whereas for French women, the proportion was lower – 72 per cent (Table 2, p. 486). However, only 5 per cent of French women had reached the level of cadre (manager) – although there were no British women at this level at all.

It would appear, therefore, that the employment patterns of French women (full-time working, no career breaks) *had* resulted in their achieving rather higher levels within the financial sector than the predominantly young, short-term female employees characteristically found within British banks. For example, Povall (1984) had argued, in her commentary on the comparative evidence then available that: 'The practice of recruiting young people only (ie, in the British banks) . . . whilst not directly discriminatory, effectively precluded women who had left to rear families from recommencing any sort of career later. Only in France (where three years maternity leave is provided, childcare facilities are reasonable and leave is available for children's illness) had moderate numbers of women progressed' (p. 35). Nevertheless, the achievements of French women have been rather modest, and this became more apparent as we pursued our detailed comparisons.

In banking, the differences between the grade levels of French and British women are greatest at the lowest level – proportionately fewer French women are on the lowest clerical grades. These differences are less marked at the highest occupational levels. In the British clearing banks, the managerial grade structure proper begins at the level of Appointed Officer – although there are, of course, many supervisory and lower-level administrative positions immediately below this. The proportion of Appointed Officers in British banks (as a proportion of all employees) is around 20 per cent (or below), although this will vary somewhat between different banks. A similar proportion of employees in French banks are at the managerial level (cadre). We were able to obtain detailed grade/gender comparisons for two comparable institutions in France and Britain: Societé D'Ivry, (a member of the Association Francais de Banques), and a major British clearer, Northbank. In 1989, in Societé D'Ivry, 5.3 per cent of female employees had reached the level of *cadre* (total number of employees, 43,000). In 1990, in Northbank, 2.8 per cent of female employees had reached the level of Appointed Officer (total number of employees, 62,000). This exercise in grade comparisons also uncovered another difference in the grading conventions in French and British banks which might explain the rather more favourable position of women in France apparently revealed in earlier reports. In France, there is a three-tier grade structure; employés, gradés, and cadres. All employés who pass the Brevet Professionel (BP) – a relatively modest occupational qualification – will *automatically* be placed at the level of gradé (such automatic progression is not the case with cadre positions). In contrast, progression, even to higher clerical grades, in British banks is through promotion. This difference in practice between French and British banks, it might be suggested, will have the effect of raising the overall level of the grade structure of French banks at the *lower* levels – indeed, in recent years, the proportion of employés has fallen, and that of gradés increased. Thus many women in France at the gradé level may not necessarily have achieved promoted positions, but their extended service, together with the BP qualification, will ensure that they are located at least at the gradé level. It is perhaps this fact which explains the relatively smaller proportion of French women at the *lowest* clerical levels in the French banks than in the British.

Given the facilities available to French women to acquire 'masculine' employment profiles – the availability of childcare, a convention of uninterrupted, full-time working, a relative lack of overt, formal discrimination such as the marriage bar, and so on – it might be considered that the proportion of French women who have achieved managerial positions in banking is in fact rather low. This fact might have practical implications for present strategies in respect of women's employment in the financial sector in Britain. In some contrast to even a decade ago, most of the major financial institutions in the UK today are anxious to attract qualified female labour, and to demonstrate that they are truly equal opportunities employers. Equal Opportunities officers have been appointed, career break schemes implemented, workplace nurseries set up in order to enable women with children to continue to work. These kinds of measures will help women to acquire the 'masculine' pattern of uninterrupted employment which has been necessary in order to develop a managerial career within large organizations. However, despite the fact that women in the banking sector in France have demonstrated such 'masculine' work patterns for a number of years, at the managerial level, the comparative data suggests that the consequences of such practices for women's achievements has not been as substantial as might have been expected. This fact might have practical implications for the kinds of strategies adopted by British employers attempting to consciously promote equal opportunities.

These possible policy implications, however, are not the major topic of this paper. At the commencement of the research we anticipated that there would be substantial differences in the career levels achieved by French and British women, and indeed, this did seem to be indicated by the aggregate level data available.

The initial process of 'unpacking' aggregate level figures, however, as revealed by our discussion of the employé/gradé distinction, suggested that the differences were not as substantial as a straightforward reading would suggest.

Research methods

In the preceding sections of this paper, we have described the aggregate level differences in French and British women's employment patterns, as well as suggesting the range of institutional factors, demographic and historical, economic and social, which have contributed to the differential structuring of women's employment in the two countries. It is being increasingly recognized within social science that the manner in which gender relations are structured within the division of labour is extremely diverse; that there is no single category, 'gender', which can be applied across a range of societies. In different nation states – indeed, in different regions within nation states – women (and men) are subject to different institutional pressures, and social contexts, which give rise to different patterns of involvement in paid work (Rubery, 1988; Jenson *et al*, 1988). Nevertheless, women and men nowhere constitute units of abstract labour, there are no empirical instances available where the labour force is not 'gendered' in some fashion or other, and the consequences of this 'gendering' usually means that women will be found occupying the lower positions (Scott, 1986). 'Macro' level constraints such as the availability of childcare, the effectiveness of anti-discrimination legislation, state and other provisions for working mothers, and so on can be called upon as explanations for the 'macro' level differences that have been described. However, we have suggested that, given the extent of the 'macro' level differences in employment patterns between French and British women, at the industry level, the differences in the proportions of women in managerial positions is perhaps not as great as might have been anticipated.

Our detailed comparison of organizational grade structures had already suggested that aggregate level data may not provide an entirely reliable account of organizational realities, thus an in-depth, micro-level approach seemed to be indicated. As Beechey has argued in her discussion of the variations in the employment patterns of French and British women:

We know far too little about the discriminatory processes which operate at the workplace level in both countries and how these are 'lived' by women. A comparative analysis of these questions would be an excellent subject for future research (1989: 375).

We already had available detailed interviews carried out with a small number of British women who had achieved managerial positions in major financial institutions. A similar number of interviews have been carried out with women on managerial grades in the finance sector in France.[6] Details of these interviews are summarised in the Appendix.

Women managers in Britain and France – work and family lives

Although this is not a random sample, and the numbers involved are very small, it is nevertheless interesting that the national level differences between the two countries were reflected amongst the women we interviewed. The relative level of academic qualifications acquired by French female school leavers is higher than in Britain, and the levels of academic qualification achieved before entering employment were generally high amongst the French women.[7] Fewer of the British women had had children (they were, on average, younger than the French women interviewed), but all of the British women except Miriam had taken a break in employment of more than a year in order to look after their child(ren). In contrast, all of the French women who had had children, with the exception of Marie-Laure, had taken only statutory maternity leave rather than an employment break.

Starting a career

The requirements for a successful career in a financial bureaucracy (indeed, in any bureaucratic organization), include full-time, continuous working as well as a high level of commitment to the employing organization. Within the sociology of work, this has been conceptualized as a 'bureaucratic' orientation to work, and as we have seen such individuals have been described as belonging to a 'service' class, bound to their organizations by the loyalty they render in exchange for a career (Goldthorpe, 1982; Abercrombie and Urry, 1983; Lash and Urry, 1987). There are a number of commonsense reasons which suggest that the majority of women do not enter employment bearing fixed and explicit assumptions relating to such a bureaucratic career trajectory. For most women, historically at any rate, marriage and children are likely to have been assumed, at least initially, to represent an alternative, specifically feminine, career. These individual assumptions have been reinforced by the actions of bureaucratic employers, who, as we have seen, have regarded women as low-level clerical workers, rather than as potential managers. Thus many successful women have been unconventional or 'accidental' careerists. This pattern was found amongst a number of the women we interviewed, particularly those born before the early 1950s.

All of the four British women in this age category had had unconventional careers. Noreen had resigned her job on the birth of her son, but her husband's low wages, together with the fact that motherhood proved to be less fulfilling than anticipated, caused her to return to work when he was two. Clare and Patricia were both divorced in their twenties, Patricia's child being from her (late) second marriage. Clare and her first husband had moved from London so that they could buy a house, and Northbank had arranged a transfer to a new branch. Remembering her new job, Clare commented:

> . . .it was a super branch, but even going to Fallowfield, I still wasn't career oriented. At the time we bought a house in Fallowfield, I was still looking for two or three years (work), and (then) starting a family.

Carole had had her children very young. Financial necessity had led to a number of part-time jobs, including routine data entry for Northbank, and it was from this tenuous base that she had begun to work her way up by acquiring qualifications. Francoise and Marie-France had both found themselves with 'breadwinner' responsibilities at a young age, and Beatrice was divorced young. Cecile has remained single, but her early decision to embark on a long-term career was itself much influenced by her father's early death and the failure of the family business. After having worked to support her student husband whilst he qualified, Marie-Laure found herself divorced with a young child:

> I was married to someone who was still a student. I had a little boy and I thought that this (the bank) was something that would

last until my husband qualified and then I'd pick up my studies. That's how I started at the bank. At the beginning I really saw it as something temporary.

Monique found herself deeply dissatisfied with her job as a secretary, and took the decision to develop a career some years after entering employment.

In some contrast, none of the younger women (ie born after the mid-50s), in either France or Britain, had had other than relatively orthodox bureaucratic careers. Nathalie and Veronique had been recruited as graduate trainees, Helene had started work as a manager in another industry. Chantal and Therese had both worked their way up via the bank's internal examinations.[8] Similarly, Sally, Janet and Ruth had all entered employment as graduate trainees, and Jane, Elizabeth, Frances, Lucy and Nicola had all begun the process of acquiring vocational qualifications immediately after their entry into employment.

In both France and Britain, therefore, a womans' age would seem to be the major factor associated with whether or not she had had an 'orthodox' or an 'unconventional' career into management. As far as the older women were concerned, contextual constraints (often of a domestic nature) stemming from the vagaries of life appeared to have pushed them in this direction. It is of course entirely to be expected that there are at this very moment many young women who will eventually experience 'unconventional' career success in a similar fashion. However, the strategic recruitment of young women, such as those we interviewed, as potential managers and profesionals would seem to be a relatively new phenomenon, and our evidence suggests that increasingly, young women are attempting to pursue orthodox managerial careers.

Building a career

Previous research on womens' employment has suggested a complex relationship between gender and the formal and informal aspects of the organization. Formal bureaucratic rules may be used to indirectly discriminate against women – for example a formal requirement to be geographically mobile which is not absolutely necessary (EOC 1985). On the other hand, the very presence of such rules relating to appointments makes it difficult to exclude systematically individuals who possess the formal requirements attached to the position. Thus liberal feminists have always fought for equal access to bureaucratic prerequisites, such as education, professional qualifications, and so on. In recent years, there is increasing evidence that women are using the 'qualifications lever' in order to gain access to better jobs (Crompton and Sanderson, 1990). However, even for women who possess the formal qualifications for higher-level positions, informal male exclusionary barriers, deriving from the fact that historically, the higher bureaucratic positions have been held almost entirely by men, have worked to their disadvantage (Kanter, 1977).

Our interviews demonstrated the workings of all of these processes. It should be stressed that by no means all of the women had suffered from direct male discrimination – in particular, those with 'unconventional' careers, such as Francoise, or Carole, had often enjoyed useful sponsorship from a male 'mentor'. However, other women had experienced considerable frustration – and career difficulties – deriving from the masculine domination of the organizations they worked for. Cecile complained bitterly of the misogynous hierarchy at Frenchbank. She was of a generation where separate internal examinations were set for men and women (rédacteur and rédactrice), and even after she had been promoted to cadre, had suffered many petty humiliations:

> . . .even when we got managerial status, we were really considered as high-level personal assistants. I officially obtained managerial status in 1956, but up until 1977 I was working as a personal assistant. At that time even male clerks had certain prerogatives that female managers were denied. Take the keys to the safe, for example. Even today at Frenchbank, the keys to the safe represent something sacred and they were never given to women – even those with managerial status. I first got access to the keys of a branch safe in 1972/3, but only temporarily as the cashier was absent and there was no other solution. When word got out that a woman had the keys. . .it was considered quite extraordinary!

In comparison to her male contemporaries, Cecile – who, it will be remembered, has never married – considered that her career had run ten to fifteen years behind theirs. As Beatrice put it:

. . .a woman sticks out like a sore thumb against a gang of men. And so we're forced to adopt an aggressive tone. . .and I admit that we disturb, and quite rightly so, the smooth run of things . . .the sort of career that I have just described doesn't happen by accident, because I can assure you that there haven't been many helping hands along the way. . .

Monique had passed her ITB (cadre) finals in 1980. However, she was still well below managerial status five years later. She was finally promoted to managerial level just two months after attending the bank's annual management seminar where the MD had drawn attention to the notable absence of female managers at the gathering. Her sudden and rapid promotion as a 'token woman' was not only frustrating, it also made life very difficult at work:

It caused a lot of suffering. . .before then I had put in a lot of work and made huge personal sacrifices to pass the ITB finals in order to get managerial status and how did I finally get there? Simply by accompanying my regional director to the annual conference!. . .that was really hard to take because, as you can imagine, the unions were up in arms. . .and it made things really difficult with the female employees I was working with.

If anything, managers in the finance sector in Britain seem to have been even more confident that organizational careers were not really suitable for women. Patricia recalled that:

. . .my sub manager said to me: 'If you'd been a boy, of course, we'd have put you on a development course, but of course they don't do them for girls'. That was the situation and you seemed to accept it.

Indeed, individual managers were often not very encouraging, to say the least:

the senior local director at the time, who interviewed me when I came up for the job, told me quite clearly that, as far as he's concerned, a woman's place is in the home having children and housekeeping (Clare)

I had a feeling that my boss in particular wasn't that struck on women. . .one of the girls was leaving to have a baby and I took the card in, he said, I can't wait for the day when they bring yours in. I said, thank you very much, do you want to get rid of me? – he said oh, no no no, I just think its where women are most fulfilled, at home having a family (Miriam)

Nevertheless, the women we interviewed had made it to managerial positions, and getting qualifications had usually played a very important part. This advancement, however, had usually involved considerable effort, and as Gauvin and Silvera (1991:39) have noted, the out-of-hours work necessary to gain such qualifications has effectively put them out of reach for many women in France.

I had to work every weekend to get my ITB – my daughter hated the time that I spent getting it (Arlette)

I had my first child two months before the exams – they required a lot of work and a lot of personal sacrifices. I often worked until 10 or 11 o'clock in the evening, and all day Saturday or all Sunday (Monique)

Out-of-hours study was also required of our British respondents:

I wrote a hundred essays in all over the time. . .and some of them I enjoyed, and some I found hard. . .Part 1 I found relatively easy. . .the second part I found difficulty in the very last paper. . .you're very much on your own, you still are. . .but my son was doing 'O' levels at the time so it wasn't too bad (Noreen)

The (IOB) exams are a slog – basically they were a slog – but that rather than extremely difficult. They were just a real slog . . .fitting it in round work so when you got in in the evening you just had to sit down and get going again (Ruth)

In summary, therefore, the picture that emerged from our interviews was of women who had worked hard and shown considerable tenacity, often against the odds. All had worked in a predominantly male environment for all of their working lives. Sometimes individual bosses (male) had been helpful, more often they had not been, although the majority of our respondents – even those who felt that their sex had been a handicap as far as their careers were concerned – felt that the situation had improved in this respect:

> When I started my job a woman wouldn't have had a chance of getting the job I've actually got now. . .I think the young women who come in now will be even more successful because they have absolutely the same possibilities as the men, they are absolutely equal (Cecile)

> . . .there are a lot more women managers today than there were ten years ago, that's certain. . .I think that developments within the (banking) sector have been working more to the advantage of women for a number of years (Helene)

Many women we interviewed (particularly in France) had achieved these positions whilst bringing up families, and even amongst women without children, the possibilities – or otherwise – of motherhood tended to loom fairly large as far as the trajectories of their working lives were concerned.

Careers and children

Practically all of the women we interviewed – married or single, with or without children – saw problems in combining a career with childbearing. Some women had decided to remain childless in order to pursue a career:

> I got to about 27–28, and got fed up training all these young boys (ie in her capacity as an experienced clerk). . .it got to the stage – what do I want to do? Do we want a family and we decided we were perfectly happy as we were and we wouldn't bother about children at all. . .the only way out of my rut was to start taking my banking examinations (Clare)

> (on having children) I think it does hinder women but its a hindrance they take on themselves. . .its not a hindrance that derives from the hierarchy of the bank (Cecile)

Other young women – for example, Janet and Ruth – thought that they would probably never have children:

I don't want children. I've spent too long getting qualified, and I'm not that way orientated at all, and I think you have to be if you really want to make sacrifices which I'm not prepared to make (Ruth)

Amongst the women who did have children, or who were contemplating motherhood as a possibility, the feeling was general that the combination of a career with motherhood was far from easy:

If the possibility existed for cadres, I would rather work part-time. . .I always suffered when I left my children to go to work . . .it's the same now they're teenagers, you can never give them enough time (Odile)

. . .it is possible to take a sabbatical leave. . .but its impossible to take advantage of possibilities like that in a job with certain responsibilities. It would be out of the question for me to take a parental sabbatical or to work part-time. For women, the ideal thing would be to reduce her hours to 80%, but for a woman manager that would be impossible, or rather the structure of the banking sector as it exists at the moment makes that impossible (Helene)

I don't think I would be able to aspire to the highest positions if I had a child. . .I see successful high-level women with a child but I think 'at what price to the child?'. . .and the same for the parents. . .we are strongly advised not to take advantage of these possibilities (ie of maternity and further leave). Let's say that it wouldn't be looked on very favourably. . .it would be taken as proof of the lack of commitment of the individual to the bank (Veronique)

In an employment context such as prevails in France, in which part-time work has not on the whole been generally used as a strategy to integrate mothers into the labour force, (O'Reilly, 1992), part-time work was nevertheless seen by our respondents as an option which *should* be possible. However, amongst the British women we interviewed, part-time work *at their level* was seen, similarly, as being out of the question, despite the fact that this type of employment is commonplace amongst women in Britain:

(I've) done about four years at (Appointed Officer) and. . .since I've decided to have a family, I've made absolutely no progress

113

whatsoever despite having worked full-time and part-time . . . I said, can you get me part-time work at the A1 level? No, there is no such thing as a part-time appointed position and, in the end, it was thought that they could give me something at Grade 4, part-time (she did take the lower-level job but gave it up in frustration) (Sally)

I think if I could, I would go part-time. Obviously here that's not acceptable. Anybody who does part-time work here is in lower grade jobs (Miriam)

I've seen people try (to work part-time). There was a woman with a baby (qualified accountant) who. . .just worked three days a week, and really she would never get promoted . . . someone said to me, she's got different priorities, you know, and her job isn't first. . .it meant that she would never really get on so much (Lucy)

Concluding discussion

Our initial interest in pursuing the Anglo-French comparison stemmed from the similarities of the employment profiles of French men and French women as compared to the very different employment profiles of British men and women. The broken employment careers of British women, together with a very high rate of part-time working, have often been cited as an explanation for their relatively low levels of material returns from employment, low levels of promotion, and so on (Dale and Joshi 1992). From aggregate level data, we know that in France, more women with children will be working full-time, and that they are likely to have had uninterrupted employment careers. These circumstances have contributed to the rather higher proportion of women in managerial positions within the finance sector in France than in Britain, although the numbers involved are still rather low. However, the picture that emerged overwhelmingly from our detailed exercise in comparison was one of the underlying *similarity* of attitude and experience amongst these women, despite the very real differences of the national employment contexts. 'Gender' may not be a universal concept, but the experiences of individual women nevertheless demonstrate important continuities.

Thus the empirical material presented in this paper could be used to develop a relatively straightforward argument relating to the question of equality of opportunity. The specific difficulties encountered by women managers in France and Britain might be used as evidence to support the critiques of liberal feminism developed by 'second wave' feminists. Liberal feminists had stressed the significance of, above all, *equality* (or 'sameness'), of the importance for women of achieving rights, terms, and conditions of employment similar to those of men. 'Second wave' feminists have continued to struggle for equality, but they have also argued that a formal equality of status for women is not in itself adequate to counter the impact of patriarchal structures and pressures in the home, in the workplace, in sexual relations as well as in the political and public arena (Walby, 1986; Cockburn, 1991). As the evidence of our interviews demonstrates, a formal equality of access is indeed not adequate to achieve a real equality of practice.

Besides the question of equal opportunities, however, our discussion relates to theoretical issues. We have already reviewed feminist criticisms of a number of supposedly universal concepts within the social sciences, including 'citizenship', 'class', and 'bureaucracy', which have been demonstrated as resting upon stereotypical practices relating to the division of labour between men and women. Changes in the gender division of labour – in particular, the increase in paid employment of married women – have not only called into question the universality of concepts such as 'class', but have also revealed their weaknesses in relation to the analysis of womens' experiences. Occupational class schemes devised with reference to mens' work do not adequately describe the pattern of womens' employment, and bureaucratic structures geared to masculine careers result in very different outcomes for women – even when men and women are in equivalent jobs. These kinds of problems have no doubt contributed to the fact that many feminist writers have rejected established strategies of 'mainstream' organizational analysis in favour of 'postmodernist' approaches which emphasise the actively-constructed nature of organizational reality. In this view, men and women within the organization are not genderless 'agents', rather, organizations are the locus within which masculinities and femininities are generated – and the 'feminine' subordinated.

Our material could be used to illustrate the manner in which establishing the 'difference' between men and women has been

115

used in strategies of subordination – for example, the mayhem that might have ensued once Cecile had been given access to the keys of the safe (the imagery of Pandora's box is inescapable here); the bosses who made it plain that women were out of place in the managerial grades, and so on. Even where women are prepared to behave as surrogate men – as were our respondents – their 'difference' was nevertheless emphasized.

An approach which views organizations as '. . . less the expression of planned thought and calculative action and more a defensive reaction to forces . . . which constantly threaten the stability of organized life' (Cooper and Burrell 1988 p. 91), does, therefore, have much to offer as far as our understanding of gender relationships within organizations are concerned. Nevertheless, women *are* bureaucrats. It is true that the formal bureaucratic model is grounded in a gender-typical division of labour, and thus bureaucratic positions have been occupied overwhelmingly by men, but in the late 20th century these processes are grounded in typicality, rather than absolute exclusionary practices. More importantly, perhaps, the bureaucratic model provides a template against which women and men have measured and shaped their actions – to suggest that it is somehow 'ideological' does not remove its impact upon human beings, male and female. The bureaucratic model is available to men *and* women, it is a source of organizational structuring, as well as an outcome. Even when their career beginnings were unconventional, the women we interviewed had usually followed an orthodox bureaucratic career path – even though this often involved personal difficulties and sacrifice. As we have seen in their attitudes (and indeed, decisions), relating to their families and children, many of these women had felt constrained to behave as 'surrogate men' – even to the extent of remaining childless. To recognize the force of 'Wollenstonecraft's dilemma', however, does not remove it, or its effects.

In conclusion, therefore, we would make a relatively straightforward argument. Even if some of the aspects of the 'critical' and 'post-modernist' critiques of classical organizational theory are accepted as valid, what is nevertheless required is a continuing plurality of theoretical approaches to the study of organizations, rather than an absolute rejection of the formal bureaucratic model. Like most human institutions, organizations embody a range of contradictions, and it is unlikely that a single theory could encompass them all. Different approaches to the study of organizations represent not so much alternatives as partial understandings of a complex whole and, in their criticisms of the inadequacies of particular models, social scientists of all persuasions should be alert to the possible danger of re-inventing the wheel.

Notes

1 The empirical research reported in this paper is part of a research project, 'Women in Professional Occupations in France and Britain', financed by the ESRC. Prof. L. Hantrais (Loughborough) and P. Walters (Salford) are co-investigators.
2 This policy was quite deliberate. In 1969, at the Institute of Bankers Cambridge seminar, G.V. Bramley said: '. . .experience has shown that it is possible to maintain an even flow of male recruits while controlling fluctuations in numerical requirements by varying the rate of female recruitment. . .if initial recruitment has been sufficiently selective possibly 75 per cent of entrants should become managers' Quoted in Povall, 1982:14.
3 See *Interim Report of the Commission's Agreement with Barclay's Bank plc*, 1987.
4 Figures taken from Association Francaise des Banques (AFB): 'Effectifs et Remunerations', March 1989, and 'Rapport sur l'evolution de l'emploi dans les banques AFB; 1987/1988.
5 Large institutions and organizations (and therefore employment units) predominate in Britain, which is the world's leading financial centre. This characteristic was even more pronounced prior to the Finance Act of 1986. In contrast, France has a relatively greater proportion of smaller financial outlets.
6 Interviews in Britain were carried out by Dr. K. Sanderson and Ms. R. Crompton. Interviews in France have been carried out by Dr. N. Le Feuvre. The research has been supported by the Economic and Social Research Council and the Joseph Rowntree Memorial Trust. Information was gathered on family background, education, career history and development, and domestic life. The interviews were unstructured. All interviews were transcribed verbatim.
7 In order to simplify the presentation of the data and thus facilitate comparison, some violence has been done to the details relating to educational qualifications. Arlette, Marie-Laure, Monique and Chantal all had a BTS, a post-Baccalaureate secretarial qualification, and had entered employment in banking on the basis of their secretarial skills. They had crossed over into 'mainstream' banking via the bank's internal examinations. In the organizations employing the British women we interviewed, secretarial jobs have, historically, been organized separately from the lower-level clerical jobs from which managers have been recruited. In France, one possible explanation of the 'crossover' is that in the late 1970s and early 1980s, French banks were faced with an excess of employees in the lower grades, due to over-recruitment during the 'guerre des guichets' in the 1970s. Extensive retraining opportunities were offered to all employees as a consequence.
8 But see note (7) above.

117

References

Abercrombie, N. and Urry, J., (1983), *Capital, Labour and the Middle Classes*, London: Allen and Unwin.

Acker, J., (1975), 'Women and Social Stratification: a case of intellectual sexism', *American Journal of Sociology*, Vol. 78: 936–45.

Allen, S., (1982), 'Gender Inequality and Class Formation' in A. Giddens and G. Mackenzie (eds) *Social Class and the Division of Labour*, Cambridge: Cambridge University Press.

Barrére Maurison, M.A., Daune-Richard, A.M., Letablier, M.T. (1989), 'Le travail à temps partiel plus développé au Royaume–Uni qu'en France' *Economie et Statistique* N.220, Avril 1989.

Beechey, V., (1989), 'Women's Employment in Britain and France: Some problems of comparison' *Work, Employment and Society* Vol. 3, No. 3, pp. 369–378.

Blackburn, R.M., (1967), *Union Character and Social Class*, London: Batsford.

Braverman, H., (1974), *Labor and Monopoly Capital*, New York: Monthly Review Press.

Cooper, R. and Burrell, G. (1988), 'Modernism, Postmodernism and organizational analysis'. *Organization Studies*, 9:1 pp. 91–112.

Cockburn, C., (1991), *In the Way of Women*, Basingstoke: Macmillan.

Crompton, R., (1986), 'Women and the "Service Class" in Crompton & Mann (ed.) *Gender and Stratification*, Cambridge: Polity.

Crompton, R., (1989[a]), 'Women in Banking' *Work, Employment and Society*, Vol. 3, No. 2.

Crompton, R., (1989[b]), 'Class Theory and Gender' *British Journal of Sociology* Vol. 40, No. 4, pp. 565–587.

Crompton, R., and Sanderson, K. (1990), *Gendered Jobs and Social Change*, London: Unwin Hyman.

Dale, A. and Glover, J., (1989), 'Women at Work in Europe: the potential and pitfalls of using published statistics' *Employment Gazette* pp. 299–308.

Dale, A. and Joshi, H., (1992), 'The Economic and Social Status of British Women'. Social Statistics Research Unit, City University.

Dex, S. and Walters, P. (1989), 'Women's Occupational Status in Britain, France and the U.S.A.: explaining the difference' *Industrial Relations Journal* Vol. 20, No. 3.

EOC (1985), *Formal Investigation Report: Leeds Permanent Building Society*, Manchester.

Erikson, R. and Goldthorpe, J.H., (1988), 'Women at Class Crossroads: A Critical Note' *Sociology* Vol. 22, pp. 545–553.

Gauvin, A. and Silvera, R., (1991), 'Effets de l'achevement du marche interieur sur l'emploi des femmes dans les Banques Francaises' Brussels: CEE.

Goldthorpe, J., (1982), 'On the service class, its formation and future' in Giddens & MacKenzie (eds) *Social Class and the Division of Labour* Cambridge: Cambridge University Press.

Goldthorpe, J.H., (1985), 'On Economic development and social mobility' *British Journal of Sociology* Vol. 36, No. 4, pp. 549–573.

Gouldner, A., (1965), 'Organizational Analysis' in R.K. Merton, L. Broom, and L.S. Cottrell (eds), *Sociology Today*, New York: Harper & Row.

Heritage, J., (1983), 'Feminisation and Unionisation: a Case Study from Banking' in E. Gamarnikow (ed.) *Gender Class and Work* London: Heinemann.

Jenson, J., (1986), 'Gender and Reproduction: or Babies and the State' *Studies in Political Economy* Vol. 20.

Jenson, J., Hagen, E. and Reddy, C., (eds), (1988), *Feminization of the Labour Force: Paradoxes and Promises*, New York: Oxford University Press.

Kanter, R.M., (1977), *Men and Women of the Corporation*, New York: Basic Books.

Labourie–Racapé *et al*, (1982), 'L'emploi féminin dans le secteur bancaire' *Gestion et Technique Bancaires* No. 416.

Lash, S. and Urry, J., (1987), *The End of Organized Capitalism* Cambridge: Polity Press.

Lewis, J., (1980), *The Politics of Motherhood: Child and Maternal Welfare in England 1900–1939* London: Croom Helm.

Llewellyn, C., (1981), 'Occupational Mobility and the use of the comparative method' in H. Roberts (ed) *Doing Feminist Research* London: Routledge.

Marshall, T.H., (1951), 'Citizenship and Social Class' in T.H. Marshall, *Sociology at the Crossroads* London: Tavistock.

Martin, J. and Roberts, C., (1984), *Women and Employment: a Lifetime Perspective*, London: HMSO.

Maurice, M. Sorge and Warner, M., (1980), 'Societal Differences in Organizing Manufacturing Units: A Comparison of France, West Germany and Great Britain' *Organization Studies* 1.1, pp. 59–86.

Mayntz, R., (1976), 'Conceptual models of organizational decision-making and their application to the policy process' in G. Hafstede and M.S. Kassem (eds) *European Contributions to Organization Theory*, Amsterdam: Van Gorcum.

O'Reilly, J., (1992), 'Banking on flexibility: A Comparison of the use of flexible employment strategies in the retail banking sector in Britain and France', Nuffield College, Oxford.

Pateman, C., (1988), *The Sexual Contract*, Cambridge: Polity Press.

Pateman, C., (1989), *The Disorder of Women*, Cambridge: Polity Press.

Perrow, C., (1972), *Complex Organizations: A Critical Essay*, Glenview, Illinois: Scott, Foresman & Co.

Phillips, A. and Moss, P., (1989), *Who Cares for Europe's Children?* (The Short Report of the European childcare network), Luxembourg: Office for Official Publications of the European Communities.

Povall, M., (1982), *Women in Banking – a Review*, Brussels: Commission of the European Communities.

Povall, M., (1984), 'Overcoming Barriers to Women's Advancement in European Organisations' *Personnel Review* 13.1 pp. 32–40.

Pringle, R., (1988), *Secretaries Talk: Sexuality, Power and Work*, London: Verso.

Rubery, J., (ed.), (1988), *Women and Recession*, London: Routledge and Kegan Paul.

Scott, A., (1986), 'Industrialization, Gender Segregation and Stratification Theory' in R. Crompton and M. Mann (eds) *Gender and Stratification*, Cambridge: Polity Press.

Stacey, M., (1981), 'The Division of Labour Revisited or Overcoming the Two Adams' in *Practice and Progress: British Sociology 1950–1980*, edited by P. Abrams *et al*. London: George Allen and Unwin.

Tilly, L.A. and Scott, J.W., (1987), *Women, Work and Family* New York and London: Methuen.

Weber, M., (1948), 'Bureaucracy' in H. Gerth and C.W. Mills (eds), *From Max Weber*, London: Routledge and Kegan Paul.

Walby, S., (1986), *Patriarchy at Work* pp. 207, Cambridge: Polity Press.

Wright, E.O., (1989), *The Debate on Classes*, London: Verso.

Table 1 France

	Employer[1]	Date of Birth	Pre-employment qualification[2]	Post-employment qualification[3]	Present personal status[4]	Previous long-term relationships[5]	Children
Cecile	Francebank	1931	Bac	Cadre	S	—	—
Francoise	Privbank	1941	Bac	ITB (1st part)	C	1	1
Odile	Credit du Chêne	1944	University	—	M	—	2
Beatrice	Credit du Chêne	1944	Bac (1st stage)	Cadre	M	2	—
Marie-France	Société d'Ivry	1945	BEPC	—	C	1	1
Arlette	Credit du Chêne	1946	University	ITB	M	—	1
Louise	Japbank	1949	Postgraduate	—	M	1	—
Marie-Laure	Credit du Chêne	1950	Bac	Cadre	C	1	1
Monique	Credit de Gex	1951	Bac	ITB	M	—	2
Chantal	Credit du Chêne	1952	Bac	Cadre	C	—	2 (+1 step)
Therese	Credit du Chêne	1956	University	Cadre	M	—	2
Helene	Société d'Ivry	1958	University	—	M	—	2(step)
Nathalie	Credit du Chêne	1962	University	—	S	—	—
Veronique	Credit du Chêne	1965	University	—	M	—	—

Table 2 England

	Employer	Date of Birth	Pre-employment qualification	Post-employment qualification	Present personal status	Previous long-term relationships	Children
Noreen	Northbank	1934	'O' level	AIB	M	—	1
Clare	Northbank	1946	'O' level	AIB	M	1	—
Carole	Northbank	1946	'O' level	AIB	M	—	2
Patricia*	Southbank	1947	'O' level	AIB (part)	M	1	1
Miriam	Royal	1952	'A' level	ACCA	M	—	1
	Bedford Insurance						
Sally*	Southbank	1954	University	AIB	M	—	2
Jane	Royal	1955	'A' level	CIMA	M	—	—
	Bedford Insurance						
Elizabeth	Northbank	1956	'A' level	AIB	M	—	—
Frances*	Southbank	1957	'O' level	AIB	M	—	1
Janet	Tower Insurance	1958	University	ICAEW	M	—	—
Lucy	Royal	1961	'A' level	ICAEW	M	—	—
	Bedford Insurance						
Nicola	Northbank	1961	'O' level	AIB	M	—	—
Ruth	Northbank	1962	University	AIB	S	—	—

*On maternity leave (career break), soon to return.

Notes

1. All names and employers are pseudonyms.
2. Pre-employment qualification: the highest qualification achieved whilst in full-time education has been recorded.

France:
BEPC: Brevet d'études du premier cycle
Bac: Baccalaureat
University: This also includes equivalent (and higher-level) institutions, e.g. Haute Ecole du Commerce; Institut d'Etudes Politiques. Only those gaining degrees have been recorded.

3. Post-employment qualification.

France:
ITB: Institut Technique de la Banque
Cadre: French banks have internal competitive examinations (Concours d'Attaché; Concours de Sous-Directeur, etc.) which qualify the individual for a managerial (cadre) position. The higher levels of these examinations are equivalent to those of external, professional level, qualifications. The younger women (Helene, Nathalie, Veronique) have been recruited directly into cadre positions.

England:
AIB: Associate of the Institute of Bankers
ACCA: Association of Chartered Certified Accountants
CIMA: Chartered Institute of Management Accountants
ICAEW: Institute of Chartered Accountants of England and Wales.

4. Present personal status.
S: Single
M: Married
C: Cohabiting

5. Previous long-term relationships: this information may be incomplete.

Women's expertise, men's authority: gendered organisations and the contemporary middle classes

Mike Savage

In the past two decades there has been a striking rise in the number of women employed in managerial and (particularly) professional jobs throughout much of the advanced capitalist world[1]. Having been excluded from these sorts of jobs for much of the nineteenth and early twentieth centuries, the apparent expansion of women employed in middle class jobs raises crucial issues about contemporary social change. From one angle the increased employment of professional and managerial women might be read as being of epochal significance, allowing women to move in significant numbers into high status occupational positions for the first time in human history. From another, however, these changes might be seen as cosmetic, as changing little the underlying patriarchal structures which continue to subordinate women to men.

This chapter is an attempt to think through some of the implications of the increasing numbers of 'middle class women', with specific reference to research on contemporary Britain. One of the central arguments, however, is that in order to understand the significance of the expansion of the female professional and managerial workforce it is essential to relate the issue to the analysis of class formation, and in particular the role which organizational hierarchies play in processes of middle class formation. I intend to show that whilst women have moved into professional and 'skilled' jobs within the middle classes – loosely defined – they have rarely been able to secure positions of managerial authority within organizational hierarchies. Women have moved into positions of high *expertise*, but not into positions of high *authority*. I will argue that it is only by registering the significance of organizational structures as elements behind class

© *The Sociological Review* 1992. Published by Blackwell Publishers.

formation and gender inequality that we can begin to understand the relationship between class and gender inequality.

This chapter is divided into three parts. I begin with a general, conceptual discussion about the relationship between class and gender, in order to show that the usual response of distinguishing class from gender fails to indicate the close connection between the two. I then indicate how by building on the ideas of Rosemary Crompton, Rosemary Pringle and Anne Witz, we can begin to think about how the middle classes are defined, in part, as male classes. I use Erik Wright's theory of class to suggest that organizational hierarchies are particularly important as vehicles of both middle class formation and male power.

In the second part of this chapter I substantiate my arguments by examining patterns of work-life mobility within the middle classes, and between the middle classes and other social classes in the years 1971–1981, using evidence from the OPCS Longitudinal Study. Here I show that women are rarely able to advance their careers within bureaucracies by climbing an organizational ladder. Instead, those women who do manage to achieve careers within the middle classes tend to pursue 'occupational' careers, usually within subordinate professional niches. Women's careers are usually based upon deepening their expertise, not on moving into positions of organizational power.

In the third part of this chapter I see how this argument stands up in the light of changes in one specific sector – banking – in the past decade. Banking has been heralded as one of the areas where women, previously directly excluded from management, are increasingly moving through organizational labour markets into positions of authority and power. I dispute this by showing that women, even women in managerial jobs, are rarely employed in positions giving them effective organizational power. The apparently dramatic rise in the number of women in managerial ranks is, I argue, largely cosmetic. I conclude by suggesting that the growing number of women in middle class jobs is not an indication that women are moving into positions of effective power but rather that, as organizations restructure, growing numbers of professionals and managers are employed in ways which do not involve them in line management.

1 Theoretical Issues

The major reason why there has been little sustained attempt to think about the way in which gender influences middle class formation lies in the way that gender processes are normally conceptually distinguished from class processes. Whilst this has the merit of allowing both gender and class inequality to be recognized, and hence in preventing gender being reduced to class, it leads to a damaging inability to comprehend the connections between class and gender inequality at anything other than a purely empirical level. This separation of class and gender is however a standard procedure. Goldthorpe, for instance, sees the project of class analysis as specifying the impact of class factors on life chances. In his eyes, class must be rigorously distinguished from gender, in order that their relative importance in affecting life chances be tested (eg Goldthorpe and Marshall, 1992). Goldthorpe's Marxist antagonist, Erik Wright, is equally keen to separate class from gender. For Wright, class structures are based on forms of exploitation, whilst gender inequalities are instances of oppression (Wright, 1985), and hence any attempt to suggest interconnections at a theoretical level is mistaken.

Both these writers sustain their arguments by appealing to a fundamental distinction between class structure and class formation. Class structure is concerned with the elaboration of unequal (usually occupational) positions within the division of labour inside the formal economy.[2] Class formation is concerned with the extent to which classes develop as recognisable social collectivities on the basis of these class positions, through such processes as social mobility and political mobilization (see Marshall *et al*, 1988, for discussion). Whilst both writers might accept that gender may affect the way in which class formation occurs – for instance when militant working class trade unionists draw upon male camaraderie to enhance their solidarity – they would claim that the crucial business of defining the class structure is devoid of obvious gender implications. This is because the class structure is composed of empty (occupational) positions defining the differing classes, and since these class positions can be filled by either male or female workers – at least in principle – gender attributes should not be used to define the class structure itself.[3]

Feminist writers have handled the relationship between gender and class in more varied ways. Christine Delphy (1984) argues that the relationship between male husbands and female wives is a class one, in which men exploit women's labour, and her views have been endorsed by Sylvia Walby (Walby, 1986, 1990). The result is to posit two overlapping sets of class relations in contemporary societies: firstly those based around capitalist forms of exploitation, and secondly those based around the patriarchal mode of production within the household. This formulation, whilst usefully recognizing the material basis of gender inequality, does however have problems. First, it does not indicate whether and/or how gendered processes operating in the labour market – paradoxically, the focus of much of Walby's attention – should be seen in class terms, and second, it does not then deal with the relationship between the two class systems, giving no guidance about how people's double class identities (one derived from their household relationships, the other from their position in the formal labour market) are related together. The result is to leave the relationship between capitalist derived class and patriarchal derived class an empirical one.

Other feminists, however, such as Rosemary Crompton and Anne Witz, have been more concerned to examine the interplay between class and gender. The alternative to emphasizing the separation of class from gender is to see class formation as in part based on gendered processes, and concomitantly, the formation of gendered collectivities as linked to class. Rosemary Crompton's work has been of particular importance in addressing this issue. In an important paper (Crompton, 1986) she argues that the 'service class' of professionals and managers is critically dependent on female labour in two crucial ways. First it relies upon the servicing of female routine white collar workers, both to carry out their routine work and to allow them ready access to senior positions themselves, since women would not be promoted to these jobs. Secondly these 'service class' men routinely rely upon their wives to service their domestic and emotional needs. The implication is that the modern service class rests upon a gendered foundation.

It is indeed noteworthy, in this context, to refer briefly to empirical studies of the middle classes, both historically and in the contemporary period, which show how gendered attributes are central to the identity and attributes of middle class groups. Historically Davidoff and Hall (1987) have shown how the emergence of middle class identity was linked to gendered processes – the idea of the housewife and the homemaker, the development of a distinction between the (male) public realm of work and (female) private realm of home. More recently it has been suggested that the increasing numbers of professional women is an essential element of the formation of a new urban middle class of gentrifying households in central London (Butler, 1992). Since professional women tend to be in relationships with professional and managerial men, these households tend to be extremely affluent, and congregate in urban locations where both can find work and have access to urban services and leisure (see also Crompton and Sanderson, 1991).

These points are pertinent but not telling. This is because one possible response to such observations is to claim that although these types of gendered processes may affect class formation and identity, they are not relevant in affecting the crucial business of analysing the class structure – the generation of class positions. It is in this context that recent feminist research has made major strides, however. Rosemary Pringle (1989) has shown how the very existence of job structures is related to gendered principles. Thus the job of secretary is defined by the types of 'feminine' traits which the female incumbents of such jobs are deemed to possess – caring, nurturing and emotional. This may appear a recondite argument, but its implications are far reaching for it questions the procedure – so central to class analysis – of assuming that the class positions which define the class structure can be specified independently of the gender of their usual incumbents. To develop Pringle's argument, the nature of managerial work, for instance, might be seen not in gender neutral terms as simply co-ordinating a complex institutional structure, but also as being defined by masculine traits of controlling and directing work. In this sense the emergence of managerial groupings could be seen as intrinsically linked to the development of forms of male power and control. It is thus not simply incidental that the vast majority of managers are male; the very creation of managerial cadres as a social grouping – I deliberately avoid the term class for the time being – is linked to their place in sustaining male forms of power and control. This is the focus of Witz's (1992) argument that the very development of the medical division of labour in the 19th century, and the professional power based on it, was linked to the exclusion of women from superordinate places within this division of labour.

So far, I have argued that there is no intrinsic reason why the types of processes leading to exploitation, closure, and possibly class formation should be seen as distinct from gendered processes. However, it is also vital not only to establish this claim at a general level, but also to show how specific classes are gendered. What I mean by this is that it is necessary to indicate how differing types of exclusion and exploitation are related to gendered processes in each case, for there may be very different connections. What I have in mind here is the differing gendered implications of the three assets which Erik Olin Wright sees as underlying the class structures of modern capitalist societies. Wright, controversially, sees class as being based around the possession of three different assets: property; organization; and skill. In each of these three dimensions we may be negatively or positively advantaged – at one extreme we may have property, be the superordinates in large organizations, and have scarce skills. At the other extreme, we may have no property, be the subordinates in organizations, and have no scarce skills. However, Wright's key point is that most of us lie between these two extremes, since we may have access to some of these assets but not others, and we may have more or less of each asset. Thus, Wright calculates that 45 per cent of the US workforce occupied some sort of intermediate position, having access to some but not all of the assets he specifies (Wright, 1985:195).

Wright's arguments have spawned immense debate, most of it critical (Marshall *et al*, 1988; Goldthorpe, 1990; Burawoy, 1989; Pawson, 1989). As I have argued elsewhere (Savage *et al*, 1992) Wright's analysis, especially his theoretical analysis of skill assets, does have severe problems. Nonetheless, Wright (1989) is correct to argue that much of the debate has been about the way he operationalizes his class categories in empirical research rather than about the theoretical adequacy of his perspective in the first place. Thus, the fact that occupational classifications derived from his class theory do not fare as well as those devised by John Goldthorpe, in accounting for variation in life chances and attitudes, is not in itself a critique of his theoretical framework. Contra research in the Goldthorpe vein (see eg Marshall *et al*, 1988) there is more to class analysis than being able to account for variation in a range of dependent variables: as one of the most eminent American quantitative researchers has phrased it: 'it is premature to think about variability in an event before knowledge is developed about the fundamental cause of the event itself. Explanations of a variable's variation should not be confused with an explanation of the event or process itself' (Lieberson 1985:115)[4].

What is exciting about Wright's analysis is his attempt to think about the way in which class formation is linked not simply to property ownership but also to organizational hierarchy and forms of skill[5]. It is at this point that I wish to develop the vital argument which the rest of this paper will substantiate: that there are fundamental differences in the gendered implications of each of these assets[6]. Organization assets, because they draw upon male forms of solidarity and on gendered patterns of subordination, are intrinsically vehicles of male power. The reasons for thinking that organizational hierarchies are linked to male power are developed in other papers in this volume and I do not wish to defend this idea at length here. One particularly powerful demonstration of this point is Rosabeth Kanter's (1977) work on the way in which male managers rely on 'homosociality'. She argues that the job of co-ordinating and managing only have to deal with managers of the same gender (and ethnicity, age and class). This allows them to get on with the job at hand, whereas if other managers are from different social groups, then preliminary 'work' of establishing a rapport has to take place. It hence makes 'economic' sense to rely on managers from the same background.

Skill assets, however, are less intrinsically gender biased. Women have historically been excluded from the acquisition of credentials but once the portals are opened, following feminist pressure, it is difficult to stop women with the appropriate cultural resources from acquiring credentials. The result is that women can gain expertise but not power and authority. Women's careers depend upon enhancing their expertise, making themselves 'indispensable', whilst men have the additional resource of being able to wield authority within organizational hierarchies. And while the possession of expertise may prevent a woman from being demoted from an expert job, it is not a precondition to advancement or promotion.

These points have established a case. However, they remain speculative. Indeed, it is no easy matter to test whether organizational assets and skill assets have different social implications for men and women, because most existing ways of analysing occupational change draw upon 'class schemas'[7] which do not allow these two assets to be distinguished. Today an unfortunate orthodoxy has emerged which claims that there is a 'service class' of professionals and managers at the top of the occupational hierarchy of western capitalist societies (Goldthorpe, 1982; Lash and Urry, 1987). Since this service class consists of individuals drawing upon both skill and organizational assets, analyses tend to neglect to examine the salience of any distinction between the two assets.

In Section 2 I therefore present a new analysis of occupational mobility which is designed to examine whether my theoretical arguments hold up. The aim is to see whether women are able to move up organizational ladders in the same way that men are, and to see what types of routes are followed by 'successful' women and how they compare with 'successful' men. If the views outlined above are correct, women would be less likely to pursue organizational careers and more likely to pursue occupational ones, in comparison to men. Women would tend to specialize within a particular occupation, possibly in the professions, in areas which do not necessarily convey power and authority within the wider organization.

2 Work-life Mobility in Britain 1971–1981

Although there is now extensive research on gender segregation in the labour market, research examining work life mobility between occupational positions is still comparatively rare (though see Dex, 1987; Dex (ed.), 1991; Crompton and Sanderson, 1991). There are particular problems also in obtaining data to examine the issues I have raised in this paper. Since I am interested in quite small sub-groups within the population (men and women working in professional and managerial occupations), a random survey would not throw up enough cases to be reliable. However, the OPCS Longitudinal Study is a major resource which can be profitably used[8]. The LS matches together the Census records of 1 per cent of the 1971 population with their records for 1981, so allowing the paths that people have followed in this ten years period to be recorded. Although 1 per cent may not sound very much, it means that it can pick up the paths of almost 25,000 men who were in professional and managerial occupations in 1971 and over 10,000 women. These high figures mean that it is possible to sub-divide the sample into smaller groupings, more meaningful for our purposes than either the Registrar General's Class Classification, or Goldthorpe's class schema, both of which incorporate varied groups into the same class. Furthermore, since the Census has an extremely high response rate – higher than any survey – we can also be sure that the reliability of the data is better than in other sample surveys. Finally, because the Census records full information on all individuals, it is an easy matter to analyse the mobility of men and women, in ways not possible if the sample is directed at men, or heads of households, as continues to be a frequent practice in studies of social mobility.

The amount of information which can be derived from the LS is immense, and I will only show two simple tables here (for more discussion see Savage *et al*, 1992). These tables compare the mobility of men and women from their 1971 origins to their 1981 destinations. The occupational categories used are of two types. Firstly, within the 'service class' of professional and managerial workers individuals are divided into six SEGs (socio-economic groups). These SEGs are useful because they distinguish workers relying on managerial authority (SEGs 1.2 and 2.2) from professional expertise (SEGs 3, 4, and 5.1), permitting me to examine whether men and women have different career routes within and between these two groupings. I should emphasize here that the use of these SEGs to distinguish professional from managerial workers, and so empirically to separate those relying on skill from those relying on organizational assets, is an operational procedure necessary to investigate the issues I have raised empirically, but I am not claiming that this is perfect. It is not true by definition that professionals rely on skill assets and managers on organizational assets, simply that given the way these jobs have developed historically some such association does exist (see Savage *et al*, 1992), and this way of operationalizing these concepts of class assets allows some access to the issues raised in this paper.

Second, for those occupations outside the broadly defined 'middle class', individuals are grouped into four broad categories: those in self employment (PB – petite bourgeoisie); routine clerical work (PWC – proletarian white collar); manual work (PBC – proletarian blue collar); and the unemployed (UE). These four groups are much broader than the middle class ones. My main interest lies in mobility within the middle classes and general patterns of mobility into different middle class groups from outside, hence I am not concerned here with examining patterns of differentiation outside these ranks in any detail.

A lot of information is contained in Tables 1 and 2. My prime focus is on the comparison between men's and women's patterns. Here a number of points can be established.

If we first examine the distribution of respondents into different middle class groups, it is clear that men are fairly evenly divided between professional and managerial groupings, whilst women are overwhelmingly confined to professional groups, and in particular SEG 5.1, the so-called 'semi-professions'. 48 per cent of "service

Table 1 Outflow table: men's work-life mobility, 1971–81

1971 SEG	1.1	1.2	2.2	3	4	5.1	All SC	PB	Others*	N=
1.1	3.7	9.3	13.0	3.7	–	5.6	35.2	25.1	15.6	54
1.2	0.0	32.6	17.6	4.2	3.4	3.8	52.7	3.1	18.1	5,008
2.2	0.0	13.6	34.4	0.5	1.8	2.8	53.2	9.8	21.6	6,790
3	–	1.0	3.0	55.5	12.6	4.5	76.6	3.7	2.7	1,118
4	0.0	9.3	8.6	5.6	40.0	11.1	74.4	2.0	13.3	5,497
5.1	–	10.9	4.4	0.4	8.6	41.6	65.9	2.1	16.9	6,373
All SC	0.0	15.2	16.2	4.1	12.8	14.8	63.1	4.5	16.9	24,849
PB	0.0	0.7	6.2	0.3	0.3	1.6	9.3	50.2	22.7	10,671
PWC	0.0	7.7	9.5	0.3	3.0	4.9	25.4	4.2	50.6	17,062
PBC	0.0	1.5	2.3	0.0	0.9	1.7	6.5	4.7	69.8	69,170
UE	–	1.0	2.6	0.3	1.1	2.2	7.3	6.5	62.3	4,528
Total LM	0.0	5.0	6.3	0.9	3.5	4.7	20.4	8.5	61.1	126,277

*Others in different labour market groupings (PWC, PBC, UE).

Notes: (a) For a 1% sample of men in England and Wales who were in the labour market in 1971.

(b) Percentages do not match to 100%, since the balance have left the labour market between 1971 and 1981 (usually through retirement).

(c) Classification:
1.1 = Large employers
1.2 = Managers, large establishments
2.2 = Managers, small establishments
3 = Self-employed professionals
4 = Professional employees
5.1 = Ancillary workers

PB = Petite bourgeoisie, (SEGs 2.1, 11, 13)
PWC = White collar proletariat (SEGs 5.2, 6, 7)
PBC = Manual working class
UE = Unemployed
Total LM = Total labour market

Source: LS ASTF011 (Longitudinal Study 1990).

Table 2 Outflow table: women's work-life mobility 1971–81

1971 SEG	1.1	1.2	2.2	3	4	5.1	All SC	PB	Other	N=
				1981 SEG						
1.1	–	–	–	–	–	–	–	–	33.3	3
1.2	–	17.4	8.3	–	0.8	8.0	34.6	1.3	19.3	827
2.2	–	4.1	16.0	0.1	0.4	4.7	25.4	4.3	25.5	1,607
3	–	1.0	3.3	37.0	14.1	7.6	63.0	4.3	7.6	92
4	–	3.3	7.0	3.8	18.4	16.6	49.1	1.7	16.7	603
5.1	–	3.3	1.3	0.0	1.3	47.1	52.9	1.1	11.4	7,566
All SC	–	4.5	4.4	0.6	2.2	35.6	47.2	1.7	14.4	10,698
PB	0.0	0.6	3.5	0.0	–	2.5	6.7	23.9	21.6	2,845
PWC	0.0	1.3	2.0	0.0	0.1	2.6	6.1	1.6	47.7	39,100
PBC	–	0.3	0.6	0.0	0.1	1.6	2.7	1.1	47.8	21,666
UE	–	0.7	1.4	0.0	0.3	6.1	8.5	1.7	36.1	2,477
Total LM	0.0	1.4	1.9	0.1	0.4	6.4	10.6	2.3	40.5	76,696

Notes: (a) 1% sample of all women in England and Wales in the labour market 1971.
(b) Otherwise as for Table 1

Source: Table ASTF014 (Longitudinal Study 1990).

class" men were in managerial groups in 1971, whilst only 23 per cent of women were. 71 per cent of women were in SEG 5.1, whilst only 26 per cent of men were. These totals are not surprising, but they confirm expectations that relatively few women are employed in managerial jobs and that, insofar as women do gain entry to middle class work, it is through entry to subordinate professional ranks.

Patterns of mobility between 1971 and 1981 allow me to develop this observation in a number of ways. Firstly, men and women in professional work (SEG 3, 4 and 5.1) in 1971 had greater chances of staying in the middle classes in 1981 than their counterparts in managerial work (SEGs 1.2 and 2.2). Thus 77 per cent of men in SEG 3 in 1971 were still in professional or managerial ranks in 1981 but only 53 per cent of men in managerial work were still in these ranks. For both men and women, professionals were more secure than managers, with fewer experiencing downward mobility. *However, this is especially true for women.* Table 2 shows that only a quarter to a third of women managers in 1971 were in 'service class' jobs in 1981, whereas over half the male managers were still in the service class. Women professionals, however, had relatively good chances of staying in professional employment – figures considerably higher than their managerial sisters.

Consider now mobility into the category marked 'other'. This represents movement into jobs outside the middle class between 1971 and 1981 and is hence indicative of downward mobility. Amongst men, only 3 per cent of the professional self employed experienced downward mobility, a figure which rises to 22 per cent amongst managers. Amongst women, the numbers moving into this category 'other' are remarkably similar, and for SEG 5.1 – the so called 'semi-professions' such as teaching and nursing – *fewer women experienced downward mobility than men!*. Only 11 per cent of women in SEG 5.1 in 1971 had moved into jobs outside the service class in 1981, but 17 per cent of men had[9].

If we turn to movement within the 'service class' it is clear that considerable numbers of male professionals in 1971 moved into managerial work in 1981 (see also on this movement, Goldthorpe, 1982; Savage *et al*, 1992). 18 per cent of SEG 4, and 15 per cent of SEG 5.1 moved into managerial work in this decade: professional men seem able to move horizontally, from professional to managerial work. However, the number of women making the equivalent transition is much smaller – 10 per cent for SEG 4, and 5 per cent for SEG 5.1. In other words, women with expertise in professional employment have much lower chances than men of subsequently moving into managerial – organizational – careers.

Finally, if we examine the prospects of those from outside the middle class in 1971 moving into the middle class in 1981 we also find striking results. No less than one quarter of men employed in routine white collar work in 1971 entered professional and managerial work by 1981: the figures for women being only 6 per cent. This confirms the argument of Crompton and Jones (1984), and Crompton (1986) that men gain promotion to professional and managerial jobs in reasonable numbers because women are often deemed unpromotable. What is also interesting, however, is the destinations of these new entrants. 17 per cent of the male clerical workforce in 1971 entered managerial work, whilst only 8 per cent entered the professional groupings (mostly in SEG 5.1). Only 3 per cent of white collar women moved into managerial work however, a similar figure to the 3 per cent who entered professional ranks. Hence men seem to find it quite possible to enter managerial work from outside the 'service class' but women find it much more difficult to make the equivalent transition.

There are lower rates of promotion out of manual work, but the proportions respectively entering professional and managerial work were similar. 6.5 per cent of manual men in 1971 moved into the 'service class', 4 per cent to managerial ranks, 3 per cent to professional. Only 3 per cent of women manual workers moved into the service class, only 1 per cent of these moving into managerial jobs.

It is now possible to sum up these findings. For men, movement into managerial work is relatively easy both from below (PWC), and from the side (from SEGs 4 and 5.1). Equally, men in managerial jobs have reasonable prospects of remaining in these jobs. Managerial work is both open to men and it is reasonably secure. For women the picture is very different. Far fewer women move into managerial work from either below or from the side. For those few women in managerial work in 1971 there is a very high rate of exit from it by 1981.

However, for professional workers the gender inequalities are, in most ways, less marked. It is difficult for both men and women to move into professional work from other occupations – an indication of the importance of pre-entry qualifications for most branches. Almost as many women as men stayed in professional jobs between 1971 and 1981. In some cases women professionals seem better able to resist downward mobility than men. The main difference between men and women professionals is that men can move out of professional work into managerial work, whilst women cannot – a point which relates to our analysis of managerial work, above.

In short, women who enter the middle classes tend to do so in professional positions in which they can practise their expertise, but they have very limited chances of climbing a bureaucratic hierarchy through movement into managerial work. Women are confined to what Crompton has called 'niche' jobs, which help insulate them against downward mobility, but do not permit easy upward mobility either. 24 per cent of men in SEG 5.1 have moved into other service class jobs by 1981, but only 6 per cent of women have.

The data from the LS strongly support the argument which I have developed in this paper. However there are a number of problems with relying exclusively on the LS. Firstly, although it is useful to distinguish managerial from professional groupings, this is still a very broad, and in some ways unsatisfactory, procedure. Job titles do not always specify clearly how workers fit into patterns of organizational hierarchy. It would be misleading to assume that professional workers do not also have super-ordinate positions within organizations. As Larson (1977, has shown, it is wrong to assume that professional power is separate from organizational power. And, secondly, workers defined as managers may not necessarily have significant organizational power – in some cases the job title is a consolation prize for lack of effective power! In some organizations – banks, for instance – all senior jobs are defined as managerial, even if the workers are carrying out professional functions.

The LS also currently stops in 1981, which means that possible changes in the position of women in the last decade cannot be discerned from it. In the third part of this paper I therefore change tack a little, by presenting detailed evidence of the gendered division of labour in one leading British bank.[10]. This case study allows me to probe issues further. It is a particularly important case study since the bank concerned is often held up as a striking case of change where women have made remarkable strides at moving into managerial jobs. I intend to show that the apparent movement of women into managerial jobs in the 1980s has coincided with a major restructuring of management itself, and that as a result women managers have rarely moved into positions of significant organizational authority.

3 Gendered change in banking 1970–1991

On the face of it, changes in the gendered division of labour in banking have been quite dramatic. Banking was, until the late 1960s, marked by particularly intense gendered division of labour, with male and female staff being recruited into different grades. Female staff grades had ceilings for increment increases earlier than male staff grades (usually at around age 27, compared to 31 for men), were not of pensionable status, and women were expected to retire on marriage. Most importantly of all, prospects for women being promoted out of the specifically female clerical grades were virtually non existent (Llewllyn, 1981; Heritage, 1982; Crompton and Jones, 1984; Crompton, 1989; Savage, 1992).

This situation has changed rapidly since then, at least on the surface. There is now formal equality of opportunity amongst all the banks and openly discriminatory practices have been abandoned. Men and women now work on the same employment grades and all the banks have some degree of formal commitment to equal opportunities policies, though there are considerable differences between the banks in their commitment to it. This has caused some writers, notably Rosemary Crompton, to argue that women have succeeded in moving into senior positions within banking.

Crompton's first analysis of banking, carried out with Gareth Jones (Crompton and Jones 1984) in 1981 as part of a comparative analysis of male and female clerical work in banking, life insurance and local authority work pointed to the continuation of discriminatory practices in banking. 46 per cent of women clerks reported that their managers had not encouraged them to put themselves forward for the vocational credentials necessary for promotion (Crompton and Jones 1984:155). She also pointed to the fact that male upward mobility to senior positions depended upon the exclusion of women from promotion, so hinting at the vested male interests which continued to depend on women's exclusion from promotion: 'the male career rests on the continuing subordination of non manual females' (Crompton and Jones, 1984:243).

Crompton also argued, however, that significant changes were taking place. She paid particular attention to the growing desire of women clerks themselves to gain credentials relevant to bureaucratic careers, which might mean a growing number of women earning promotion to managerial posts. Crompton was careful to emphasize that this tendency was not likely to be widespread, but did suggest that it was possible that it would upset the gender hierarchy: 'even if only a very small minority actively seek, and gain, promotion, then the male career structure will be seriously threatened' (Crompton and Jones, 1984:247).

In her more recent work, Crompton has returned to consider the prospects in greater detail. She has pointed to a number of developments likely to enhance the position of women. Firstly the banks have increasingly turned to tiered entry, where significant numbers of senior workers are recruited with pre-entry qualifications, often degrees. This combines with the second development – the growing number of women with pre-entry and post-entry qualifications – to increase the number of women in more senior positions. She calls this the use of the 'qualifications lever'. A third factor, the role of feminist pressure, has also been important, particulary with the EOC investigation of Barclay's Bank in the mid 1980s, which in turn encouraged the bank to introduce tiered entry (Crompton, 1989). All these developments have led to an 'important change', in which 'women have been given access to the middle and upper tiers of employment in the finance sector' (Crompton and Sanderson, 1990:129).

Crompton is careful to recognize that any change is not straightforward. In particular – despite her reference to the rise of women at upper tiers – she also stresses that the rise of women in previously male jobs is most marked in senior clerical and junior supervisory jobs. 'The knowledge and experience of female clerks is no longer entirely trapped in frustrating, dead end jobs: rather women can now aspire realistically to middle level supervisory positions without having to follow through the prerequisites of a career modelled on linear, male "breadwinner" experience' (Crompton, 1989:20). More generally, Crompton and Sanderson (1990) have drawn attention to the fact that qualified women frequently move into 'niche' occupations, where their skills are rewarded, but where career mobility to more senior jobs is difficult. Crompton's view of these niche occupations is also ambivalent. At one level she seems to endorse them, since they seem to offer an alternative to the linear male career. They allow a qualified worker to specialize but also take time off for childcare or other domestic labour and return in a part-time mode. Yet she also recognizes the potential marginality of such workers within the decision making of the organization. Despite her slight equivocation, Crompton's work suggests that women have had some successes at moving into positions of authority and power within the bank, and that this process is likely to continue. I will argue, however, that Crompton's recognition of the significance of 'niche' employment for expert women undermines the apparent optimism of her earlier argument.

There is no doubt that figures on the proportion of women in management do suggest a major influx of women into management since the 1970s, in line with Crompton's arguments. In Natwest the percentage of female 'appointed officers' in managerial jobs rose from 11.7 per cent in 1980 to 14 per cent in 1985 and 22.3 per cent in 1990. The aggregate figures for Midland Bank are even more striking: in 1985 7.9 per cent of managers were female, a figure which had risen to 19.9 per cent by early 1991.[11]

Nonetheless, my argument will be that these figures should not be taken as evidence that women are moving into positions of authority within banking. The idea I wish to develop is that the expansion of women in managerial jobs is closely associated with the restructuring of management, and that women are located in specific areas within the new management structure. These positions demand high levels of expertise but do not give important organizational authority.

The research I discuss is derived from a project examining men's and women's careers in banking, local authorities and nursing. The information I will discuss here comprises only a small part of the material gathered, and is primarily a detailed exposition of figures revealing the grades and areas of employment of men and women within Midland Bank as a whole, and in the Birmingham area in particular. In order to explicate these figures I have used a range of information gathered from detailed interviews with around thirty Midland Bank workers which throw light on how restructuring has affected the nature of managerial work within the bank.

4 Women in bank management

Traditionally, managerial jobs in banking were usually in various forms of branch management, where managers had a large degree of effective control over most activities taking place within 'his' branch, subject only to imposed lending limits and bi-annual inspections by Head Office staff (see Savage, 1992). In such a situation bank managers drew upon organizational assets, as they supervised branch staff and controlled day to day activities. There is now a considerable literature on the undermining of the autonomy of the branch manager (eg Child, 1986), and managerial jobs have changed enormously in the face of corporate restructuring. From the Second World War to the mid-1970s, banks were well placed to expand, as higher proportions of the population began to open bank accounts. From the mid-1970s, however, major restructuring has been forced on the banks because of growing competition from Building Societies and the general de-regulation of financial institutions (see Savage, 1991). This restructuring has helped bring about four major changes to the position of the bank manager.

First, there has been a diversification away from branch retailing, based upon the current and deposit account, towards other financial services, such as pensions, mortgage, insurance, credit card, and share dealing businesses. The result is that a growing number of workers and managers are employed in specialist units outside the branches – 32 per cent of Midland Bank workers worked outside the regional branch network by 1991.[12] As this type of specialist work increases growing numbers of managers do not run branches but are instead employed in specialist units, where they carry out very different sorts of tasks to the old branch manager. Only 42 per cent of managerial workers worked in the branch network in 1991, a figure which rises only to 55 per cent even if managers employed in 'group operations', running autonomous units such as Thomas Cook, are included.

Secondly, and associated with this, within the regional branch network, customers have been streamed into three groups: large corporations, small businesses, and private customers. All these types of account used to be held in the same branch; but the first two have now been hived off to specialist units, either working out of the larger branches or out of Regional Offices. As a result, branch managers have lost responsibility for the biggest and most prestigious accounts.

Thirdly, management has been restructured around a division between 'lending managers' and 'operations managers'. Lending managers are employed to sell products and organize loans to customers but have little role in organizing other staff or administration. Their importance within the bank testifies to the rapid emergence of a 'sales culture' which encourages workers actively to sell their portfolio of financial services to customers, rather than to wait for clients to approach the bank. Operations managers, by contrast, are responsible for the administration and staffing of branches and units but tend not to deal with customers. The traditional branch manager's job has effectively been divided down the middle. Alongside this, managerial gradings have been radically altered, with jobs which were previously regarded as 'accountants' jobs', intermediate between clerical and managerial grades, now being placed in junior categories of management. Indeed, the number of managerial workers has increased so that by 1991 no less than 27 per cent of Midland Bank workers were of managerial rank.

Finally, management has increasingly been subjected to a series of controls which reduce autonomy and discretion. The best known of these is credit scoring, which allows routine loans to be offered or refused according to standardized criteria rather than management discretion (Child, 1986). Another important change is the imposition of management objectives, whereby each manager is given annual objectives (specific sales targets, or operational targets), which the manager must meet, regardless of circumstances, and on which performance-related pay is based. Finally, personnel departments have grown in significance for staffing decisions and have undercut the role of branch managers for staff promotion.

The general result of these trends is to uncouple skill from authority. Managers tend to work in highly specified and specialized areas, where they are put under pressure to meet stated objectives but where they tend not to have significant power over other workers or bank resources, other than those specifically earmarked for them. There are some exceptions to this: the branch managers of large branches continue to enjoy significant power since they tend to have a team of managers working to their remit; Regional Management teams and above all senior Head Office management also continue to exercise discretion.

The implications, however, are clear. The influx of women into management may be linked to the changing structure of management itself, with women managers having little effective organizational authority within a massively expanded managerial hierarchy. Instead, women may be recruited into those positions which demand high expertise and skill. This argument can be borne out by examining Table 3.

Table 3 shows the proportions of women in the differing managerial grades within Midland Bank in January 1989 and January 1991. The table indicates, unsurprisingly, that women tend

Table 3 Proportion of Female Managerial Staff, 1989–1991

	M93	M94	M95	M96	M97+
% female 1989	23.1	6.5	3.6	2.6	0.7
% female 1991	28.8	13.7	7.9	5.8	2.6
% total mgrs in grade 1991	52.1	24.8	14.9	5.9	2.3

Grades: M93 manager of small branch (−15 workers) or equivalent
M94 manager of medium branch (15–70 workers) or equivalent
M95 manager of large branch (70+ workers) or equivalent
M96 regional manager or equivalent
M97 senior manager

Source: information provided by Equal Opportunities, Midland Bank.

to be found in junior levels of management, especially in the lowest grade, M93. The M93 grade is used to specify junior management jobs and these are jobs which, historically, have been seen as outside management. Although they have been regraded into management grades in 1987, many managers I spoke to argued that it was only when managers reached the M94 grade that they had 'really' obtained managerial status (Ms Foster, Ms Leese, Mr Brown[13]).

There is an interesting shift between 1989 and 1991, as shown by Table 3. In 1989 the proportion of women in M93 was well above that in the next grade, M94 (23.1 per cent compared with 6.5 per cent). By 1991 there is evience that considerably more women had moved into higher managerial grades: whilst the proportion of women in M93 had increased by only a modest amount, from 23.1 per cent to 28.8 per cent, the numbers in M94 had risen from 6.5 per cent to 13.7 per cent, and in M95 from 3.6 per cent to 7.9 per cent. The proportion of women in the top grades remained very small however, and of the 42 most senior managers in the bank, graded M98 and M99, none were women.

According to Table 3, women have not reached senior management but have moved into middle management in some numbers. The question is, however, in what sorts of area? Are they typically found in positions which might be highly graded and highly skilled but which do not convey organizational authority? Table 4

Mike Savage

Table 4 Gender and Managerial Employment within Midland Bank 1991

Sector	% mgl jobs female	% jobs in sector which are mgl	% emp in sector female
UK BANKING			
Central Region	13	18	66
London	15	18	58
Midlands	11	16	64
North	10	17	61
South	13	15	61
West	9	16	64
Sub total – regions	12	17	62
First Direct	35	53	49
Head Off UK banks	36	69	47
Pers Financial Ser	21	67	42
UK Corporate Bank	12	82	25
Sub total – other UK	28	68	44
Midland Montagu	25	72	37
Access	32	15	67
Group Operations	24	39	47
Group Head Office	27	61	38
Sub total – other	25	47	44
Total – Midland	20	28	56

Notes: full time workers only. Almost 10,000 part time staff (95% of whom are female) are employed on top of this, nearly all in clerical grades.

Source: Figures made available by Equal Opportunities, Midland Bank.

indicates the sectors in which women managers are typically located.

Table 4 shows that whilst 20 per cent of the bank's managers are female, there is a fundamental difference between the branch network in the regions, where a lower proportion are managers, and the specialist units, where most report considerably higher proportions of women managers. The point to emphasize is that, with two exceptions, it would appear that the greater the proportion of the staff which is employed in managerial grades, then the greater the proportion of women managers. In the regions, where much of the work is routine cashier and data processing duties, the proportion of the workforce which is managerial is 17 per cent and the proportion of these managers who are female is also low – around 12 per cent in the regions as a whole, which rises to 15 per cent in London. On the other hand, where the proportion of the workforce on managerial grades rises above 50 per cent of total employment, as it does for most of the specialist units, then the proportion of the female managerial workforce also rises, to up to 36 per cent in the case of Head Office UK Banking.

Within the regions women are also typically located in subordinate managerial jobs. Detailed research on the Birmingham area (Savage 1991) shows that there are no women managers of large branches or in senior levels of regional management. Women managers in this area tend to be operations managers in branches (jobs which until 1987 were not regarded as managerial), rather more senior managers in lending management (which, whilst highly skilled, conveys little organizational power within the bank) or junior managers in Regional Offices. All the leading positions within Regional Management and in the larger branches are held by men.

The findings from both Birmingham and the country show that where women are employed as managers in large numbers they tend to work in a unit where there are many managers. It is hence unlikely that they are in positions of significant power within that unit. On the other hand, in those sectors where there are fewer managers compared to other, clerical, workers and hence where line managerial power might be relatively greater, there are fewer women managers.

There are two exceptions. In UK Corporate Banking there are a very high proportion of managerial jobs (82 per cent), but a low proportion of women managers (15 per cent). This is a very interesting finding, since Corporate Banking enjoys the highest status of all the different banking services, and managers in this area enjoy the greatest discretion in dealing with their clients. The other exception is Access, where there is a low proportion of managers in the workforce, but a high proportion of women managers. However, further scrutiny of evidence for Access shows that all the women managers in this sector are employed on the lowest managerial grade, M93.

The evidence suggests that whilst women have entered managerial grades in significant numbers, *they have not moved into the sorts of sectors where managerial discretion is important, or where they are likely to be in charge of a specific unit*. They have been more likely to have moved into professional or specialist type jobs within large managerial departments, in which they remain subordinate to predominantly male managers.

Mike Savage

One final way of checking this argument is to examine the location of the very small proportion of women graded in the higher managerial grades, M96 and M97. There were 47 women managers in these two grades in 1991. Of these, 22 were in Midland Montagu, the merchant banking arm of the bank, where the need to retain staff able to command high market salaries forces Midland to have a very large number of high graded managers (there were 310 managers graded M96 and above, more than in the entire retail banking side of Midland!). Another 15 women were located in Head Office functions, where, even though highly graded, they continue to have even more highly graded men above them. In other words, these figures suggest that only a handful of women in the bank, probably less than ten, are in positions conveying any sort of meaningful discretion or power.

These figures for Midland Bank indicate that the expansion of women in managerial grades should not be seen as evidence for women moving into positions of line managerial authority. As management has expanded and diversified women have been recruited into lower levels of management, but continue to work alongside male superiors.

Conclusions

Some of the evidence presented above might appear slightly indigestible. I have however felt it important to persevere because the conclusions are important. Rosemary Crompton's optimistic picture of women moving into superordinate positions within the bank does not fully register the way in which women are confined to specific areas of the managerial hierarchy in which they lack serious power. Although women have moved into specific types of managerial and professional employment in some numbers in the past decade, it would be misleading to think that it will simply take 'one more heave' for them to move through into senior management. Women tend to move into those areas of professional and managerial employment where they may be able to exercise high levels of skill and expertise but have little effective organizational discretion. Whilst women are increasingly gaining entry to jobs demanding high levels of expertise, they are only rarely translating these into jobs with high levels of authority and organizational power – a point which also stands out from my analysis of the Longitudinal Study. From this perspective the increasing numbers of 'expert' women in the labour market should not be seen as evidence that women are moving into positions of organizational authority but rather that, as organizations re-structure, there is increased room for women to be employed in specialist niches, subordinate to senior management although enjoying a degree of autonomy from direct control.

This relates to a wider point about the contemporary significance of organizational assets for class formation. Organization assets proved an important feature for middle class formation in the early and mid 20th century, when organizational hierarchies relied on human discretion to operate effectively. However, as a series of social and technical innovations allow organizations to co-ordinate activities and staff without recourse to human intermediaries, large numbers of middle and junior managers who have previously drawn upon organizational assets are by-passed. Managerial jobs are redefined, and the currency of organizational assets for many groups of workers devalued.

One way of thinking about the historical transition which this argument suggests is to consider Chandler's (1977) account of the rise of managerial hierarchies. Chandler argues that the modern business corporation, which began to develop in America from the late 19th century, depended upon the creation of managerial hierarchies in which senior, middle and junior managers enjoyed specific areas of jurisdiction within the organization. This jurisdic-tion was, however, normally defined spatially (being in charge of a particular unit, branch, or part of a factory), or in terms of process (for instance, being a production manager). In both cases managerial work involved diverse tasks. As a result, the managers concerned enjoyed a measure of autonomy and discretion about the implementation of organizational policy and control of staff and resources within their particular unit. In particular the weak specification of managerial work in terms of tasks and functions allowed managers discretion in juggling resources and staff within their unit. As Hannah (1982) noted, the prime control over managers was an accounting one. So long as the books were properly kept and pointed towards profitability, no-one inquired about how the units were run.

However, this particular set of arrangements has been eroded by the tendency, evident within banking but by no means confined to it, to differentiate managers according to function and task, rather than according to spatial criteria. Differentiation of personnel, financial, selling, production, and operations management is standard. Greater specification of managerial work tasks makes it easier to assess whether these tasks are being achieved. However, alongside this trend to the diversification of management functions at intermediate and low levels, power at the top continues to be highly centralized and mediated by human – nearly always male – contact.

These arguments suggest that the influx of women into professional and managerial jobs indicate not that women are moving into positions of power and authority, but rather that these positions are being redefined and restricted. Senior managers are better able to draw upon organization assets than previously. No longer need they trust their subordinate managers to do their job, and as a result their power and discretion has increased massively. But senior management remains overwhelmingly male and very few women have moved into these areas. The reasons, I would suggest, are clear, that senior management continues to rely on the 'homosociality' seen by Kanter as inherent to managerial work.

To conclude, the growing numbers of women in professional and managerial work may well be of far-reaching significance. However, their real importance is not that they are an indication that women are gaining access to the middle classes for the first time, but rather that the middle and upper classes themselves are undergoing transformations.

Notes

1 Versions of this paper have been delivered to seminars at the Dept of Geography, University of Sheffield; and Dept of Sociology and Social Anthropology, University of Hull. I am grateful to participants for valuable comments. I must particularly thank Rosemary Crompton, Susan Halford and Anne Witz for comments on the first draft of this paper.
2 The restriction of class positions to the division of labour in the formal economy is not actually mentioned by Goldthorpe, who instead refers to the 'division of labour' as whole. However, since he nowhere discusses the role of domestic labourers within the division of labour, and does not include them in his class classification, it seems that he actually means the formal economy.
3 Marshall *et al*, 1988 come close to questioning this in statements such as 'the manner in which the class structure is (at least in part) constituted through relations between sexes is, in our view, fundamental to class analysis'. However in more recent work Marshall seems to have retreated from this view – which has very serious implications for the viability of the Goldthorpe approach to class analysis which he generally endorses. See Goldthorpe and Marshall, 1992. For a fuller discussion of these issues see Savage *et al*, 1992, Appendix 1.

4 This paragraph has advanced a number of controversial ideas about class analysis which there is no space to justify here. Suffice it to say that it is only by adopting a realist theory of social class (see Sayer, 1984; Keat and Urry, 1975) that class analysis can move away from a rather sterile, positivist, concern with correlation, to a more fruitful analysis of the causal powers of social classes (see Abercrombie and Urry, 1983; Savage *et al*, 1992, Appendix 1, for discussion).

5 This is not the place to enter the debate about Wright's theory of class (see Savage *et al*, 1992). However, I would simply add that in my view Wright's rather problematic concept of skill assets – the problem being that it is difficult to see how those with skills can exploit those without skills – can be put on firmer ground by relating them to Bourdieu's (1984) analysis of cultural capital as an axis for class formation.

6 My focus in this paper is on organizational and skill assets rather than property. This is because the middle class groups which I discuss are largely employees. However, the theoretical points I have established can be equally applied to those drawing on property assets.

7 I deliberately use the term class schema, in accordance with the terminology of Goldthorpe (1980), Marshall *et al* (1988), and others. However, it should be emphasized that the classes distinguished in a class schema are not necessarily social classes (see Savage *et al*, 1992; Crompton, 1992).

8 I would like to thank Tony Fielding for his help in extracting this data, and the Social Statistics Research Unit at City University, London, for their support.

9 The reason why the proportions of women not staying in the service class is higher than men, but that women do not seem to suffer as much downward mobility is that more women have left the labour market by 1981, presumably to enter domestic work. This is one area where the LS becomes less useful, since it is not possible to know what type of jobs these women move into on their return to the labour market.

10 This research forms part of a wider ESRC funded project 'Gender, Careers, and Organisations' involving Dr Susan Halford at the University of Sussex and Dr Anne Witz at the University of Birmingham.

11 These figures provided by Personnel Departments from the two banks.

12 This does not mean that 68 per cent worked in the branches. The regional branch network includes regional and area offices, district service centres and management centres from which no retail banking takes place. Taking these into account, only slightly over half the bank workforce work in branches providing counter services to the public.

13 These are all anonymous names of respondents who were interviewed by the author.

References

Abercrombie, N. and Urry, J., (1983), *Capital, Labour and the Middle Classes*, Basingstoke: MacMillan.

Burawoy, M., (1989), 'The limits of Wright's Analytical Marxism and an Alternative', in E.O. Wright *et al The Debate on Classes*, London: Verso.

Butler, T., (1992), *The Service Class in Hackney*, unpublished PhD thesis, Open University.

Mike Savage

Chandler, A.,(1977), *The Visible Hand: The Managerial Revolution in American Business*, Harvard: Harvard University Press.

Child, J., (1986), 'Information technology and the service class', in K. Purcell *et al* (eds), *The Changing Experience of Employment*, Basingstoke: Macmillan.

Crompton, R., (1986), 'Women and the Service Class', in R. Crompton and M. Mann (eds), *Gender and Stratification*, Cambridge: Polity.

Crompton, R., (1989), 'Women in Banking', *Work, Employment and Society*, 3, 2, pp. 141–156.

Crompton, R., (1992), 'The fragmentation of class analysis', *Sociology*, forthcoming.

Crompton, R. and Jones, G., (1984), *White Collar Proletariat: deskilling and gender in clerical work*, Basingstoke: MacMillan.

Crompton, R. and Sanderson, K., (1990), *Gendered Jobs and Social Change*, London: Unwin Hyman.

Davidoff, L. and Hall, C., (1987), *Family Fortunes: Men and Women of the English Middle Classes*, London: Hutchinson.

Delphy, C., (1984), 'The Main Enemy', in *Close to Home*, London: Hutchinson.

Dex, S., (1987), *Women's Occupational Mobility*, Basingstoke: MacMillan.

Dex, S. (ed.), (1991), *Life History Analysis*, London: Routledge.

Goldthorpe, J.H. *et al*, (1980), *Social Mobility and the Class Structure in Modern Britain*, Oxford: Clarendon.

Goldthorpe, J.H., (1982), 'The Service Class; its formation and future', in A. Giddens and G. MacKenzie, *Social Class and the Division of Labour*, Cambridge: Cambridge University Press.

Goldthorpe, J.H., (1990), 'A Response', in J. Clark *et al* (eds), *J.H. Goldthorpe: Consensus and Controversy*, London: Falmer.

Goldthorpe, J.H. and Marshall, G., (1992), 'The promising future of class analysis: a response to recent critiques'. *Sociology*, 26, 3.

Hannah, L., (1982), *The Rise of the Corporate Economy*, London: Methuen.

Heritage, J., (1983), 'Feminisation and Unionisation: a case study from banking', in E. Garmarnikow *et al* (eds), *Gender, Class and Work*, Basingstoke: Macmillan.

Kanter, R., (1977), *Men and Women of the Corporation*, New York: Basic.

Keat, R. and Urry, J., (1975), *Social Theory as Science*, London: Routledge.

Larson, M., (1977), *The rise of Professionalism; a sociological analysis*, California: University of California Press.

Lash, S. and Urry, J., (1987), *The end of Organised Capitalism*, Oxford: Polity.

Lieberson, S., (1985), *Making it Count*, California: University of California Press.

Llewellyn, C., (1981), 'Occupational mobility and the use of the comparative method', in H. Roberts (ed.), *Doing Feminist Research*, London: Routledge.

Marshall, G., Newby, H., Rose, D. and Vogler, C., *Social Class in Modern Britain*, London: Hutchinson.

Pawson, R., (1989), *A Measure for Measures*, London: Routledge.

Pringle, R., (1989), *Secretaries Talk*, London: Verso.

Savage, M., (1991), *Gender, Careers and Organisations: background paper on banking*, mimeo.

Savage, M., (1992), 'Career Mobility in Banking', in A. Miles and D. Vincent (eds), *Building European Society*, Manchester: Manchester University Press.

Savage, M., Barlow, J., Dickens, P. and Fielding, T., (1992), *Property, Bureaucracy and Culture: middle class formation in contemporary Britain*, London: Routledge.

Sayer, A., (1984), *Method in Social Science: a realist approach*, London: Methuen.

Walby, S., (1986), *Patriarchy at Work*, Oxford: Polity.
Walby, S., (1990), *Theorising Patriarchy*, Oxford: Blackwells.
Witz, A., (1992), *Professions and Patriarchy*, London: Routledge.
Wright, E.O., (1985), *Classes*, London: Verso.
Wright, E.O., (1989), 'Rethinking, Once Again, the Concept of Class Structure',
    in E.O. Wright *et al*, *The Debate on Classes*, London: Verso.

Strategies

Feminist change in a patriarchal organisation: the experience of women's initiatives in local government and implications for feminist perspectives on state institutions

Susan Halford

Over the last decade the issue of equal opportunities for women has been placed on the agenda of an ever increasing number of British local authorities. More than half of all authorities have now devised policies which fall within the broad field of equal opportunities, whilst a smaller proportion of these have chosen to set up specific structures such as Women's Committees and Equal Opportunities Communities to address equalities issues on a general and on-going basis (Halford 1989a). To varying degrees all these local councils have recognized the implicitly gendered nature of existing policies and practice and appear to have made a commitment to introducing new policies and practices which promote positive alternatives for women.

This explicit intervention by certain local governments into the field of gender politics raises some important questions. Most commonly these concern the extent to which feminist social change can be brought about via the institutions of the state. More specifically, how far can Women's Committees and similar initiatives actually bring about changes in the policies and practices of local government? The foundation for these concerns lies with a tradition of feminist analysis which locks state institutions into a broader analysis of gender inequality, and emphasizes the ways in which state actions reflect and reinforce the dominance of men and the oppression of women. How then are we to interpret a situation where these very institutions, defined as patriarchal, are apparently pursuing feminist policies?

In this chapter I shall argue that feminist perspectives which view 'the state' as a functional tool in the hands of patriarchal (and/or capitalist) interests paralyse our understanding of local government women's initiatives and, more widely, of the relationship between gender relations and the state in contemporary Western society. Instead, I shall argue, we must turn our attention inwards and examine the organizational forms and social relations *within* state institutions. In what follows I will briefly summarise some feminist theoretical debates on the relationship between gender relations and state institutions. This establishes the general principle of the patriarchal state, but also demonstrates some major weaknesses in the debate to date. Following on from this I will describe the interaction of women's initiatives with local state organizations using empirical material from two local authorities. Women's initiatives have encountered a number of *general* features common to local government organizations which make the implementation of *any* change difficult. In addition there are specifically *gendered* structures and relations within local government organizations which make the implementation of positive changes for women especially difficult. I will conclude by drawing out some of the wider implications which this chapter holds for understanding the ways in which organizations are gendered as well as for feminist perspectives on the state.

Theoretical perspectives on the state

There is of course a long and diverse history of theoretical perspectives concerning the nature and role of state institutions and their relationship to wider society. Despite well debated differences between the more influential perspectives – from liberal to variations of Marxist analysis to the new right – they nonetheless share certain common features. First, few contain any analysis of gender. Second, and at the same time, most have gendered assumptions and implications embedded firmly within them (see Franzway *et al* (1988) for an excellent review).

Feminists reject this gender-blind view of state institutions on both empirical and theoretical grounds (see Showstock-Sassoon 1987; Franzway *et al* 1988; Walby 1990). Historical and contemporary analysis of state policies and practices demonstrates beyond question that these have had – and continue to have – gendered implications on a day-to-day basis, in everyday life. For example, policies on childcare, employment, policing and taxation all have different implications for men and women, reinforcing gender roles which are not only distinct but are also unequal (Wilson 1977; Barrett 1980). The theoretical basis for rejection of gender-blind perspectives on the state lies with rejection of the common idea that society can be divided into distinct and discrete public and private portions. Layers of connected dichotomies are embedded within this division: public/private; social/natural; political/apolitical; male/female. Were this to be accepted, women would be confined to the private sphere, where they naturally belong, away from politics and the state. Conversely, politics and the state would have no connection to women, or more properly to gender relations, or to supposedly private matters such as sexuality, domestic violence or childrearing. Feminist theory exposes this distinction, as an artificial and patriarchal construction (Gamarnikow, 1983; Elshtain, 1984).

The implications of this revelation for theoretical perspectives on the state are two-fold. First, state policies can be seen to enter the supposedly private sphere and to shape supposedly natural gender roles in this sphere. For example, the division of labour in the household whereby women are largely responsible for domestic labour and childcare is shaped, inter alia, by government's choice not to provide affordable childcare. State policies and practices also affect gender divisions in the public sphere. Here the childcare example is important again, as is successive governments' relucance to set 'equal pay for equal value' or 'comparable worth' precedents for women's pay (Equal Opportunities Commission, 1988). Second, and at the same time, state policies and practices maintain a false division between public and private. A clear example of this is state policy on violence against women. Domestic violence is still widely seen as a private matter, whilst women are literally confined to the private sphere through fear of attack on the streets arising, in part, from police advice to women to protect themselves by staying at home and from inadequate policing on the streets (Hanmer and Saunders, 1984).

Beyond this theoretical foundation, feminist perspectives on the state diverge, most commonly as a result of disagreement over theorization of gender inequality, but also arising from differences in the theorization of the nature and role of state institutions themselves. The potential combinations of these two prerequisites for any feminist conceptualisation of gender *vis-à-vis* the institutions of the state creates the possibility for a vast number of possible positions. However, those which have been most commonly developed are outlined below.

Liberal perspectives view gender inequality as the result of individual cases of discrimination combined (sometimes) with the existence of sex-role stereotyping in education and the labour market. Through the removal of these stereotypes, and legislation outlawing discrimination, it is believed that the state will be able to fulfill its proper function as the upholder of equality between all citizens. The introduction of women's initiatives into local government could be a prime strategy for the achievement of this objective. Once women's interests are properly represented at the level of the state the male bias will be successfully redressed. Most other perspectives reject the essentially atomistic conception of gender inequality in liberal theory, as well as the notion that the state is, in principle at least, a neutral arbiter over conflicts in society. Instead, both marxist-feminist and radical feminist perspectives call on an analysis of socio-economic power relations and integrate the role of state institutions into the longterm survival of capitalism, or patriarchy, or both. Whilst marxist-feminism and radical feminism differ fundamentally in their analysis of gender inequality, both perspectives view state institutions as instruments in the hands of a dominant interest, be it capital or men.

Whilst this kind of perspective may be more satisfying than liberal positions, since it is based on an understanding of power relations between social/economic groups and embeds the state *in* these power relations rather than somehow *above* them, there are nonetheless some major difficulties. These stem from the functionalism of such perspectives and the drawbacks inherent in this are well exemplified when we turn to analyse local government women's initiatives. Functionalist perspectives pay little attention to political struggle, and assume that 'the state' is a monolithic, all-seeing, all-knowing corpus, which will always act in the most advantageous way possible for existing power relations. In practice, complex and competing political pressures are constantly levelled at state institutions (Walby, 1990). Dualist perspectives on gender inequality point to the tension between capitalism and patriarchy, and the competing pressures which this creates on the state (Eisenstein 1984; Walby 1990). There are also competing pressures from within capitalism and patriarchy themselves, from trade unions and employers, from feminists and anti-feminists. All these competing pressures may, under certain circumstances, influence state policies and practices. Local government women's initiatives were set up largely as the result of pressure from feminist women organized in the Labour Party (Halford, 1989b). Thus they provide an example of successful political pressure put on the state by feminists. The functionalist retort would point once more to the long term interests of patriarchy (and/or capitalism) claiming that apparent 'gains' are in fact simply a part of a long term strategy to mollify subordinate groups.

Thus far then, we either hail women's initiatives as the end of the male-biased state (the liberal view) or we must reject them as a patriarchal strategy (the functionalist view). In fact, most feminist commentators have not done either, preferring instead to adopt a 'wait and see' stance towards women's initiatives (see *Spare Rib*, April 1983). This is symptomatic of the truly problematic nature of the state for feminists. On the one hand the implication of state policy and practice in gender inequality is irrefutable. On the other, many feminist goals can only be met by state institutions. Think for example of the provision of affordable childcare, abortion on demand, free contraception, action on violence against women, and there are many more examples. It was in recognizing the power of the state to address these issues that feminists organized in the Labour Party pressured for change and the setting up of women's initiatives in local government (see Halford 1989b). Thus,

> It [the state] becomes stripy, partly good, partly bad. It is a case of now you see it now you don't. The dominant interests slither mysteriously about. (Rowbotham 1989:150)

Is it possible to move beyond this? In order to do so we have to accept that it is simply not credible to view the diverse set of institutions which comprise the modern democratic state as unitary or rational and nor do they pursue clearly defined single strategies. State policies and actions are 'not simply a reflex response to the functional needs of a system' (Franzway *et al* 1988:35) but rather should be seen as the outcome of specific social struggles. State institutions *themselves* are the result of social struggles. But the outcomes of social struggles over time have been unequal. There have been some policies and laws which benefit women (for example, extension of the franchise, legalization of contraception and abortion or the Equal Pay and Sex Discrimination Acts). But overall the modern state represents the institionalization of male power arising from a history of social struggle. This allows us to reject functionalism without recourse to pluralism.

Taking the point further, the institutionalization of male dominance does not simply mean that state policies and practices reflect gender relations which only exist somewhere else ie in society outside the state. Rather, gender relations (and those of class and race) are articulated *within* state institutions (cf. Franzaway *et al* 1988). In this sense, state institutions are themselves a node in the network of gender relations (Franzway *et al* 1988).

Where does this revised perspective leave us as far as women's initiatives are concerned? We would still not expect that action by certain local governments will bring about the end of patriarchal gender relations, since gender inequality is not caused solely, or even mainly, by state actions. However, moving away from functionalism we can see that local state institutions may *in principle* bring about some positive changes for women. Whether they do or not is another question. The ability of particular women's initiatives to implement change is shaped by a variety of factors including resources, political commitment and leadership and the degree and nature of political mobilization in the local area. In particular, however, my research has shown the extensive and powerful influence which local government organizations have in shaping the implementation of change by women's initiatives. In part this lies with a general tendency to resist *any* change, although women's initiatives have suffered particularly from this because of the organizational form which they have taken. Beyond this however there is clear evidence of powerful, pervasive and *specific* resistance to positive policies for women. This lies in the gendered dynamics of local government structures and cultures. Paradoxically however, both general and gendered dynamics in local government may, under certain circumstances 'flip-over' from resistance to *support* for positive gender policies. This is not common, but I will discuss the possibilities as they arise.

The place of women's initiatives in local government organizations

Women's initiatives (WIs) have been set up to promote the interests and welfare of women. This means analysing the gendered content of existing policies, devising new positive policies and implementing them. Sometimes the initiatives are restricted to looking at employment by the local authority, but more often they are charged with examining all areas of local authority activity covering both employment and service delivery. The scope which most WIs have been given clearly means that they are not able to devise and implement all the policies alone. Most commonly, WIs have been placed in central, co-ordinating locations within both councils and local authority organizations. From this position WIs may devise policies for implementation elsewhere in the authority and/or act as co-ordinators and monitors of current practice and new policy developments across the authority. WIs themselves have no responsibility for actual employment (beyond the handful of women's officers employed) or for service delivery (beyond sometimes the administration of small grants to voluntary sector women's groups). This means that WIs have to get the *rest* of the local authority to change. The degree to which different WIs are able to achieve this varies. In what follows I will describe the dynamics of change and resistance to change in local government organizations using material from case study research carried out between 1988 and 1990.

In total ten case studies were carried out[1] and my argument below draws generally on material from all these studies. But I shall refer in detail to the two major studies: the London Borough of Haringey and Manchester City Council. These two studies were chosen to explore in detail the dynamics of policy implementation by local government WIs. Case studies comprised extensive analysis of committee minutes and council reports tracking the overall development of the initiatives since their inception, as well as detailed activities, recommendations, policy development and results. The processes underlying these outcomes were explored through in-depth interviews with a range of key informants in each study including officers, councillors, trade unionists and feminist activists. Individual versions of events and analyses obviously varied for a number of reasons and it is not my intention here to present a composite version of 'the truth'. However, in each interview the organizational dynamics surrounding the WI were discussed in depth producing a complex, sometimes contradictory, picture which is interpreted below.

First I shall outline the meaning of the term 'bureaucracy' – so often applied to local state organizations – as a background for describing and analysing the interaction of WIs with bureaucratic local states.

Susan Halford

Local authorities as bureaucratic organizations

The emergence of the term 'bureaucracy' was closely connected to the development of modern state organizations. Over time definitions of bureaucracy multiplied but the association with the power of public officials over citizens remained constant (Albrow, 1970). Successive debates concentrated on the political and philosophical implications of this, and not until the late 19th century was 'bureaucracy' distinguished as just one form of organization, distinguished by particular technical characteristics. The best known and most influential account of these characteristics was produced by Max Weber. Weber's model emphasized the following features:

— a specialized division of labour;
— a hierarchy of authority with a clearly demarcated system of command and responsibilities;
— a formal set of rules and procedures governing operations and activities co-ordinating behaviour in a predictable, uniform and impersonal manner;
— a body of full-time, permanent officials, appointed according to technical competence, trained in specialized tasks, paid according to rank in the hierarchy and who may develop careers on the basis of their ability and seniority.

(Jackson, 1982; Abercrombie *et al*, 1989). Since Weber presented these characteristics as part of an ideal-type model they could be more or less pronounced in a range of more or less bureaucratic organizations. Weber regarded bureaucracy as the most *efficient* and *rational* form or organization, stressing the virtues of:

> . . . precision, speed, unambiguity, knowledge, continuity, discretion, unity, strict subordination, reduction of friction and of material personal costs. (Weber, 1968:973)

Weber's ideal type identifies many significant characteristics which remain strongly associated with state organizations, including local government organizations, today. This leaves us with a problem. If local state organizations function in the efficient and rational manner identified by Weber, how can we explain the widespread yet qualitatively uneven influence which these organizations have on the implementation of positive policies for women?

Ever since Weber's account was published, criticisms have been developed (see Albrow, 1970 and Jackson, 1982 for reviews). Two major criticisms are as follows. First, the features identified by Weber do not necessarily equal 'efficiency'. Second, Weber's concentration on the formal organizational characteristics of bureaucracies misses the informal dynamics which exist, and without which we cannot understand the operation of bureaucratic organizations. Arising from this Morgan (1986) helpfully suggests that Weber's 'machine' model of bureaucracy is just one metaphor with which to approach the study of organizations. Morgan presents alternative perspectives under the headings of seven further metaphors (for example organizations as 'organisms', as 'brains', as 'political systems' and so on). He argues that we cannot choose one approach as the right one, and reject all others. Rather, different perspectives should be critically employed as appropriate, in order to analyse different questions and different organizations. Hence, although local authority organizations *do* undoubtedly bear a strong resemblance to Weber's ideal-type bureaucracy, it is to the criticisms and alternative metaphors that we must turn in order to analyse the processes of organizational support and resistance in the implementation of positive policies for women.

Introducing change into bureaucratic organizations

Bringing about change in bureaucratic organizations is not easy. Resistance to organizational change is endemic and empirical research on major changes in large organizations has clearly shown this to be the case even after a number of years (Argyris, 1967; Johns, 1973). It is suggested that the more bureaucratic an organization, particularly the finer the division of labour and the more hierarchical an organization is, the more there will be resistance to change (Crozier 1964). The experiences of WIs provide evidence of two *general processes* of organizational resistance to change: empire building and organizational inertia.

Empire Building

In both Haringey and Manchester it was widely suggested that centralized WIs have had difficulties influencing the activities of other authority departments. This is partly due to the physical

163

distance of central policy units from other departments, and the generalized nature of WIs compared with day-to-day departmental work. Making inroads into departmental work in this context is difficult. However, these general problems are compounded by the prevalence of 'empire building'. Functional specialism, a fine division of labour, is one of the fundamental characteristics of a Weberian bureaucracy and is a significant feature of local authority organizations today. Weber regarded this as a path to efficiency. However, functional specialism

> . . . creates a structure that is supposed to be a system of co-operation, but often turns out as a system of competition.
> (Morgan, 1986:37)

Empire building means competition between departments. This may have multiple causes. In the context of limited funding, competition arises for resources. Individual departments naturally want to secure as many resources as possible in order to fulfil their function. However, what is sensible behaviour for one department does not necessarily benefit the whole organization, as competition for resources results in insularity and low levels of co-operation (Morgan 1986). A further cause of empire building stems from the career strategies of managers within particular departments. The hierarchical organization of local authorities is also a career ladder for employees. Towards the top of the ladder opportunities diminish. Building up the size and responsibilities of a department increases the opportunities for career development and is therefore in the interest of career-minded officers. Furthermore, empire-building increases the power, control and status which managers have. This status may be within the authority itself, or may stretch beyond the confines of the organization to status in the eyes of professional peers.

Professionalisation of administration is another of Weber's bureaucratic characteristics. Local authority management largely remains the province of professionals: individuals trained and awarded qualifications by major professional associations/institutes (for example the Law Society, the Royal Institute of British Architects and the Chartered Institute of Public Finance Accountants). Kudos amongst peers in these associations and institutes may be one reason for empire building. The dominance of professionalism is further relevant. These professionals tend to have little training in management or public administration, placing faith in their own particular specialism. The local authority professional:

> . . . like all professional experts . . . will tend to believe that his ability and expertise enable him to provide solutions to all the problems with which he is confronted and he will be reluctant to accept that experts in other disciplines, or for that matter councillors, have anything useful to contribute to the solution of these problems. (Elcock, 1982:96)

Local authorities have therefore tended to '. . . remain in essence loose confederations of semi-autonomous empires.' (Smith, 1966: 29). This makes the implementation of corporate policy rather difficult.

Other research has shown that the most 'successful' organizations are those where professional differences are minimized and common standards introduced (Morgan 1986:127). This hardly applies to local authorities. Rhodes (1989) has demonstrated how sub-national government in Britain became increasingly dependent on professional expertise during the post-war expansion:

> In short, policy-making in British government became characterised by professional bureaucratic complexes based on specific functions. . . (1989:206).

Given this general situation, it is likely that empire building is a common feature of most British local authorities. Certainly it was present to some extent in all the ten authorities researched by this author (Halford 1991). But in the London Borough of Haringey the level of empire building was particularly severe and widely cited as a major problem for the WI (interviews with author 1988–9). Departments in the organization are highly insular, with little communication between them. Indeed an internal report into management problems in the borough concluded that the authority was suffering from a 'policy vacuum filled by bargaining and fiefdom' (Lansley, 1990:115). The central position of the women's unit makes it difficult to get information. What communication there is, is distrusted since:

> Information is power. No-one wants to tell anyone anything else. If you *do* hear something you assume it's false. (ex-chair of Haringey women's committee, June 1988[2]).

The WI rarely gets reliable information and its ability to analyse the situation across the authority, and what action should be taken, is severely impeded. Information is crucial to the successful implementation of any corporate policy. Yet empire building ensures that barriers to the spread of information are put up, since information equals power and control (Jackson 1982).

Departments are resistant to intervention by the centrally located women's unit for several reasons. Fundamentally, where an empire is under construction demands that it be built differently are not welcome! In Haringey the demands came from a unit with few resources, and therefore low bureaucratic status. Women's units may be further weakened by the non-professional status of women's officers. This may undermine the respect with which professional managers (are willing to) regard women's officers. There is also the objective problem that altering the policies and practices of particular departments may require detailed, professional knowledge. But women's officers cannot be expected to have detailed knowledge of all areas of the authority and must rely on departmental experts to some extent. Arguments from the departments that women's officers don't know the details of policy implementation may simply indicate an unwillingness to co-operate. In Haringey the women's unit was deliberately located in the chief executive's department, supposedly the nerve-centre of a local authority. But in this case the department was weak and ineffectual. The problem was so bad that one chief officer remarked:

> If you have people in that location then you set them up to fail
> . . . If you'd set out to chart a way to make something start out as
> badly as possible, that's how you'd do it. (December 1989).

However, empire building in Haringey has also *led* to some departmental initiatives on women's equality. Paradoxically these developments confirm the operation of departmentalism. In-department initiatives have taken place unevenly in Haringey, but *always independently* of the WI. Thus women's equality work has itself become an empire-building strategy. Whether or not this happens depends on whether the issues are seen to enhance departmental status. This may be within the authority, where managers might seek to identify with a particular political position, or more widely within the relevant profession field. The major departmental initiatives in Haringey have taken place in the

Planning and Housing Departments. Both are professions which were radicalized in the 1970s and in which women's equality work may have some status (see further discussion of gender and professionalism below).

The take-up of women's equality work in Manchester City Council's departments was also uneven. Most developments have taken place in the Education Department, largely as the result of committed individuals in a supportive professional context. Manchester experimented with departmental equal opportunities officers for a short time, whereby extra equalities officers were located in mainstream departments in order to encourage departmental ownership of equal opportunities. The results are instructive. Apart from Education (where a Women's Education Team of three officers was set up) the results were minimal. Different explanations are suggested for this. At a general level these concern the inability of one isolated officer to change a department, especially in those cases where there was open hostility to the promotion of women's equality work. In one case opposition was so fierce that the officer was badly harassed and resigned after a few months. Haringey too sited women's officers in departments following re-organization in 1988, but here this was achieved through the break up and decentralization of the women's unit. Early results were mixed, being largely dependent on the individual departmental contexts into which individual women's officers were moved. It is worth noting however that the mechanism for the decentralization of officers entailed putting them up for bids from departments, since there were not enough women officers for each department simply to be allocated one. In the first five months only two departments had made a bid (Housing and Community Affairs) and following this women's officers were simply placed by central decision and not departmental bid.

Bureaucratic Inertia

The second general explanation for resistance to change within local authorities is the *inertia* which exists in large bureaucratic organizations. Some writers go so far as to suggest that organizations noted for their security and stability of work functions (which despite major upheavals still included local government in the 1980s) will attract employees

. . . motivated by the desire for security and stability, qualities clearly associated with personal rigidity and resistance to innovation. (Johns 1973:68)

These so-called mechanistic personalities may be one explanation for bureaucratic inertia, although it seems unwise (not to mention inaccurate) to assume that all local authority workers fall into this category! A more satisfactory explanation lies with the problems of educating people to change their behaviour and the fear of failure both of which pervade bureaucratic structures. WIs require officers to revise the way they discharge their functions and take the initiative in adapting policies and practices to take account of the interests of women. However, bureaucratic structures do not provide a good context for this kind of evaluation and learning process. Morgan (1986) suggests three explanations. First, in highly fragmented structures information and knowledge are restricted both horizontally (as we have seen with empire building) and hierarchically. Yet without information and knowledge people are unable to learn and re-evaluate. Johns (1973) makes the point:

When told they must change, people often become stubborn and defensive, particularly if . . . the orders are not accompanied by adequate explanations. (Johns, 1973:45)

Second, the accountability placed on individuals in the division of tasks produces defensiveness, making people unable to deal with uncertainty. Anything new is 'strange and threatening, surrounded by uncertainties' (Johns 1973:50). In a context where information and knowledge are restricted and people are uncertain as to what is actually expected of them, the tendency is to oversimplify. Thus people are 'interested in problems only if there are solutions at hand' (Morgan 1986:90). The development of women's equality work is unlikely to be compatible with this simple task orientation. Last, where there is uncertainty the impulse may be to claim action where there is none. This may be a strategy to cover up in the face of failure. Thus individuals may

. . . engage in diversionary behaviour consciously, or unconsciously, as when threats to a basic mode of practice lead an individual to deflect blame elsewhere and to tighten up on that practice rather than questioning its nature and effect. (Morgan, 1986:90)

This process can be seen in operation when departments are asked to include 'gender comments' on their reports to committee. It is common to claim that there are *no* gender comments. Thus the impression is that the issue has been considered and resolved. This may well not be so. For example, on the report which recommended abolition of the Women's Education Team in Manchester the gender comments paragraph contained the comment 'none'!

However, organizational inertia should not be acepted as inevitable. Morgan cites practical strategies which can be employed to overcome organizational learning difficulties. Unfortunately, overcoming inertia is not simply a technical question. By concentrating on the ability of organizations to learn and initiate (the 'brain' metaphor) Morgan warns:

> . . . there is a danger of overlooking important conflicts between the requirements of learning and self-organisation on the one hand and the realities of power and control on the other. (*ibid* p. 108)

Allowing officers to re-evaluate their work and initiate change threatens the power of those in control. Further, changing an organization means changing attitudes and values. This cannot be a simple technical matter. Organizational inertia is reinforced by those attitudes and values which currently prevail. An essential element of this concerns the *gendered* attitudes and values which are present in local authority organizations. Bringing about *any* change in a local authority bureaucracy is difficult. Bringing about changes which challenge the gender order of local authority organizations is far more difficult still. It is to these points that we now turn.

Gender relations in bureaucratic organizations

Weber suggested that impersonality, an emphasis on technical competence in the appointment of staff, and the presence of rules and procedures would rid organizations of social and individual biases and prejudices. For him

> . . . bureaucracy is progressive in that it breaks down old patriarchal structures and removes the arbitrary power held by fathers and masters in traditional society. (Pringle, 1989:84)

Weber stressed the removal of personal attributes placing the emphasis instead on skills and standardized rules and procedures. This remains a common conception of how bureaucracies function and has been employed as a lever by liberal feminists in their campaigns for equal opportunities. Equal opportunities employment policies emphasize above all the importance of excluding personal considerations, preconceptions and prejudices based on race, gender, sexuality or physical ability, in favour of the impersonal application of uniform rules of assessment. Where it is assumed that local authorities *should* function in this impersonal way, claims for modifications to iron out aberrations can be difficult to reject.

However, this is one of the planks of Weber's perspective which has been most thoroughly and convincingly criticised. Generally, it has been widely argued that the personal attributes of employees continue to shape bureaucratic organizations, and that even the most rule-bound structure allows scope for personalized actions and judgement. But, despite the widespread acceptance of these points, most organizational theory continues to treat *gender* as marginal and/or incidental to the workplace (Pringle, 1989). In what follows I will argue that gender relations and gendered interests are in fact thoroughly embedded in local authority organizations, and that it is only by re-conceptualizing local authority organizations in this sense that we can understand the operation of organizational resistance to implementation of positive policies for women.

Formal and Informal Structures

The formal structure of local authority organizations is not depersonalized in the way Weber suggested. Pringle (1989) suggests that the dominant discourse of 'rationality' in the formal structure of organizations is one important aspect of this. Weber's view of bureaucracy implicitly relies on a public-private division of society. He separates

. . . the public world of rationality and efficiency from the private sphere of emotional and personal life. (Pringle 1989:86)

Feminist exposure of the patriarchal basis of this dichotomy provides a specific foundation on which to build a model of bureaucratic organizations which includes gender relations. Furthermore, Pringle argues that the concept of rationality itself

> . . . can be interpreted as a commentary on the construction of a particular type of masculinity based on the exclusion of the personal, the sexual and the feminine from any definition of 'rationality'. The values of instrumental rationality are strongly associated with the masculine individual while the feminine is associated with the world of chaos and disorder. This does not mean that men are in fact 'rational' or that women are 'emotional' but rather that they learn to recognise themselves in these conceptions. (Pringle, 1989:88–9)

Belief in the discourse of rationality and separation of the so-called 'private' from the supposedly 'public' local authority may be one basis for resistance to women's equality work. WIs explicitly challenge the 'public' rational image of local authority organizations, making it clear that gender is a significant dimension of all areas of organizational life. This makes people uncomfortable. WIs challenge conventional notions of what local authorities should be involved in. A common response to WIs is that it is unnecessary for them to get involved in women's equality, and not what local authorities should spend their time and money on. The term the 'loony' left is indicative. Some people literally think it is 'mad' for local authorities to be involved in such issues. Women are frequently embarrassed by WIs – embarrassed to be 'picked out for special treatment' in the workplace. Of course, some women might oppose women's equality work on political grounds. But others may feel it is best to leave things the way they are even if they know only too well of the ways in which the organization is gendered, for example sexist language, harassment, the operation of old boy networks and so on.

In fact it is common knowledge that all sorts of informal practices and events take place within the supposedly formal and rational structure of organizations. Indeed it is now widely accepted that in addition to the formal structure of bureaucracies elaborated by Weber, all organizations have *informal* structures (Selznick 1964). Looking at the formal structures alone will not expose all the dynamics within an organization nor enable us to explain particular organizational outcomes. Selznick argues that in every organization goals are modified (abandoned, deflected or elaborated) and that this is effected through the informal structure. An informal structure arises partly from the inability for *any* organization to specify rules and procedures down to the *n*th degree. Organizational rules are incomplete guidelines within which individual judgement must operate (Bendix, 1949). This element of 'individual judgement' is absent from Weber's model but bureaucrats are not depersonalized automatons! As Albrow appropriately puts it:

> The official has characteristics as a social being beyond those which the administrative code specifies. Like other men he has interests prejudices and fears. (Albrow 1970:55)

Interests, prejudices and fears shape the actions and practices of officials in the absence of complete guidelines. Furthermore even when specified rules and procedures do exist:

> . . . in practice, staff may adapt their action to suit circumstances and needs of individuals. (Frances and Stone 1956; discussed in Albrow 1970:56)

So what *are* the interests, prejudices and fears which shape the actions and practices of employees in bureaucratic organizations? Once we accept that staff bring their personal interests into organizations, and that these shape the way they discharge their functions, we must also accept that *gendered* perceptions, practices and attitudes will be present too. To varying degrees, women's initiatives challenge the patriarchal gender relations within local authority bureaucracies. In the rest of this section I will consider in more detail the ways in which male interests are embedded in local authority organizations and the ways in which this affects the implementation of positive policies for women.

Individual Interest in Organizations

Morgan (1986) suggests that decoding the personal agendas underlying informal actions and activities in organizations depends on understanding the way in which the following three areas of interest interconnect. (See Figure 1). The implementation of women's equality work may interfere with any of these interests. The introduction of positive policies for women requires that individuals re-evaluate their actions and practices. Thus the 'organizational' task is altered, requiring new and/or extra work perhaps over a long period of time. The interest of individuals in

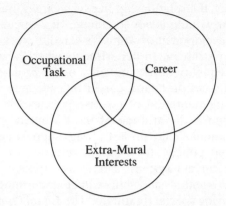

Figure 1: *Individual interests in organizations*
Source: Morgan, 1986.

an organization – both men and women – may well be against such alterations, particularly the need to take a long-term and overall perspective rather than ticking off specific tasks to be carried out.

Second, there is the question of career interests. Hierarchical local authority organizations are also career ladders. The pyramid shape of the hierarchy means that the number of opportunities diminish towards the top. The typical pattern of men's and women's employment in local authorities displays a strong tendency for women to be concentrated towards the bottom of the hierarchy whilst the top echelons are almost exclusively male (Stone 1988). Normally, then, the competition for promotion up the career ladder takes place between men and this intensifies towards the top of the ladder. Equal opportunities employment policies aim (amongst other things) to increase the numbers of women competing for senior jobs. Thus, a successful equal opportunities employment policy would intensify competition, diminishing opportunities for individual men even further. Men's career interests may be served by opposing the entry of women into senior jobs. Crompton and Jones further this point, claiming that '. . . the male career rests on the continuing subordination of . . . females.' (1984:243). A similar argument can be made concerning male opposition to the entry of women into manual crafts and trades. This has been another equal opporunties employment policy pursued by WIs – Haringey in particular – and has met with considerable resistance (see the *Guardian*, 11/4/90).

However, the relationship between career interests and positive policies for women is not so simple. In particular we should note that the development of women's equality work may become *part* of a career strategy. In departments where a positive attitude to women's equality work prevails, or in professions which have taken the issues on board, career mileage may actually be gained by the implementation of positive policies for women. Another complication is the attitude of those women who are already in senior positions. They do not always support equal opportunities employment policies for women, referring to their own success under the current system. There also appears to be a fear that women's credentials and skills will be undermined if they are seen to be receiving special treatment. The Equal Opportunities Officer at British Rail has commented recently on difficulties in getting women to go on training courses for these very reasons (*In Business*, Radio 4, 29/9/90).

The third and final area of individual interest in Morgan's model is 'extra-mural' activities. This is a catch-all category for everything that is neither an organizational task nor directly related to careers. In many ways it is also the most interesting category. Equal opportunities employment policies often make direct links to 'extra-mural' activities/responsibilities, in particular childcare. It is recognized that because of the sexual division of labour in the household, women will not be able to compete in the workplace without childcare provision. Thus WIs promote policies which enable women to combine career and extra-mural activities as well as a variety of policies and campaigns which challenge women's inequality in all areas of life and encourage women to fight inequality. Because WIs may challenge gender relations in all areas of life they may well also challenge the extra-mural interests of men. Johns argues that

> People oppose change if their social relationships, their status or their security are threatened. (1973:60)

and that employee reaction to organizational change will be affected by 'any perceived threat to his status in the family' (ibid p. 62). By encouraging women to fight inequality, along all dimensions of patriarchal gender relations, WIs may be perceived as a threat to male status in the family and civil society more generally. An example of this came from one officer in Haringey who described a common male reaction to the WI as fine so long as their wives didn't find out about it!

Thus we can see that WIs may run counter to the individual interests of men or women in any of the three interest categories described by Morgan. This is a useful starting point but is rather simplistic and requires development in a number of ways.

Organized male interests in bureaucracies

There are three principal forms of organization through which collective male interests tend to be represented in local authority organizations. These are the trade unions, the professions and the senior managers group which (supposedly) co-ordinates all authority activity.

The role which trade unions have had as representatives of organized male labour is now well documented (see Walby, 1987). Although women are increasingly unionized, they remain less likely to hold official posts and the particular interests of female-dominated occupations and of women generally remain less likely to be addressed. The response of local authority trade unions to positive policies for women varies by union and by geographical location. In general, manual unions are less supportive and white collar unions more so. Where there is a strong and recent tradition of organized male labour dominating local politics there is also likely to be more resistance to equalities policies (see Halford, 1989b, on Sheffield). Trade unions can disrupt the adoption of new policies during negotiations over changes to employment practice. Particular sticking points have been the introduction of disciplinary procedures for cases of alleged sexual harassment, and banning of page 3 pin-ups. Unions have also impeded consultation with women workers by failing to pass on information. The situation appears to improve when women take on official posts, as the unions' national organizations begin to address equalities issues, and as new generations of members, particularly women and black people, begin to make new demands on the grounds of race and gender.

Professionals dominate local authority management (Elcock 1982). The term 'professional' implies objectivity, rationality and technical occupational expertise. However, this hides a gendered reality. This is true in a double sense. First, professionalism is a means by which entrants to an occupation can be controlled. Witz

(1990) argues convincingly that we must abandon any generic notion of profession as a state, and refer rather to professional projects. She continues:

> It is my contention that the generic notion of profession is also a *gendered* notion as it takes what are in fact successful professional projects of class-priviledged, male actors at a particular point in history and in particular societies as the paradigmatic case of profession. (1990:675)

Witz shows how medical occupational groups dominated by women, for example midwives, engaged in professional projects but were denied the status by male-dominated state institutions. Furthermore, she argues, seeking professional status has often been a project of occupational exclusionary closure with gendered dimensions. For example, the history of law and medicine professions show clearly that professionalization deliberately excluded women. Not all professional projects are exclusionary closure strategies of this sort. There are other informal ways in which professions effectively exclude women. Training may take many years, requiring extensive evening and weekend work and often takes place when the trainee is in his/her 20s. Of course it is absolutely possible for women to undertake this commitment. However, since women may well have children at this stage in their lifecycle, the likelihood of having time for professional training is less than is the case for men who tend to bear less domestic responsibility.

Paid work typically performed by women is less likely to have achieved professional status; women have been formally excluded from occupations with professional status; and gender divisions of labour make women less likely to be in a position to achieve professional status. Thus, it is hardly surprising that the numbers of women amongst local authority managers, who are overwhelmingly professionals, is low.

As well as regulating entrants to occupations, professional institutions regulate the *practice* of professionals in the field. They are trained to perform tasks in certain ways, prioritize particular factors and so on. The creation of professional practices and norms is gendered too. For example, separation of the so-called 'private' and 'public' spheres of home and (paid) work became one of the key principles of landuse planning in the post war period. This rested on inherent assumptions about the households and the division of labour. In particular, that there would be a full-time paid worker and a full-time domestic worker. In fact this

> . . . organization of urban landuse tends to benefit employed
> men with wives, at the expense of both married and single
> women struggling to run homes, care for children and, in greater
> and greater numbers, also manage a part-time job. (Women in
> Geography Study Group, 1984:46)

Women's employment opportunities are limited by physical accessibility and compounded by the planning of transport routes around full-time workers making simple home to work and back again journeys, not the complex routes women perform in order to combine paid and unpaid work (Pickup 1984). There are numerous other examples of the way in which professional norms and practices institutionalize gender differences and assumptions (see for example McKinnon (1983) on law; Matrix (1984) on architecture).

However, professions are not static in terms of members or practices and norms. The numbers of women in professional occupations is increasing. Furthermore, the nature of professions is changing. I have already referred to variations in the nature of professions as a significant factor in the development of, and resistance to, women's equality work. It is certainly the case that some professions particularly associated with local authorities became radicalized in the 1970s. According to Gyford (1985) these professions formed a crucial element of the 'new left' which emerged around local government in the early 1980s.

At a general level, equal opportunities developments are more likely in some local authority departments than in others. Engineering, Environmental Health and Direct Works (dominated by crafts not professions) are all unusual sites for development. By contrast, developments in Housing, Social Services and Education are far more common. There is, however, no guarantee that transformations in a profession will be uniform across all local authorities. Whether or not new professional discourses are taken up depends on whether managers have had exposure to new ideas (connected to age) as well as on personal dispositions and council politics.

A final grouping of male interests present in local authorities is rather different from the previous two. Each local authority department has a chief officer. Usually these chief officers meet on a regular basis to discuss corporate policy. The power of individual senior managers is multiplied in this group which forms the very heart of the organization. According to one of Weber's early critics, every organization is in fact run by a few leaders. Michels spoke of the 'iron law of oligarchy' and argued that this small group of leaders

> . . . will put their own interests first and work to preserve the bureaucratic procedures which have all the character of efficiency and certification and which keep them at the top. (Smith *et al*, 1982:187)

Of course, there is no rule that chief officers *have* to be men or that they must all be hostile to equality policies! Indeed the number of female chief officers is on the increase. However, in 1985 there were only 50 women chief officers in the whole of the UK (Stone, 1988[3]). As well as usually being male (and white, and middle-class) chief officers are at the peak of their career. They are commonly older and less likely to have been affected by the new professional ideas discussed above. The chief officers' group can therefore represent the very bastion of organizational resistance to change. Whether this is in fact the case will vary according to individuals, council politics and the ability of council politicians to control the chief officers' group.

Gendered cultures

It is not credible to suggest that all individual men consciously or explicitly pursue the patriarchal career and/or extra-mural interests described above. Some may do, but focusing on strategic individual interests will not illuminate all the gendered processes which exist in organizations. In order to understand patriarchal resistance to organizational change, we need to consider more subtle gender dynamics than these. One way of approaching this is to consider organizational culture and in particular the way in which the culture of organizations is gendered. The masculine bias of 'rationality' as a basis for organizational culture is one aspect of this. Indeed some have even suggested that the discourse of rationality which surrounds bureaucratic organizations makes for a more stable form of male domination than other forms of patriarchy which rely on power being vested in the hands of individual men in the household. It is the apparent neutrality of bureaucracies hiding the gendered interests served by them which bestows this potency (Pringle, 1989).

Perhaps surprisingly a well-documented aspect of this concerns the nature of sexuality in organizations (Hearn and Parkin, 1987; Hearn *et al*, 1989; Pringle, 1989). A Weberian perspective leads us to believe that sexuality is private and hence absent from the public workplace. This line of argument simply cannot be sustained. Brenda Jones sums this up well:

'Sex is like paperclips in the office: commonplace, useful, underestimated, ubiquitous.' (quoted in Pringle, 1989:84)

Feminist exposure of the widespread occurrence of male sexual harassment of women in the workplace is the most obvious example of the gendered power of sexuality in organizations. The naming of sexual harassment at work has simply made public and a legitimate cause for complaint what most women have always known. Sexual harassment can take place in varying degrees and it can be argued that there is an almost seamless join with broader organizational culture as this comment from Hearn and Parkin claims:

Male managers with female subordinates may use sexuality, harassment, joking and abuse as a routine means of maintaining authority. This may be thoroughly embedded in the taken-for-granted culture of the organization. (1987:93)

(Hetero)sexuality is embedded within organizations in a diversity of ways not just through harassment (see Cockburn, 1991; Adkins, 1992). But sexuality is not the only gendered aspect of organizational culture. We need also to consider the gendering of status, power and control both formally and informally as well as the presence of wider ideological constructions of masculinity and femininity.

Where individuals are able to use their own judgement and make decisions independently of specified procedures – in the informal structure – it is likely that they will rely on informal 'norms' based on shared meanings, understandings and values (Morgan, 1986). These do not appear from nowhere but are shaped by the cultural context in which the organization exists. In this case, a patriarchal society. For example, where two candidates are equally qualified for a job/promotion after the formal procedures have been exhausted, the decisions as to who to appoint will depend on such nebulous factors as 'will this person fit in?' or 'can I work with this person?' Discussing careers in the civil service, Cockburn (1991) describes this phenomenon thus:

> . . . what a reporting officer wanted to see in a budding professional was someone of whom he could say 'I was just like that at his age'. White men had simply been reproducing themselves. (1991:54).

A study of executive life in the Swedish public sector demonstrates clearly the way in which male norms operate at this stage, when it is men who are making the decision (Ressner, 1987). For example, in executive life the communication of information is essential. Ressner's study shows male executives to be more satisfied communicating with socially uniform people. Women, Ressner argues, are therefore not 'legitimate and natural recipients of information' (*ibid* p. 48). A similar point is made in Figure 2.

Figure 2: *Equal Opportunities?*
Source: *Guardian* 9/10/90.

Ressner's study provides an excellent basis for understanding the hidden hierarchy of gendered informal structures in organizations. In particular she illuminates the way in which the operation of the hidden hierarchy varies at different levels within organizations. In contrast to the executive example above, she shows how the lack of a career ladder and development prospects affects low level office workers, who are almost exclusively female. This is partly a problem for the formal structure of organizations, which could be altered to provide more opportunities. However, Ressner also shows how the existing formal structure affects women's self-esteem. Lack of change makes them afraid of change, therefore less likely to apply for new jobs and therefore less likely to build successful careers. Ressner quotes one women worker:

> The treatment you get as a clerical worker doesn't improve your self confidence, it does just the opposite . . . If you're a clerical worker, you're marked for life – you behave like a skivvy because you're treated like one, and this narrows you down. It's a vicious circle. (1987:25).

Ressner draws our attention to variations in the nature of gendered attitudes and practices throughout an organization. This point is also important in respect of departmental differences. Both the intermediate and major case studies described in this paper showed some departments in particular local authorities to be especially reactionary or sexist, whilst others were especially progressive or innovatory. Commenting on *sub*-corporate cultures Morgan says:

> In organizations there are often many different and competing value systems that create a mosaic of organizational realities rather than a uniform corporate culture. (1986:127)

Why do differences exist in the gendered culture of different local authority departments? One explanation may be difference in the degree of male dominance in department personnel. Direct works and engineering departments, which are usually almost exclusively male, are also usually identified as particularly sexist and in-transigent. Another reason may be the level of staff turnover in a department. A common reason cited for Haringey Personnel department's lack of interest in equal opportunities was that the same managers had been in post for many years. Thus they were stuck into a pattern of doing things and had not been affected by recent changes in the Personnel profession which incorporate equal opportunities as 'good professional practice'. This suggests that the nature of professions may be important in shaping the differences which exist between departments in the take-up of women's equality work.

Conclusions

The story of organizational resistance and opposition to change in the two local authorities described above is not an unusual one. Research in a further eight local authorities *and* a national survey of all local authorities with women's initiatives have both clearly pointed to organizational resistance and opposition as major problems in the implementation of new policies to address the needs and interests of women (Halford, 1989a; Halford, 1991). What implications do the experience of women's initiatives in local government have for broader understandings of gender, bureaucracy and the state?

Weber's ideal type retains a power, despite ultimately convincing criticisms, since many of the features he identifies are still commonly assumed to describe modern bureaucracies. Impersonality, rationality, technical specialism and the dominance of rules and procedures are characteristics still closely associated with bureaucratic organizations (especially local authorities) both by the public and even those who work within them. Yet gender is centrally located even within the confines of this Weberian perspective, for example within notions of rationality and/or the definition and operation of technical expertise. Furthermore, few non-Weberian perspectives on bureaucracy recognize the implicitly gendered nature of *all* the alternatives they suggest. Feminists have not been blind to the gendered nature of bureaucracy. Some have suggested that feminism and bureaucracy are inherently in opposition to one another (Ferguson 1984). More pragmatically, women's initiatives have often been set up to work according to non-bureaucratic principles, following from the women's movement, and creating a feminist space within male local authority bureaucracies. On a day-to-day basis this objective has met with some success – at least in the operation of women's initiatives themselves. In challenging the broader bureaucratic structures there has been far less success. This is not surprising. If a major obstacle to change lies with structure and practice of local government organizations, then trying to change those organizations will meet with certain resistance.

Understanding the gendered nature of bureaucratic local government organizations is essential to any consideration of the potential which local government women's initiatives have to implement change. Dismissing women's initiatives as a functional strategy by 'the patriarchal state' to demobilize and disempower feminism is not credible. Some politicians and officers may indeed behave in a tokenistic manner and/or hope that they can 'co-opt' feminist activism into local state structures and thus silence independent criticism of policy and practice. But 'the state' as a whole has neither clearly defined goals to this end nor the textbook strategies to achieve them as implied by the more functionalist perspectives. Conversely, all the empirical evidence demonstrates that state institutions are not monoliths blindly serving particular interests. However, this is clearly not to say that it is simply an empirical matter whether WIs implement change, or that state institutions are in some way 'up for grabs'. A revised organizational perspective demonstrates the operation of gendered power relations within state institutions, and it is in this sense that those institutions can be understood as patriarchal. The historical form of the organizations, the people who work in them and the political structures, too, cannot be separated from the social relations of gender (and those of class, and race and sexuality) which exist in society more generally. *But* what happens in state organizations is not simply a *reflection* of what happens outside. The scope of activities which local state institutions are involved in, for example education, planning and design and health, mean that policies and practices also *shape* gender relations.

This perspective transcends the functionalism of pioneering feminist theoretical perspectives. It allows proper consideration of the complex and contradictory nature of political struggle and the modern democratic welfare state *without* rejecting the operation of gender power relations within those institutions.

Acknowledgements

This paper is based on research funded by the Economic and Social Research Council and on my PhD thesis. I would like to thank Simon Duncan, Tony Fielding and Mike Savage for their advice and support during the production of my thesis. Thanks must also go to all the people who agreed to be interviewed during the course of my research, especially those in Haringey and

Susan Halford

Manchester, and to all who helped with finding and interpreting council minutes and official reports.

Notes

1 These were: Cambridge City Council, London Borough of Camden, Derbyshire County Council, London Borough of Haringey, Kirklees Metropolitan District Council, Manchester City Council, Nottingham City Council, Redditch District Council, Sheffield City Council and the London Borough of Wandsworth.
2 Unless otherwise specified all local authority interviews were carried out by the author.
3 Considering that there are 500 plus local authorities in the UK, each with at least six chief officers, this is a miniscule number.

References

Abercrombie, N. *et al*, (1988), *Contemporary British Society*, Oxford: Blackwell.
Adkins, L., (1992), 'Sexual work and the employment of women in the service industries' in Savage, M. and Witz, A., (1992), *Gender and Bureaucracy* Sociological Review Monograph.
Albrow, M., (1970), *Bureaucracy*, London: Pall Mall Press.
Argyris, C., (1967), 'Today's problems with tomorrow's organisations' in *Journal of Management Studies* February 1967.
Barrett, M., (1980), *Women's Oppression Today*, London: Verso.
Bendix, R. *Higher Civil Servants In American Society* University of Colorado Studies, Colorado.
Cockburn, C., (1991), *In the Way of Women: Men's resistance to sex equality in organisations*, London: Macmillan.
Crompton, R. and Jones, G., (1984), *White Collar Proletariat*, London: Macmillan.
Crozier, M., (1964), *The Bureaucratic Phenomen*, London: Tavistock.
Eisenstein, 2 (1984), *Feminism and Sexual Equality*, New York: Monthly Review Press.
Elcock, H., (1982), *Local Government: politicians, professionals and the public in local authorities*, London: Methuen.
Elshtain, J. (1984), *Public Man, Private Woman: Women in social and political thought*, Oxford: Martin Robertson.
Equal Opportunities Commission (1988), *From Policy to Practice: a strategy for the 1990s*, EOC: Manchester.
Ferguson, K., (1984), *The Feminist Case Against Bureaucracy*, Philadelphia: Temple University Press.
Franzway, S., Court, D. and Connell, R., (1988), *Staking a Claim: Feminism, bureaucracy and the state*, Cambridge: Polity.
Gamarnikow, E., Morgan, D., Puvis, J. and Taylorson, D., (eds) (1983), *The Public and the Private*, London: Heinemann.
Guardian, 11.4.90, 'Building a better future for women?'

Gyford, J., (1985), *The Politics of Local Socialism*, London: George Allen and Unwin.

Halford, S., (1989a), 'Local authority women's initiatives 1982–8: the extent, origins and efficacy of positive policies for women in British local government' *Urban and Regional Working Paper 69*, University of Sussex.

Halford, S., (1989b), 'Spatial divisions and women's initiatives in British local government' *Geoforum*.

Halford, S., (1991), *Local Politics, Feminism and the Local State: Women's initiatives in British local government in the 1980s* Unpublished PhD thesis.

Hearn, J. and Parkin, W., (1988), *'Sex' at 'Work': the paradox of organisation sexuality*, Brighton: Wheatsheaf.

Hanmer, J. and Saunders, S., (1984), *Well Founded Fear*, London: Hutchinson.

Hearn, J. *et al*, (1989), *The Sexuality of Organisation*, London: Sage.

Jackson, P., (1982), *The Political Economy of Bureaucracy*, London: Phillip Allen.

Johns, E., (1973), *The Sociology of Organisational Change*, Oxford: Pergamon.

Lansley, S. *et al*, (1990), *Councils in Conflict*, London: Macmillan.

MacKinnon, C., (1983), 'Feminism, marxism, method and the state: towards a feminist jurisprudence' *Signs* 8,4.

Matrix Book Group, (1984), *Making Space: Women and the man-made environment*, London: Pluto.

Morgan, G., (1986), *Images of Organisation*, London: Sage.

Pringle, R., (1989), *Secretaries Talk*, London: Verso.

Ressner, U., (1987), *The Hidden Hierarchy: Democracy and equal opportunities*, Aldershot: Avebury.

Rhodes, R., (1989), '"A squalid and politically corrupt process?" Inter-governmental relations in the post-war period' in Anderson, J. and Cochrane, A., (1989), *A State of Crisis: the changing face of British politics*, London: Hodder and Stoughton.

Rowbotham, S., (1989), *The Past is Before Us: Feminism in action since the 1960s*, London: Pandora Press.

Selznick, P., (1964), 'An approach to a theory of bureaucracy' in Coser, L. and Rosenberg, B. (eds) *Sociological Theory*, New York: Macmillan.

Showstack-Sassoon, A., (ed.) (1987), *Women and the State*, London: Hutchinson.

Smith, M. *et al*, (1982), *Introducing Organisational Behaviour*, London: Macmillan.

Spare Rib (April 1983), 'Takeover Town Hall' No. 129 pp. 6–8.

Stone, I., (1988), *Equal Opportunities in Local Authorities*, London: HMSO.

Walby, S., (1987), *Patriarchy at Work*, Cambridge: Polity.

Walby, S., (1990), *Theorising Patriarchy*, Oxford: Blackwell.

Weber, M., (1968), *Economy and Society*, Berkeley: University of California Press.

Wilson, E., (1977), *Women and the Welfare State*, London: Tavistock.

Witz, A., (1990), 'Professions and patriarchy: gender and the politics of occupational closure' *Sociology* 24,4.

Women and Geography Study Group of the IBG (1984), *Geography and Gender*, London: Hutchison.

Femocratic feminisms

Sophie Watson

This chapter compares British and Australian feminist interventions in the state arenas, locating these within feminist theory which has both influenced and derived from these interventions. Australia provides an interesting point of comparison with Britain since feminist theory has developed in rather different directions. Indeed it can be argued that the much more extensive involvement of feminists in the arenas of the state in Australia compared to Britain has made possible recent feminist work on the state which engages with feminisms of difference and poststructuralist debates.

The state has been theorized in countless different ways by liberals, Maxists and feminists with shifting concerns, disagreements and common ground. However, building on recent experiences of feminist intervention in the state bureaucracy as well as on the poststructuralist framework of Foucault, Australian feminists have begun to reconceptualize 'the state' in feminist theory. The tendency in much previous writing was to pose the state as a unitary, monolithic and intentional actor, which acts according to a fixed set of interests. Instead Rosemary Pringle and I (1990) have argued that it is more useful to conceptualize the state, not as an institution but as a set of arenas and a collection of practices which are historically produced and not structurally 'given'. This is not to say that there is no intentionality or purpose, but what intentionality there is comes from the success with which various groupings are able to impose themselves and is always likely to be partial and temporary. Whereas previous feminist writings on the state tended to posit a view of coherent interests which exist outside the state and which can either influence the state or are represented by or embodied in it, we suggest that group interests do not pre-exist, fully formed, to be simply 'represented' in the state, but have to be actively forged and, arguably, it is in the domain of the state that they are formally constituted. In a more recent work (Pringle and Watson, 1992), the emphasis is on the lack of coherence of the arenas which constitute the state and the discourses which construct it. Our analysis concurs with Anna Yeatman's (1990) view of the state not as an actor or object but as a 'plurality of discursive forms'. Franzway, Court and Connell's (1989) book on feminism, bureaucracy and the state similarly emphasizes the practices that construct the state rather than taking its structures as given.

This recent feminist work on the state meshes with Foucault's 'bottom-up' analysis of power. The general drift of discourse analysis is away from 'grand theories' of power, particularly 'top-down' ones that see power as a unity residing in the state. Instead it stresses the omnipresence of power, as being produced in every social relationship. Foucault (1980) warns that we should not assume that 'the sovereignty of the state, the form of the law or the overall unity of a domination are given at the outset; rather, these are only the terminal forms power takes'. He treats power as exercised rather than possessed by individuals or groups, and as existing in the complex network of relations that permeate every aspect of life. 'The state' is an overall effect of all these relations and cannot be assumed to act coherently as the agent of particular groups. In particular Foucault shifts the emphasis away from the intentionality of the state; so rather than posing questions about how 'it' intervenes in the wider society, he is concerned with its techniques and apparatuses of regulation. Power is diffused throughout society, it operates as a network, not as a collection of isolated points, and each specific and localized struggle potentially has serial effects on the entire network. Power now more typically operates through representations, norms, forms of language, definitions of who we are and in what we should find pleasure.

Such an approach contradicts much Marxist theory of the state which, though recognizing that the state is not a blunt instrument of the ruling class and that the divisions between and within classes are actually inscribed in its structures – with frequent conflict between different state apparatuses as a result – nevertheless posited the state as acting coherently and political power as unified. In stressing that 'the personal is political', feminists emphasized the continuities between men's power in the state and in other domains. However when feminists have focused on the patriarchal nature of state structures, they have tended to see the state as a reflection of what exists elsewhere rather than an important site for the construction of gendered power relations.

If the state is to be perceived as an object of feminist theory and strategy, it requires an analysis which avoids the different functionalisms of the past. This will be one which examines the ebb and flow of power, its twists and turns, nodes and concentrations. It will not place the state at centre stage but will situate it amongst the variety of strategies employed by men in constructing their interests and, indeed, amongst the various strategies and counter strategies deployed by women who, as we shall see, in the case of the Australian state, have constituted their interests at the level of the state arenas.

Feminism and the state in Britain

In Britain the early feminist texts sought to marry feminist with Marxist paradigms, reflecting the dominance of Marxist theory within British academe at the time, particularly within sociology, where many of the feminist writers were located. It also reflected the dominance of class divisions economically and culturally within British society and the tendency of radicals to construct inequality and oppression in terms of class. Perhaps inevitably therefore, gender has been treated as subordinate to what is constituted as the 'real' struggle – that between the classes. Within this paradigm a feminist analysis of social reproduction, the family and gender was grafted on to an analysis of the capitalist state which was seen as acting primarily in the interests of preserving the dominant class relations and assisting the accumulation of capital. The family was theorized as the necessary site of reproduction of labour power and as maintaining existing social relations.

Gender domination, in this account, is assumed to be functional to capitalism. Thus in 1978 Mary McIntosh writes:

> Capitalist society is one in which men as men dominate women; yet it is not this, but class domination that is fundamental to the society. It is a society in which the dominant class is composed mainly of men; yet it is not as men but as capitalists that they are dominant . . . the state must be seen as a capitalist one. (McIntosh 1978, p. 259)

McIntosh reflects what was a dominant view amongst activists and feminists engaged in the various areas of the welfare state during the 1970s. The influential text 'In and Against the State' written by activists and state workers in 1979 characterizes the state as a form of social relations which acts in the interests of capital, which defines and delimits our needs and lives, and which obscures class divisions. Although there is discussion of working within the institutions, we are exhorted to build a culture of opposition. Attempts to work within the state arenas were viewed with suspicion and likely to be regarded as co-option. The liberalism that characterized feminism in other parts of the world was never more than marginal to British feminism. This standpoint was dominant during the 1970s in Britain, with lasting implications for feminists and activists. As a result, less energy was put into trying to enter the bastions of power, in particular the Civil Service or the trades unions.

What might have been achieved in these arenas is impossible to assess. There certainly was an absence of a party in government that was committed to progressive reform. It is also the case that, until recently, influential policy positions in the British Civil Service have been gained by rising up through the fast track system and there has never been a moment at which feminists have been brought in to develop women's policy issues as has been the case in Australia. A recent study (Watson, 1992) found that, despite the adoption of comprehensive equal opportunity policies, the fast track system remains a potent force in bringing a certain kind of 'sensible chap' to the top. The point is that during the 1970s a strategy of working within institutions was not employed and the structural marginality of feminists and activists was assumed. Little attempt was made to challenge this discursively or in action.

After the election of the Thatcher government in 1979 there were important shifts in feminist involvement within the bureaucratic and political institutions of the state although these took place at the metropolitan and local rather than central level. Thatcherism provoked innovative as well as defensive responses, with many local authorities expanding their traditional role as providers of urban, education, and social services to include economic development, race relations and women's issues. The largest and most publicized radical Labour council was Greater London Council. This was the first Council to set up a Women's Committee in 1981 and it provided a model that was adopted by a number of authorities in the following years (eight by 1984). The committees varied in form and status but all were characterized by a commitment to alternative modes of operation, consultation and accountability (Button, 1984:5). Drawing on feminist ideals of democracy and equal participation, there was an attempt to set up structures which were non-hierarchical and which encouraged women from outside of the bureaucracies to be involved. In the GLC, for example, open meetings were held and working parties were set up on employment, lesbian women, women with disabilities, ethnic and black women, childcare etc. A budget of £500,000 was allocated to the committee to set up a women's unit and to fund voluntary organizations in the community (Goss, 1984: 112). Particular efforts were made to secure the representation of black, disabled, older and lesbian women, thus challenging the notion of homogeneous women's interests. Inevitably the small amounts of money given to groups establishing innovative projects for women in London quickly became exaggerated in the press, with evening paper headlines like 'GLC gives thousands to lesbians for gym mats' and other such 'scandals'.

By 1982 the influences of feminism were beginning to be felt within the Labour Party. A specific commitment to women in the Labour Party's programme emerged. The borough elections in May 1982 gave rise to several new Labour administrations who were committed to equal opportunities and women's rights. Women's Committees were set up, without the usual departmental structure beneath them, with the broad terms of reference to achieve 'fair and equal treatment for women'. The idea was that they should act as municipal watchdogs examining policy and practice in a wide range of areas to protect women's interests as consumers and workers (Button, p. 6). The women's units were also set up outside of the traditional departmental structures sometimes attached to the Chief Executive's Office. On the one hand this gave them the autonomy to consider inter-departmental matters, and on the other the non-hierarchical and non-traditional structures reinforced their marginality and ineffectiveness.

Reflected in these attempts to apply feminist methods of organizing and feminist ideals of participation and democracy to local government is the earlier notion that the 'state' has the capacity to taint our ideals and that compromises should be avoided. There was thus a strong desire to adhere to feminist principles and less of the pragmatism that characterized Australian feminist interventions. The workers in the units thus tended to have equal access to decision making, equal pay and were responsible for their own administration, although one woman appointed was usually appointed as the head. Problems inevitably arose since this form of organizing proved to be incompatible with the existing bureaucracy. The feminist ideals of anti-élitism, self-realization, sisterhood and authority of personal experience clashed with a bureaucracy characterized by a system of rules, impersonality, a career-based employment structure and a hierarchy of authority (Button:42).

Feminist interventions into the arenas of local government in Britain have been conceptualized in a number of ways. There has been some degree of mistrust and suspicion between the women's movement and local government workers and concerns about the issue of accountability. Roleoffs (1983), while welcoming the open nature of the GLC women's committee, argued that little account was taken of the views of open meetings on crucial occasions and that the elaborate democratic structures obscured the ultimate power of the labour councillors. On the other hand the open or co-ordinating meetings were susceptible to domination by well organized groups like Wages for Housework. Goss (1984:127) suggests that the groups were inevitably self selected, attracting women who were more articulate, could travel around London and had no childcare responsibilities.

What is raised here is the question of interests. Those women co-opted on to committees as lesbian or black women and those who went to the open meetings found themselves having to represent the interests of women from their respective constituency or local area. Membership of a particular group thus allowed a speaking position as say, lesbian, which had a direct impact on the way certain policies were formulated. In some instances this meant that one woman could define the issues for the group in question with little or no accountability to her own constituency. When demands were seen to be unreasonable the politicians tended to dismiss them by drawing distinctions between the feminists and the 'ordinary women' (Goss, 1984:127). The definition of interests of a particular group was thus constructed out of a shifting set of alliances, individuals, political expediencies, temporary connections and so on.

The experience of feminist interventions at the level of the local state in the British context throws up a number of questions which need further research and analysis. When does participation mean consultation and when does it mean power? Elaborate democratic structures can hide the lack of effective power. Can feminist structures ever be incorporated into bureaucracies in their current form? In Britain there seems to have been some confusion between the local authorities and the wider women's movement.

The more effective role for the women's units appears to have been in terms of funding women's activities outside rather than trying to shift the focus of employment policies inside, and to alter the framework of service provision. In the long run new forms of local authority organization are needed to deal with women's issues rather than adding on committees and units that have little power. Goss (1984: 129) argues that it is essential for the Women's Committees to have more political power and more support from the local government administration as a whole. Otherwise there is a danger of ghettoization and marginal access to power.

Overall the continuing framework for understanding these interventions tends to characterize the state from a Marxist- (or quasi-Marxist) feminist analysis. There is, however, increasing interest in social democratic type reform through the Labour Party which reflects a more liberal feminist analysis, similar to the analysis which was prevalent in Australia during an earlier period.

Femocracy: feminism and the Australian State

Australia offers a stark discursive and political contrast to Britain. Here, feminist philosophers and political theorists have tended to have a greater impact on feminist thought than have sociologists, and the Marxist tradition has held less sway. The specifically gendered, as well as capitalist, nature of the state has been widely discussed and debated. As in Canada (Weir, 1987) extensive engagement within state arenas has inevitably contributed to the debates and provided the groundwork for evaluating what these interventions have meant. Practice has informed theory which, in turn, has informed practice. Unlike Britain there has been a long tradition of expecting the state to be concerned with the welfare of its. citizens and to act as arbitrator in conflict. The state has been perceived as more open and less under the control of the establishment.

Australian feminists have drawn creatively on French, British and American writing to generate their own analyses. The lack of dominance of Marxist-feminist perspectives in Australia and a more diverse academic feminism combined with the political culture to create a space where feminist interventions were possible and not immediately subject to widespread criticism. Instead, over the twenty years of considerable feminist engagement with the state, there has been constructive debate between feminists working as bureaucrats within the state arenas (known as the femocrats), feminist academics and activists, a debate that has enabled both sophisticated theoretical work and innovative policy to be developed simultaneously. The relationship between feminism and the femocracy, between co-option and issues like dressing for success were addressed at an early stage (Lynch, 1984).

Australian feminist interventions into the political and bureaucratic arenas date from the early 1970s. Of importance was the development of a form of feminism which fell within a tradition of liberal democratic and political reform. In 1972 the Women's Electoral Lobby (WEL) emerged as an organization of women who were dedicated to entering and changing the mainstream political arenas. The strategy was to put the six demands of the Women's Liberation Movement onto the political agenda. By the end of the campaign WEL had established important contacts with the major political parties and dramatically changed the nature of public debate by and about women. When the Whitlam government was elected in 1972, committed to a platform of progressive reform, WEL was well placed to lobby for the appointment of a woman's adviser, anti-discrimination legislation, equal opportunity programmes, an integrated childcare policy, supporting mother's benefit, abortion legislation and so on.

The strength of WEL in this early period is key to understanding the form of Australian state feminism and the construction of feminist interests. Many of the personal links made in the 1970s have been maintained and developed. The channels of intervention reflect the players and their connections. Which interests are represented and what policies are initiated as a consequence can often be traced to the political concerns of the femocrat involved, her own work, political history and feminist constituency. This is not to deny the equal importance of feminist pressure groups and networks outside. The specific interests that have been taken up within the political sphere have been those where the lobby outside is particularly strong and organized, either through the trade unions, campaigning groups, or associations of state workers or voluntary sector workers at local or state level.

The form of the Australian state is also crucial. The Whitlam government was committed to opening up the public service and creating bureaucratic structures which reflected changing community needs. New commissions and committees of enquiry were established, policy advisers with appropriate skills and sympathetic to the government were brought in. A number of feminists were appointed to the staff of several ministers and in 1973 a political adviser in women's affairs to the Prime Minister was appointed, signifying a commitment to introduce feminist ideas into government decision-making processes and to begin planning for more permanent feminist representation in the bureaucracy (Ryan 1989). In contrast to Britain, the bureaucracy in Australia was less entrenched in tradition and exclusionary practices.

By the time Whitlam's government fell in 1975, a Women's Affairs Section had been established in the Welfare Division of the Department of Prime Minister and Cabinet, a considerable budget had been set aside for pre-school and childcare services ($75 million), and major political and financial support had been committed to the International Women's Year, which spawned a plethora of feminist cultural, political, activist and community projects around the country. The adviser on women's affairs and the head of the Women's Affairs Section, were concerned to place feminist policy making in the main stream of the bureaucracy and the sphere of the Prime Minister rather than marginalized in a separate women's affairs department. Their aim, reflecting the influence of WEL thinking, was to raise the consciousness of other government departments to women's issues. This early focus had important legislative and practical effects in the ensuing years. In 1975 an Equal Employment Opportunity section was established in the Public Service Board, the policy maker and implementer of employment practice for the Commonwealth Public Service; and a recommendation was made to establish women's units in key government departments. The latter was implemented by the Fraser Liberal government in 1976 (Ryan 1989).

Since the Whitlam government was dismissed in late 1975, the political complexions of the federal government have changed twice. In the same period the states have undergone similar political shifts with inevitable consequences for the strength of women's units in different departments, the possibilities of legislative reform, policies for women, women's services, funding, and local feminisms. Because of its federal structure Australia is typically governed by a mixture of political parties at any one time. Any generalization is thus problematic. Feminist aspirations can be tenuously linked with the fortunes of political leaders or parties, alliances are fragile, and the identities of the players in the game can have significant effects. Nevertheless, despite the presence of a conservative federal government in power for eight years during this period, several hundred feminists entered a range of bureaucratic structures at Commonwealth and State level, equal opportunity programmes were initiated and women's programmes gained funding.

The election of the Hawke Labor government in 1983 marked the beginning of another distinctive period in the history of feminist interventions. This was a Labor government committed not so much to the radical reform which characterized the Whitlam era but to change through the mechanisms of tripartitism and consensus. One of the main mechanisms was the Accord, a prices and incomes policy struck between the government and the trade union movement, which included some social wage provisions and which sparked considerable debate in the feminist movement. The relatively high rates of unionization of women in Australia and the increasingly active participation of women within the Australian Council of Trade Unions during the early 1980s meant that trade union women have played an important role in developing women's policies. Those in broad sympathy with the Accord argued that the social wage area had significant redistributive effects which benefited women, that female full time employment had increased and that female adult unemployment had dropped during the first years of the Accord, which should therefore be supported. Feminists who were critical argued that the Accord was negotiated primarily by men, or that it didn't deal specifically with women's issues, and that the centralized wage fixing system maintained existing relativities between particular industries and occupations (Booth and Rubenstein, 1989). The fanfare of the Accord was accompanied, in the early years at least, by a commitment to developing policies for women, building up the rather dwindling women's policy areas in the federal bureaucracy, and introducing Sex Discrimination and Affirmative Action legislation. The women's areas in government were strengthened. In 1984 the Public Sector Reform Act was passed, making discrimination unlawful on a range of grounds including sexual preference, and establishing Equal Opportunity programs. By 1986 women constituted approximately six per cent of the senior executive level of the federal public service – not a huge proportion but a notable increase from the 1.3 per cent in 1979. Considerably more women were appointed to positions of influence at slightly lower rungs in the hierarchy. Similarly, feminists were taken on as consultants to draw up new legislation and advise ministers on policy in both mainstream and women's areas. The same pattern held for many of the states, particularly where there was a labour government in power.

The impact of femocratic feminisms over more than a decade is apparent in policy reforms, changes within the bureaucracy, legislative changes, and in the growth of women's services in the non-government sector. Policy reforms include the development of housing programmes for women (Watson, 1988), changes in the training of nurses, labour market policies directed at single parent families, the increased provision of childcare and the introduction of Equal Employment Opportunity Legislation. Like the Australian working class, feminists have placed great emphasis on the need to establish women in a secure and well-paid work force as a prerequisite to autonomy and independence. This is particularly the case in the current period. Women have fought to gain citizenship as workers rather than as welfare recipients. This shift in the construction of women's interests makes sense in the context of Accord type politics. Important here have been key feminists in positions of influence within the bureaucratic and union arenas where alliances have been made. Frequently it is the feminist bureaucrats who have argued for, and formulated, a policy which they have persuaded their minister to accept rather than vice versa.

Even though femocrats have experienced greater power in Australia than many other countries this is still limited. The relative exclusion of women continues due to such factors as masculine control in the selection of candidates, the routines of party life, and the skills and the forms of behaviour valued in public officials. Certainly in Canberra, the women at the top levels of the political and bureaucratic arenas tend to be without dependents and rarely in conventional marital relationships. Drinking after work and working at weekends is an unspoken prerequisite for high-level positions. Forms of masculine dominance and behaviours are the ascribed norm referred to by Canberra feminists in the bureaucracy as 'playing the boys' games'.

Workers in the institutions of the state inevitably have to negotiate a path of contradictions, conflicts and dilemmas, particularly if they see themselves as feminists (Franzway, 1985). There is no one pattern of how feminists have negotiated their positions of political and bureaucratic power. Neither is there a distinctive category of 'femocrat'. Women working in the 'femocrat' areas – in the women's policy units in the prime minister's office and in other government departments – face different problems and contradictions from the women working in the mainstream areas of departments. Femocrats can find themselves marginalized in women's policy areas with little impact on economic and social policy formulated elsewhere, but at the same time deriving their strength and coherence from this separate relation. Feminists working in mainstream areas, who are less likely to be referred to as femocrats, can find themselves formulating policies which may have a negative impact on some groups of women. Policy-making may involve responding to conflicting demands, from politicians, other bureaucrats, and a whole range of diverse feminist interests outside the bureaucracy and facing the constraints of government expenditures, directives, legal structures, within a prescribed bureaucratic framework. Feminists are thus likely to adopt different strategies at different times and in different places. Uneasy alliances are made and broken.

Bureaucracies operate on closed systems of favours, shared perspectives and values, deals, hierarchies of knowledge, and mystification. Loyalties to ministers or departments frequently conflict with policies formulated elsewhere in the women's units. Bureaucratic languages and abbreviations are quickly learned and spoken, to the fury of feminists 'outside' who feel mystified and excluded. The path followed has been reliant on an alliance with the Labour party, which has required of necessity a willingness (at least publicly) to accept the constraints of what is politically expedient.

Feminist interventions into the state arenas in Australia have received mixed reactions and inspired a range of theoretical analyses. Grass-roots feminisms have met the femocracy on both lively and destructive terrains. The inevitable characterization of one side as the true revolutionaries and the other as corrupted by power and prestige has occurred, but the divisions are by no means stark. Whatever the debates and conflicts, the femocrats played an important part in securing funding for a range of women's services. Even if this has often involved tensions for the feminist groups involved, who try to maintain feminist principles while being accountable to the funding authority, the mutual engagement has tended to be constructive. Not least, femocrats have been continually reminded of the constituency from which many of them came and of the women to whom their policies are directed. Notions of the 'real women' out there, whose needs must be met are invoked and contested.

Taking stock of 'femocracy'

There is no single discourse or account of feminist interventions. In Australia theory has evolved over the last two decades from more traditional Marxist or liberal feminist perspectives to theory which engages with feminisms of difference on the one hand and poststructuralist thought on the other. It is suggested that these more recent developments in part were possible precisely because feminists had much more involvement in the arenas of the state than feminists in Britain.

Lesley Lynch (1984) has considered whether femocracy constituted a strategic transference of the struggle to a key arena of influence or an undermining of the women's movement. Although not explicit in its theoretical underpinnings, some of the more 'purist' tendencies of British feminist theory of the late 1970s are reflected in Lynch's analysis. Using the metaphor of 'bossism and beige suits' she identifies the femocrat phenomenon with an increasing dominance of careerism and conservatism. Three issues are discussed. One is the notion that femocrats have been co-opted or sold out, which derives in part from their resistance to discussing their work, their claims to be unable to tell the real story, their high salaries and the pressures on feminist bureaucrats which undermine their capacity to function as feminists. The second issue is that of conformism. The difficulties of maintaining a high profile as a radical activist, the inability to publicize work issues and the pressure to 'dress for success' all generate pressure to conform. Femocrats' conformity in fashion is linked with effectiveness at the job, rather than as ambiguous and contradictory. The third issue is that of rejection, the sense that femocrats have of being maligned or misunderstood on the one hand, and arrogant or critical of the women's movement's naivety and unwillingness to compromise on the other.

Feminists operating with a liberal feminist view of the state have offered a more optimistic assessment of the femocrat phenomenon than Lynch. Liberal feminist ideas have been important in feminist writing in Australia since at least the mid 1970s. This approach sees the state as something like the neutral arbiter or at least potentially principled agency of pluralist liberal theory that could be called upon to improve women's position. Within this framework, equal rights for women are both possible and desirable. The aim is to win reforms to improve women's position and in particular to give them equal standing to men in the public sphere. Liberal feminism tends to play down sexual difference and deny the lived experience of biology. The body appears as of little relevance.

This more 'positive' liberal feminist view of the state has been particularly significant amongst feminists involved in the political and bureaucratic spheres particularly those associated with affirmative action, equal employment opportunity and anti-discrimination. Although such engagement has often been branded by Marxists and radical feminists in Australia as leading to reformism or co-option, feminists working within the state arenas have suggested that the state can be made 'to work for women'. Thus, Hester Eisenstein in 1985 wrote:

> I think it is inaccurate to say that 'the state is male' but it is accurate to say that up to now the state has been male if by that we mean that until recently public power has been wielded largely by men and in the interest of men . . . The possibility of altering that fact may now lie within our grasp.

Other feminist writers in Australia have developed feminist assessments of femocracy which cannot neatly be inserted into a liberal or Marxist or radical (in the British sense of the word) feminist framework. More recently in Australia feminisms of difference and critiques of degendering have been applied not only in the cultural sphere but also to assess equal opportunity policies and other policies to improve women's position. This has resulted in a focus on the gendered nature of the public sphere and a critique of universal categories such as the individual. It has been argued (cf Patemen and Grosz, eds, 1987) that individuality is not a unitary abstraction but that individuals are both feminine and masculine, and that it is necessary to reconceptualize the distinctions between the social and the political and the private and the public. The two spheres only gain their meaning in relation to the other.

These issues assume particular relevance in an assessment of practically based policies of Affirmative Action, equal employment opportunities and sex discrimination since arguments for sex equality underpinning these rely on a degendered notion of equality – an assumption of similar natures which if treated equally will result in equal performance (Thornton 1987). However, if the possibility of distinct natures for the sexes is considered, we then substitute an argument that men and women should be equally enabled to develop their *different* capacities and that their different performance will be both complementary and of comparable value. Barbara Sullivan (1989) demonstrates that sex discrimination legislation tends to impose a norm of male life experiences on all participants in the public sphere so that women have to deny the lived experience of a female body in their public lives. The implications of these feminisms of difference for an assessment of equal opportunity policy are that equality and an end to discrimination is not enough, and that a recognition of gender differences (social or biological) implies the need for new solutions which will enhance women's potentialities, and create the preconditions for full liberation.

A dominant theme in these assessments of equal opportunity policies is that the universal standing in society for which we have been fighting is illusory and misguided because 'apparently universal categories, such as the individual, the worker, the social or the political, are sexually particular, constructed on the basis of male attributes, capacities and modes of activity' (Pateman, 1986). The issue of sexual difference within feminist struggles, especially those taking place in the state arenas, tends to be either denied or have attempts to lessen its impact minimized. Since so much of women's exclusion from the public and political spheres has been premised on our physical difference, then arguments for sexual equality which seek to minimize difference can seem to sit uncomfortably with arguments for women's liberation which has 'sought to envalue and develop what have been perceived as women's gender-specific potentials and capacities' (Thornton, 1986). The questions posed by the difference versus equality debate are beginning to be discussed amongst the women who work in the bureaucracy on women's policy areas in Australia. The implications of this discussion for pragmatic feminisms which seek to develop policies for women within the political and bureaucratic arenas is of serious concern, since the appeal to women's gender-specific potentials and capacities still underlies most opposition even to formal equality.

Finally, a feminist post-structuralist approach to understanding femocracy raises different questions. In posing the state as a set of complex and erratic arenas and collection of practices, or as a 'plurality of discursive forms', and in posing interests as constituted in the domain of these arenas, the notion of evaluating the success of femocracy is challenged. Rather than trying to evaluate the femocrat phenomenon in terms of what femocrats have done to improve the position of women, new questions are raised. Instead of seeing the entry of women into the bureaucracy as necessarily supporting and furthering a linear progress towards sex equality and the improvement of women's position, the femocrat phenomenon is analysed in terms of the strategies, tactics and resistances deployed by the players in the political and bureaucratic arenas. Such an approach allows questions to be raised as to how men perceive femocracy and build feminist policy goals into their concerns, and as to what are the multiple strategies and games that bureaucrats and politicians play and so on.

If we take this approach we do not have to worry about why the state acts contradictorily or assume in advance that it will act uniformly to protect certain interests. The outcomes of particular policies will depend not purely on the limits placed by 'structures' but in the range of discursive struggles which define and constitute the state, and specific interest groups from one moment to the next. Thus Hester Eisenstein's (1989) evaluation of equal employment opportunity legislation becomes interesting as a story about how the heads of departments in the bureaucracy started to compete with each other in relation to their equal employment opportunity plans to advance their own standing. To analyse these events solely in terms of how the plans advanced the cause of women would be to miss the complexities.

Similarly, Rosemary Pringle and I (1990) have shown how in Australia in the late 1980s, the shifting of women from supporting parents benefits to unemployment benefit once their youngest child was sixteen, illustrated the conflicts and compromises between different players in state arenas, including the femocrats. The policy was represented as a gain for feminism, since social security provisions were seen as reinforcing women's dependence and militating against women's entry into the labour market. The policy was formulated and femocrats were left defending a package which left single parents the hardest hit in the budget package. It is impossible to know if the presence of the femocrats had in part legitimized the changes or if in their absence, the policies would have been worse. In a sense, what happened was that the feminist arguments and discourses were incorporated and thrown back in a distorted or qualified form.

In examining the strategies deployed, the discourses used and the operations of power, a new light is shed on old debates. Thus in her analysis of the affirmative action programme in Australia Marsha Rosengarten (1992) looks at how evaluations of these programmes contribute to and affirm what she calls the deployment of the construct 'the employable productive woman'. She argues that the discourses intersecting to produce this construct presume and deploy a notion of power as repressive and negative. The evaluations are operating within a set of normative assumptions and power/knowledge relations where the success of the programme is seen in terms of creating women as economically productive. She suggests that it is more fruitful to focus on how those positioned as 'in need of employment', or 'needy' have come to be so by the effects of forces embodied in this construct. She suggests that it would be more useful to look at the different arenas of policy making, programme delivery and parliamentary politics concerned with Affirmative Action to see how they incorporated and struggled with different sets of interests. Again the shift is away from evaluating the direct success or failure of a particular policy.

In conclusion I have attempted to explore the significant differences between British and Australian feminisms and their relation to the arenas that constitute the state. What is clear is that feminist interventions in these two countries have differed at the level of both practice and theory. It is suggested that feminist theory and discourse has both influenced and derived from these interventions, so that theory has defined practice which has in turn defined theory. Of particular interest are the recent applications of feminisms of difference and poststructuralist debates to questions of feminism and the state. The former approach throws into question the very equality that women have been striving for, while the latter approach asks questions which shed new light on the phenomenon of femocracy and on how we might evaluate its success. I have argued that such a focus is useful since it reveals and allows for the complexity of practices, strategies, tactics and discourses that construct and are constituted in the arenas of the state. It also acknowledges the omnipresence of power in every social, bureaucratic and political relationship. Such an approach frees us from trying to evaluate the success or failures of feminist policies and allows us to see the multiplicity of outcomes and effects which will certainly be complex and which may or may not be beneficial to women.

References

Allen, J., (1989), 'Does Feminism need a Theory of the "State"?' in Watson, (ed.).

Booth, A. and Rubenstein, L., (1989), 'Women in Trade Unions in Australia', in Watson (ed.) 1989.

Button, S., (1985), 'Women's Committees – A Study of gender and local government policy formation'. School for Advanced Urban Studies. Working Paper 45.

Eisenstein, H., (1985), 'The Gender of Bureaucracy' in Goodnow, J. and Pateman, C. *Women, Social Science and Public Policy* Sydney: Allen and Unwin.

Eisenstein, H., (1989), 'Femocrats, Official Feminism and the Uses of Power' in Watson (ed.).

Foucault, M., (1980), *History of Sexuality*, Harmondsworth: Penguin.

Franzway, S., (1985), 'With Problems of their own: Femocrats and the Welfare State'. Australian Feminist Studies No. 3.

Franzway, S., Court, D. and Connell, R., (1989), *Staking a Claim*, Oxford: Polity.

Goss, S., (1984) 'Women's Initiatives in Local Government' in Boddy, M. and Fudge, C. (eds) *Local Socialism*, Basingstoke: Macmillan.

Laclau, E. and Mouffe, C., (1985), *Hegemony and Socialist Strategy*, London: Verso.

London Edinburgh Weekend Return Group, (1979), *In and Against the State*, London: Pluto Press.

Lynch, L., (1984), 'Bureaucratic Feminisms: Bosses in Beige Suits' Refractory Girl May.

MacKinnon, C., (1982), 'Feminism, Marxism, Method and the State: An Agenda for Theory' Signs 7, 3. pp. 515–44, 1982.

McIntosh, M., (1978), 'The State and the Oppression of Women' in Kuhn, A. and Wolpe, A.M. (eds) *Feminism and Materialism: Women and Modes of Production*, London: Routledge and Kegan Paul.

Pateman, C. and Grosz, E., (eds) (1986), *Feminist Challenges*, London: Allen & Unwin.

Pateman, C., (1988), *The Sexual Contract*, Oxford: Polity.

Pringle, R. and Watson, S., (1989), 'Fathers, Brothers, Mates: The Fraternal State in Australia' in Watson (ed.) 1989.

Pringle, R. and Watson, S. (1992), 'Constructing Women's Interests', in Barrett, M. and Phillips, A., *Contemporary Feminist Debates*, Oxford: Polity.

Roleoffs, S., (1983), 'GLC Women's Committee – Democracy of Feminism' Labour London Briefing, April.

Rosengarten, M., (1992), 'Double Trouble in "the Employable Productive Woman"', Masters thesis, University of Technology, Sydney.

Ryan, L., (1989), 'Feminism and the Federal Bureaucracy 1972–1983' in Watson (ed.).

Sullivan, B., (1989), 'Sex Equality and the Australian Body Politic' in Watson (ed.).

Thornton, M. (1986), 'Sex Equality is not enough for Feminism', in Pateman and Grosz.

Watson, S., (1988), 'Accommodating Inequality: Gender and Housing', Sydney: Allen & Unwin.

Watson, S., (ed.) (1989), *Playing the State: Australian Feminist Interventions*, London: Verso.

Watson, S., (1992), 'Is Sir Humphrey Dead?' The Changing Culture of the Civil Service', Bristol: School of Advanced Urban Studies Working Paper 103.

Weir, L., (1987), 'Women and the State: A Conference for Feminist Activists' Feminist Review 26.

Yeatman, A., (1990), *Femocrats, Bureaucrats, Technocrats*, Sydney: Allen and Unwin.

Theories

Sexual work and the employment of women in the service industries

Lisa Adkins

This chapter will consider factors which structure sexual relations between men and women in the labour market. It will show that gendered employment relations contribute to the production of compulsory heterosexuality for women because, in order to have access to employment (to be employees), women must participate in male-initiated and male-dominated heterosexual interactions. They must provide various kinds of sexual servicing[1] for men, both as customers and as co-workers. This will be shown using material drawn from a study of two British tourist operations, which included detailed and in-depth exploration and observation of work relations between men and women in various employment situations[2].

When this research was begun in 1987, the question of the importance of sexual relations for the gender dynamics of employment had received scant attention. Most if not all labour market theory, including that produced by feminists, had either completely ignored sexuality or considered it thoroughly unimportant for the gendered operations of the labour market – and indeed for the construction of gender *per se* (see for example Hartmann, 1979; Walby, 1986). Some of this theory seemed in fact to deny that sexual relations actually operated in the labour market – despite work by radical feminists on the sexual harassment of women in employment which clearly questioned this assumption (see for example MacKinnon, 1976; Stanko, 1985, 1988); and despite a great deal of feminist research which showed just how important sexual relations are for controlling and shaping all aspects of social reality for women – for creating gender inequalities generally. In all such radical feminist research, the extent to which sexuality is male controlled and defined was made clear (see eg Russell, 1984; Hanmer and Maynard, 1987; Kelly, 1987).

Some five years later, however, there seems to be a gradual realization that 'sexuality' can no longer be left off the agenda when it comes to thinking about the gendered dynamics of employment. There are now a few studies which are either completely (Hearn and Parkin, 1987; Pringle, 1988) or partially (Cockburn,1991) dedicated to exploring the relationship between sexuality and employment. They all, correctly, point to the manner in which sexuality has previously been ignored in labour market theory. However, they themselves still do not address some fundamental questions about sexuality and the relationship of sexual relations to the labour market. Although they claim to have engaged with the significance of sexuality in terms of gender relations, they actually continue to miss the substantive point about the relationship between sexuality and gender. They do not see that sexuality is a *structuring process of gender*.

That is to say, even though the authors of these new studies *claim* that they *do* understand the relationship between sexuality and gender, when we look closely at the forms of sexual relations their studies consider, and examine the ways in which they understand these relations to be constituted, it is evident they do not understand sexuality and gender as fully socially constructed phenomena. In particular, we can see that their view of the construction of sexual relations in employment is taken for granted and/or short-sighted. They treat heterosexuality as a social phenomenon only when it involves direct coercion.

Taking sexuality seriously?

The most straightforward example of a recent study of sexuality and employment which actually does not problematize sexuality but rather treats it in a taken-for-granted manner can be found in Hearn and Parkin's (1987) study of sexuality in organizations: *'Sex' at 'Work'*. They argue that 'organizational sexuality' can be understood as a by-product of what they define as capitalist labour market processes. But, in arguing this, they simply take male-dominated heterosexual relations for granted. They argue, for instance, that the sexual harassment of women by men in employment can be understood as a product of alienating work conditions. These conditions incite men to harass. They base this claim on an assertion that sexual harassment is particularly endemic in industries characterized by alienating work conditions, where men lack control over the product and the act of production.

This argument is highly dubious. It assumes either that it is only men who experience alienation from their work, or that it is only men who can react to such conditions. Ethnographic studies of women's experiences of the labour market, which have revealed the various strategies women develop in response to alienating work conditions, clearly problematize both these assumptions (see for example Pollert, 1981, Westwood, 1984). Women in fact both experience and 'react' to alienation in the labour market, which clearly undermines the argument that the sexual harassment of women by men within the workplace can be understood in terms of alienation. If both men and women experience alienation, then why should this lead men to harass women? The argument does not address the gender specificity of harassment (that it is men who harass women).

As well as attempting to explain sexual harassment by alienation, Hearn and Parkin also reduce other 'instances' of sexuality in organizations to what they see as capitalist labour market processes. For instance, they see displays of pornography in the workplace by men as also deriving from men's boredom with their work. Pornography is a way to escape boredom (Hearn and Parkin, 1987:85). Alternatively they suggest the labour process can alienate men from their sexuality – men who work night shifts may have a disrupted sexual life outside of the workplace (Hearn and Parkin, 1987:89) – and this constitutes an alienation which may lead men to refuse to work such shifts. Or again, the gender division of labour within organizations (which itself is posited to be an outcome of capitalist processes, since Hearn and Parkin[3] believe women form a functional reserve army of labour for capital) is also seen to produce 'organization sexuality'. They argue that gender divisions of labour are reinforced by gender divisions of authority and power; both authority and power are expressed through organization hierarchies; and hierarchical organizational structures in turn construct hierarchical inter-personal relations between people – including sexual relations. Hearn and Parkin thus suggest, for example, that the higher valuing of men than women in organizations parallels the tendency to value men's sexuality more highly than women's (Hearn and Parkin 1987:92). In this rather tortuous argument, men's sexuality is associated with the properties of more highly valued labour and higher positions in the hierarchy – with, for instance, control, activity, physical power and emotional distance.

What I see as particularly problematic about Hearn and Parkin's argument is that in reducing sexuality to a by-product of capitalist processes, they simultaneously naturalize and essentialize hetero-sexual relations. For instance, when they assume that the sexual harassment of women by men is produced by alienation, or that men's sexuality is valued more highly than women's in organiza-tions because women constitute a reserve army of labour for capital, they assume male dominated heterosexuality. The same applies to all their other instances of 'organization sexuality'. As a consequence of their reducing, eg, sexual harassment to alienation in this way, they completely obscure the ways in which, through sexual harassment, men control women; and moreover, they take men's ability, power, and desire to sexually harass women to be simply a (natural, essential) characteristic of male sexuality.

But why should capitalist hierarchies call into being a sexuality in which women are sexually exploited by men? To assume this ignores both the ways in which men (rather than capital) currently benefit from heterosexuality, and also the ways in which patriarchal agents actively produce and maintain gender divisions within organizations and within sexuality (see for example Hartmann, 1979; Cockburn, 1983 and 1985; Summerfield, 1984; Walby, 1986; Rich, 1983; MacKinnon, 1987 and 1989). Reducing sexuality to the dynamics of capital thus completely ignores the gendered power relations of sexuality. More specifically, it pushes male-dominated heterosexuality (and indeed the whole of gender) into the realm of the extra-social.

But although Hearn and Parkin's approach to sexuality is the most obviously problematic among recent publications, some of the other new studies are equally, if less self-evidently, worrying. These assume that heterosexuality only contributes to the pro-duction of gender, *and* is only structured by gender inequality, when explicit male coercion is evident, notably in the case of sexual harassment. Outside of coercive practices, heterosexuality is treated as a spontaneous and mutually satisfying relation between two naturally given groups, men and women. Hetero-sexuality is thus only treated as a *social* phenomenon when it is 'forced'.

Both Pringle (1989) and Cockburn (1991) share this misunder-standing of heterosexuality in their analyses of the relationship between sexuality and employment. At first sight this may not be apparent, for both agree that 'men control women not only through rape or through forcing them to do what they want [them] to do, but through definitions of pleasure and selfhood' (Pringle, 1987:165 cited in Cockburn, 1991:158). But in the analysis of her material on secretaries, Pringle assumes that heterosexuality is only male *dominated* and *unequal* when men impose sexual attention on women by force. Outside of this, she views heterosexuality as being largely voluntaristic, negotiable and flexible for women. In fact, outside of coercive sexual relations, she sees heterosexuality as a source of pleasure and power for women. This is evident in her thesis that feminists' focus on the coercive elements of sexuality in relation to the workplace has been detrimental to a consideration of the positive elements of sexuality for women. Thus she argues:

> Rather than assuming . . . that secretaries are always the
> pathetic victims of sexual harassment, it might be possible to
> consider the power and pleasure they currently get out of their
> interactions with people [sic] and how they get what they want
> on their own terms (Pringle, 1987:101–2).

What is important here is that Pringle is not simply making a distinction between different kinds of heterosexual interactions (ie coercive and non-coercive). She is also assuming that these are constituted differently; that they are fundamentally different sorts of heterosexuality. Coercive interactions make women powerless victims, while non-coercive heterosexuality may afford women power and excitement. Put simply, it is only forced heterosexuality which is a bad thing for women, and Pringle sees only this sort of heterosexuality as a problem.

Cockburn also makes the same distinction between different sorts of heterosexual practice. She locates the sexual harassment of women by men in employment as 'a male intervention for the assertion of power' (Cockburn, 1991:142), and she shows, for instance, how male sexual banter and sexual innuendo act as a means of control of women. But she then goes on to say that 'sexual harassment shows only the negative side of organization sexuality' (Cockburn, 1991:152). On the 'positive' side, for instance, she points to the opportunities that employment affords both women and men for sociability, since 'work can be a path to pleasure too' (p. 151). Hence, she says, 'women as well as men have a stake in the degree of openness and sociability in the organization' (Cockburn, 1991:152). The fact that a large proportion of marriages 'are made at work' provides part of Cockburn's evidence for such a claim. But since when did feminists see getting married as unambiguously advantageous for women? Isn't the family one of the key institutions of patriarchy (eg Freidan, 1965; Barrett and McIntosh, 1982; Delphy, 1986)? Isn't it the place where a variety of unpaid labour is extorted from wives (Delphy and Leonard, 1992)?

Although Cockburn is at pains to point out that sexual pleasure, sociability, and openness are all risky for women, compared to men, because of the power relations of heterosexuality, she nonetheless still sees these power relations as being substantially negotiable and flexible for women, and certainly so compared to directly coercive sexual relations with men. This is evident in her concluding comments on sexuality and employment, where she agrees with Pringle that strategies for change involve:

> being bold in knowing and asserting our likes as well as our dislikes. Opposition to sexual harassment is only one component of a sexual politics in the workplace. It needs to be supplemented with analyses of the ways in which sexual pleasure might be used to disrupt male rationality and to empower women (Cockburn, 1991:159).

Here Cockburn, along with Pringle, clearly sees heterosexual relations which are not 'harassment' as chosen ('liked') and as even potentially a threat to men's power. Sexual harassment requires direct opposition, but definitions of sexual pleasure are so fluid that their meaning can be subverted by women to such an extent that they can empower them in the workplace. For both Cockburn and Pringle, then, coercive sexuality is male dominated; but non-coercive heterosexuality, understood in terms of desires, whilst it may be subject to the power relations of gender, is *not necessarily* constituted by or through male power. Women can have a lot of 'say' in heterosexual relationships. They may even 'determine' them. Non-coercive heterosexuality in the sphere of employment is thus negotiable. It is a site where women can assert choice and control, in ways which are impossible in coercive situations.

But both Pringle and Cockburn neglect to consider the ways in which heterosexuality is (made) compulsory for women; and hence they neglect the ways in which this compulsion lies behind both explicitly coercive *and* non-coercive ('chosen') sexual practices. They ignore the ways in which *both* of these are structured by male dominance.

In the following section I shall look at cases of gendered work relations and the construction of sexual relations in tourist operations, and show how Cockburn and Pringle's understanding of sexuality in employment has a limited view of how heterosexuality is made compulsory for women. In particular I shall show how male dominance and inequality structures both coercive *and* 'non-coercive' heterosexual interactions between men and women in employment.

The sexual condition of women's employment

The research upon which this section is based was a study of men and women employed in two tourist operations: a hotel and a leisure park. Both operations shared the same regional location, were of similar size in terms of the number of employees, had a similar ratio of men and women employees (roughly equal), and both had a highly gender segregated occupational structure. But there were some differences between them. In particular the hotel was owned by a multinational leisure and tourism corporation whereas the leisure park was owned by a private local company; and the hotel relied upon the national and international conference/business trade for its custom, while the leisure park relied upon a highly localized market in the form of day-trippers from across the region in which it was located.

As part of the general study of the construction of work relations between men and women, the forms of control to which workers were subject, and the different kinds of work which men and women were engaged were examined in both these operations[4]. The last aspect – the study of the different kinds of work – involved not simply a study of the gender differentiation of jobs or occupations, but rather, a study of the different types of work men and women actually carried out within and across occupations – work which was not necessarily specifically linked to the occupation in which employees were located. In fact, rather than being determined straightforwardly by occupation, the kinds of work carried out by employees at the two workplaces was found to be gender specific. Or more precisely, the kinds of work men did was occupationally specific, whereas *part* of the work women did was not, *for women employees had as a condition of their employment the requirement to provide sexual services for male customers and male employees.*

The actual kinds of 'sexual work'[5] women carried out within the workplaces will be discussed later in this chapter. First, the issue of how the obligation to provide sexual services formed a condition of women's employment needs to be addressed. This was unravelled primarily through studying recruitment and the forms of control exercised in relation to employees. This revealed that, for women to have access to employment and to remain in it, they must fulfil the condition of being sexualized actors. In other words, there were requirements operating in relation to women's employment which served to commodify them sexually and to reduce systematically their employment status in relation to that of men.

At both workplaces, in order to be recruited as employees, regardless of the jobs they applied for, women had to fulfill criteria of visual attractiveness. At the hotel, being attractive was a requirement for all the occupations in which women were clustered (for example waitresses, housekeepers and chamber-maids). It did not, however, operate in relation to *any* of the occupations in which men were clustered (for example, barmen, kitchen hands, porters, and chefs/cooks). In fact there were *no* parallel requirements which operated in relation to men as a group in the way attractiveness operated for women. (All employees had to be well groomed, see on, but women *also* had to look good.) Requirements for men operated only at the level of specific occupations. Being attractive was, then a requirement *specific to women as a group* at the hotel, regardless of the occupation.

This becomes clear if the task content, the requirements and the gender constitution of two comparable occupations at the hotel – bar staff and waiting staff – are considered. Both occupations were highly gender segregated, with men constituting by far the majority of bar staff and women the majority of waiting staff. The task content was very similar: both were high customer contact jobs, involving taking orders from customers and serving them with drinks and/or food. Given these similarities, it would seem likely that the personnel specifications for the occupations would require similar worker qualities. In certain respects this was the case. In both occupations workers were required to be helpful and enthusiastic; but bar staff, unlike waiting staff, were required to be 'strong', 'smart' and to have 'good communication skills', and these were requirements which were specifically for this occupation. Waiting staff, on the other hand, were required to be 'attractive' and 'caring', and these were requirements common to all occupations in which women were clustered.

These differences in occupational specifications cannot be adequately explained by the differences in the requirements or needs of the occupations themselves. Why, for example, was 'strength' a requirement for bar staff and not for waiting staff, when delivering food to tables all day required just as much physical stamina/strength and was just as physically demanding and exhausting as lifting crates and changing barrels in bar work? Why were waiting staff required to have a 'caring' attitude (towards customers), when bar staff needed to be 'good communicators' (with customers)? Why were bar staff required to be (only) 'smart' when waiting staff were required to have a visually attractive appearance, given that workers in both these occupations (and in fact in all the hotels' occupations) were required to wear clean, pressed smart uniforms, and polished shoes? Everyone had to be 'smart' so the requirement to be attractive was an *additional* specification. The occupations were so similar that these differences in personnel specifications made little sense in terms of the occupations themselves.

But these specifications were in fact related not to occupational requirements, but to the gender of the occupants. Specifically, what was at issue in the differences in requirements was the way in which, to have access to employment, women had to fulfil specific criteria relating to their looks which men did not.

A similar scenario was also found at the leisure park. Here, too, in order to be employed, women had to look attractive. They were recruited, across occupations, not simply on the basis of the particular skills or resources needed for particular jobs (that is, on occupational requirements, eg knowing how to pull a pint or add up a bill or make sandwiches), but rather on what they as women needed if they were to be given a job at all. They had to look 'right'. In the words of one manager, women had to be 'attractive and fresh' to be employed. Recruitment to the various occupations in which women were clustered at the leisure park was *primarily* based on this and a number of women were *not* offered employment there because their appearance was not up to standard. Examples of this included a woman who was not recruited because she looked 'weird' (she wore a scarf tied around her head), and a number of women who were not offered jobs because they were 'too ugly' and/or 'too manly'.

For men at the leisure park, as at the hotel, recruitment was based solely on specific occupational requirements. There were no additional criteria they needed to fulfil as a group of workers to be employees. That is, recruitment for men was based exclusively on (constructions of) what was needed for the occupations in which they were clustered. Eg, recruitment to the occupation of park ride operator was on the basis of what kinds of skills/qualities were thought to be required to operate the rides.

In addition, women not only had to fulfill criteria related to appearance to *enter* into the two workplaces, they had also to *maintain* this 'correct', 'attractive' appearance as a condition of remaining in employment. At the leisure park, a strict regulative regime was in operation through which such appearance main-tenance was turned into a condition of employment. Women employees were instantly warned if their appearance deviated from the prescribed standard and, if they failed to correct such appearance problem(s), they were dismissed. Examples of such forms of control included warnings about looking tired, having chipped nail varnish, wearing 'weird' make up, and looking 'sloppy'. In all these cases management reported they had 'no option' but to intervene to attempt to get the women to correct their appearance problems, and if, as was the case for some of the women, they did not respond to the warnings, the managers had 'no choice' but to dismiss them.

For men at the leisure park, no such controls over their appearance operated. Both men and women had to wear clean uniforms, but this was *all* the men had to do. Their *personal* appearance was never once the subject of intervention. Men could look tired, sloppy, or weird without their employment position being under threat. They simply had to wear their uniforms.

Since women not only had to look good to be employed in the leisure park in the first place, but also had to stay looking good as a condition of remaining there, and since, across occupations, women had no choice but to adhere to certain standards of appearance, it could be said that *part of the job* for women, consisted in looking good.

This was also the case at the hotel. Once employed, women in all occupations were obliged to conform to a plethora of standards relating to their personal appearance in ways which men were not. Women employees were given strict guidelines on the way they should look, including how they should wear their hair (to ensure facial display), how to wear make-up, and in what manner to wear their uniforms (which included sheer stockings and shoes with heels). Failure to adhere to these standards again led to forms of management intervention, including warnings and the possibility of dismissal.

Men at the hotel, however, were subject to no such appearance standards. Again, the most they had to do to conform was to wear a uniform. Thus, men's looks were not the subject of attention at either workplace, and being attractive was neither their entry qualification nor a condition of their continued employment. Men could thus be said to have been systematically exempt from such conditions.

Sexualizing uniforms

One particular aspect of the controls on women's appearance at both the hotel and the leisure park was the *way* the women were required to wear their uniforms. In both cases the uniforms were gender differentiated, but women and only women had to wear theirs in certain specified ways. The women at the hotel had to wear skirts and wear them at a particular length, and they had to wear sheer stockings and not only polished shoes but high-heeled shoes; while the women who worked in the bar at the leisure park were required to wear full skirted gingham dresses and these had to be pulled down over their shoulders: 'off the shoulder'.

These controls on what women should wear and how, together with all the other conditions relating to women's appearance, acted as processes through which women were sexualized – that is to say, they served to turn women into sexualized actors, or rather into sexual 'objects' for men's use. It was a condition of employment for women who worked in the bar that they wear their uniform 'off the shoulder'. They ran the risk of dismissal if they refused, even though they (and everyone else) knew this requirement sexually degraded them. The women concerned specifically said that this uniform worn in this way was a means whereby the manager 'tried to try and turn us into sex toys or something'. These uniform requirements meant the women were often subject to sexual attention from men, whether customers, co-workers or management. Indeed the women were often subject to this kind of attention from the bar manager himself. It was he who had decided that wearing the dresses off the shoulder was the correct way to wear the uniform, and he aggressively enforced the requirement, often pulling the women's dresses down into the 'correct' position, 'legitimately' paying the women sexual attention (touching their clothing and their bare shoulders), and simultaneously degrading them.

This connection between uniform requirements and the sexualization/degradation of women workers is also evident in other examples of situations which women at the workplaces had to deal with routinely. Male customers, for instance, constantly made sexual innuendoes, and/or degrading comments about how the women looked in their uniforms. In the words of one woman employee, male customers were 'always eyeing us up . . . [commenting on] the way we looked, on how they liked us in our uniforms.' Here again, the form of the uniforms – which the women had no choice but to wear – acted to turn them into the objects of sexual attraction and subordinates for men.

Other requirements relating to women's appearance – that they should be attractive – also operated in the same manner. Women were routinely sexualized by men in relation to their *personal appearance*. Male customers and co-workers at the leisure park, for instance, constantly commented on the appearance of women workers in sexual ways. They would 'judge', for instance, whether or not women would be good in bed on the basis of what they looked like and they constantly 'eyed up' women or sexually objectified them by leering. Indeed the degree of sexual attention paid to the women's appearance at the leisure park by 'fellow' employees was so marked and so routine that one woman employee compared working there to 'being in a tits and bums show'. While another said of the customers 'they seem to think we are on display for them'.

Given women needed the 'right' appearance to have access to and to stay in employment, and given this attractive appearance and the required uniforms meant they were subject to constant sexual attention from men, both customers and workers, it must be concluded that the conditions and controls operating in relation to women worker's appearance and dress acted together to *produce a sexually commodified female workforce*. This process of commodification at both workplaces occurred through attractiveness being systematically prioritized above all other requirements for women employees, and then enhanced by uniform requirements. Sexual looks were thus part of what was 'sold' by women to employers in 'exchange' for employment at both the leisure park and the hotel – and part of what employers sold to customers.

Male customers and sexual work

The fact that being sexually attractive (a sexually defined being for use in male initiated sexual transactions) was a condition of work for women was clearly revealed in the ways in which women *had* to develop strategies to cope with various forms of sexual attention from men on a routine basis. Some of the main ways in which women dealt with situations where they were sexualized by male customers included 'laughing it off' and 'playing along with it'. The women said the worst thing they could do if a man made comments to them or touched them was to get annoyed, look angry, or not respond. This would mean the men were more likely to carry on bothering them, often more intensely. Such compulsory inter-actions – such participation in male initiated sexualized interactions and the development of strategies to work situations through – was indeed so routine for the women that they regarded it as a regular part of their work.

Here it is clear that because being sexually attractive formed a condition of employment, the actual *work* the women were hired to do was, in part, the work of being, and behaving as, a sexualized actor. Women had routinely to recognize and deal with men's desire to chat them up. By having to engage in sexual interactions with male customers and having to give men (to an extent) what they wanted, women were thus routinely engaging in forms of sexualized work. When male customers chose to pay women staff sexual attention, women had to respond. They laughed/looked flattered/smiled and 'entered into it'. They therefore sexually serviced the men, and men appropriated this work. Men used and enjoyed these sexual services, and they were able to do so because of the conditions operating in relation to women's employment. It was the men customers who initiated and defined the nature of these interactions, and who were made to feel good about themselves. It was they (not the women) who got their egos boosted and their sexual thrills. The sexual commodification of women workers therefore produced a sexual power relationship (as well as the more usually recognized customer-service relation-ship) between men customers and the women workers.

The fact that women *had* to engage in/respond to sexual

interactions initiated by male customers was a condition of their work. This was made absolutely clear by a member of management at the leisure park. He said quite simply that if a woman could not cope with the men, then she was not up to working there. Knowing how to deal with men was 'part of the job'.

Thus the women at the two workplaces were not simply 'economically productive' workers for the owners and managers. They did not only stack the shelves, serve food and drinks, clear the tables, and carry out all manner of other tasks necessary for the production of goods and services for the hotel and the leisure park. They also, in addition, provided sexual services – amusement, titillation, gratification – for men customers. Moreover, they had to perform this work whenever it was required. It was compulsory if they were to have access to, and retain a job.

Male co-workers and sexual work

The sexual power relationship between men and women produced through the conditions operating in relation to women's employment was not, however, limited simply to that between women workers and male customers. It also operated between women workers and their male co-workers. Because women's employment status was defined primarily through their location as sexual workers, women were no better placed to resist sexualization from male workers than they were from male customers. There was nothing the women could do except cope with the behaviour of the male employees too. One woman manager, for instance, was dismayed that she could not prevent male employees sexualizing and harassing the women who worked in her department, not least because she lacked the power to prevent them behaving in this way towards herself.

Thus male workers, like male customers, directly appropriated forms of sexual work from women. But the sexual power relationship that existed between men and women workers also had other implications. Most importantly, it systematically undermined the status, the overall structural position, of women workers vis-à-vis male workers in the workplaces. It was part of the process of production of the structurally more powerful position occupied by male workers at the two workplaces.

Male workers occupied this more powerful position because

men and women were different *kinds* of workers in both workplaces. Men did not have to carry out sexual work in the way that women did, and their work was not exploited in the same way as that of the women. Put simply, men did not have their status as workers undermined by their status as sexual subordinates. Women did.

The fact that men and women were different kinds of workers also explains why the recruitment requirements for the occupations in which the men were clustered were variable and concerned with *specific* occupational requirements. Unlike women, men did not need something extra to be employees. Unlike women, mens' location as workers was not predetermined. Women had *always* to be sexualized actors, for this was their main employment qualification in all the jobs they occupied. The systematic prioritization of this requirement for women meant that, if they were not attractive, it did not matter whether or not they could claim to possess any other labour market resources (any occupationally specific skills) because they simply would not be employed[6].

Men, in contrast, because their employment position was not subject to any similar, or parallel, set of processes through which they were located and defined as a group of workers, were able to claim (and be seen to) possess various labour market resources, such as strength or specific occupational 'skills'. Occupations could be defined as the preserve of men by linking the occupations to specific skills and capacities, which, in the given circumstances, only men could claim to possess. For example, the highly paid work of operating the rides at the leisure park was argued to need muscular strength, although in fact it only involved pushing buttons. Moreover, because they were sexualized, women workers could never challenge this situation. Women as women were not able to possess particular occupational skills because the primary labour market resource women were recognized to possess was that of their value as sexual servicers.

The conditions and controls operating in relation to women's employment meant, therefore, that not only were male employees able to have access to sexual servicing from women employees, but the conditions and controls also created a power relation between men and women in terms of their relationship to employment/the workplace. Men were a structurally more powerful group of workers than women in both workplaces. They could claim to possess labour market resources which women could not, and they therefore dominated and participated in the creation of the

221

workplace hierarchies and gendered occupational structures in a way women could not counter.

Men as workers, men as customers, and the hotel and leisure park as employers all therefore derived considerable benefits from the construction of women as sexually differentiated and subordinate. For male workers it meant they always occupied a more powerful position than women and were able to exploit the position of women within their workplace. For the employers it meant the women served (in fact worked) as sexual attractions, satisfying male customers. And for both male workers and male customers it meant they had access to, and could appropriate sexual servicing from women workers.

The benefits that male employees got from women occupying the position of sexual workers were not, however, simply derived from the ways in which the hotel and the leisure park as capitalist enterprises sought to locate women in this position. They were also an outcome of the ways in which men themselves actively constructed women as sexualized workers. Male employees were key agents in this process. Men managers participated in the creation of the regulations on appearance which reduced women's status, and men (across occupations and all the way down the occupational hierarchy) colluded in producing the conditions in which women could be and were routinely sexualized.

In sum, the conditions and control which operated in relation to women's employment at the two workplaces – having and maintaining an attractive appearance – formed part of the process through which women workers were sexualized, and hence downgraded/degraded. Through these controls and regulations, women's status in the two workplaces was created as that of sexualized *and* subordinate actors. Women could do little to resist this process as it precisely defined and shaped their position in the workplaces. They could only be employees *if* they were sexual subordinates, and *if* they carried out sexual work. The routine sexual exploitation of women by men at the workplaces was therefore the result of *work relations which operated only for women*. Women could only be workers (they could only 'exchange' their labour) if they fulfilled the conditions of being a sexualized worker.

Heterosexuality and employment: when compulsion does not equal coercion

As has been shown, at both the hotel and leisure park, to have access to employment, women had to do sexual as well as other types of work. The fact that work or labour for women can be sexual in the context of employment requires a rethinking of the intersection of sexuality and the labour market. Sexuality has been shown to enter into and organize production. This problematizes the way in which sexual relations and the labour market have consistently been separated out in feminist labour market theory. The labour market has characteristically been defined as an economic, and sexuality as a non-economic, entity (outside of prostitution). As a result, sexuality and the labour market have become irreconcilably differentiated[7]. But far from being separate or differentiated from economic relations, sexuality, as this chapter has shown, constitutes part of (gendered) economic relations. In both the workplaces studied, sexual relations actually structured both production and the gendered organization of work. Sexual relations existed as an economic relation between men and women, and produced gender divisions. In both cases, work itself was sexual for women. Indeed, coping with sexualization from male customers and male co-workers on a day-to-day basis, as part of the job, was an outcome of the manner in which sexuality structured production.

The gendering of production in this way also *created* sexual relationships/sexuality at the two workplaces. Being a sexual worker (for example, always having to be sexually attractive) placed women in a position where they were consistently sexually objectified and used by men. The relations of production thus produced (or rather contributed to the production of) a form of sexuality which was structured in terms of male dominance.

That the sexuality produced through the sexual commodification of women workers was one structured in terms of male dominance, shows that these work relations meant women had no choice but to be 'heterosexualized' (Wittig, 1982, 1989). At both workplaces, to be employed, women had to participate in sexual interactions with men in which they were located as objects for male use. Thus, the conditions surrounding women's access to employment at the two workplaces can be seen to be part of the process through which heterosexuality is made compulsory for women (Rich, 1983). This situation, where being heterosexually available both constitutes a condition of work for women and determines the kinds of work they carry out – women have literally to work heterosexually – clearly raises important questions about the way in which sexuality in employment is viewed in the studies which were discussed at the start.

As was shown earlier, in these new studies, male-dominated heterosexuality in the context of employment is either simply assumed or else heterosexual relations are seen as male dominated, unequal and exploitative for women only when direct coercion by men is evident. When explicit coercion is not evident, heterosexual relations are treated as completely different: as if they are structured neither by male domination nor by compulsion, as if they can be equal and liberating. Non-coercive heterosexuality is thus treated voluntaristically: as something over which women have a lot of, or almost complete individual choice and control. Coercive and non-coercive heterosexual practices are, in other words, presented as if they are unconnected to each other, as if they are constituted differently.

However both these new approaches to understanding sexuality in employment are problematized by the material presented in this chapter. Hearn and Parkin's analysis is put in question because the data shows male-dominated heterosexual relations to be not simply 'a fact' about sexuality which gets acted out under capitalist work relations, but rather, socially produced relations which are maintained within, by and through (gendered) wage labour relations. Cockburn and Pringle's analysis of sexuality in employment is also questioned because both coercive and non-coercive heterosexual interactions can be seen to be structured by male power and dominance, and both are clearly exploitative for women.

At the hotel and the leisure park women interviewed *enjoyed some* of their sexualized interactions with men and found most of the rest annoying rather than threatening, in the sense that they were not explicitly coercive. In addition, in by far the majority of cases women were not literally forced to conform to the conditions attached to their employment. But all of this is not to say that engaging in heterosexual interactions with men was not compulsory, nor that these interactions were not structured by male power. The conditions attached to women's employment meant both that heterosexuality *was* compulsory for women, and that men had *power* within such heterosexual interactions. Resistance to this situation by women – eg by refusing to 'exchange' sexual labour, or their refusing to be sexually attractive – led to dismissal. Resistance was thus possible, but it carried a high social cost – indeed such a high cost that very few instances were observed during the fieldwork. Conformity was apparently achieved easily. Certainly the great majority of the women fulfilled the conditions attached to their employment.

In most sexualized interactions with men, women therefore gave the men 'what they wanted'. But this was *not* because they welcomed the men's attentions or felt that men deserved flattery! This compulsion to provide men with sexual services did, however, mean the women did not need to be directly coerced. Circumstances gave men constant sexual access to the women, and ensured that, no matter what the form of the interaction, male-female relations were always constructed by a power relation. It was always men who had the power to initiate and determine the form of the interaction, and women who had to respond.

Thus both directly coercive and non-coercive – and even pleasurable – sexual interactions between men and women were structured by the same power relations. The sexualized interactions between men and women did not fall into different categories or types – they were not separate or distinct forms of heterosexuality. They were the same basic social relations, played with variations. Heterosexuality is a socially constructed institution, and even when no direct coercion is evident in individual heterosexual interactions, this does not mean (as Cockburn and Pringle imply) that it is not social, nor that it is not male dominated, nor that it is not exploitative for women.

Work relations at the hotel and the leisure park (as probably in the bulk of women's service work – both paid and unpaid[8]) demonstrate clearly that male dominated heterosexual relations are socially produced, and that they are maintained through (*inter alia*) the way sexual exploitation of women by men is structured *at the point of production*. They also show that the exploitation of women within heterosexual relations is not simply associated with particular forms of heterosexual practice, still less is it associated with particular sorts of men. Rather work relations are one of the elements constituting heterosexual relations.

All this is not to say that women never get anything back from compelled sexual interactions with men (for example women may indeed manipulate such relations and get some enjoyment, and/or some material gain from them – sometimes considerable enjoyment and material gain). But these kinds of returns need to be firmly located and interpreted in terms of the general structuring of heterosexuality. They are not discrete phenomena existing outside of it. Nor are they voluntary for women, nor do women have overall control over them. Until this is recognized we shall remain stuck within an essentialist account of heterosexuality.

This understanding of the way in which men and women's relationship to employment at the hotel and the leisure park was formed has important implications for analyses of the labour market. One of the most significant of these is that my research shows how *production* in the labour market may itself be gendered. Men and women can be constituted as different kinds of workers because to be employees in these workplaces women had to be sexualized subordinates and carry out forms of sexual work, while men did not. In other words, men and women participated in the two workplaces in different relations of production. They were all waged labourers, but they carried out different sorts of work – women did sexual work and men did not – and one set of workers was subordinate to the other. Men occupied a structurally more powerful position in capitalist employment than women and did no sexual work.

Seeing and recognizing labour market production as gendered in this way raises some really fundamental questions for existing labour market theory. In particular it questions the previous emphasis on occupational segregation as the *key* mechanism for understanding/explaining the gendering of the labour market.[9]

Notes

1 There is often a resistance to seeing 'lighthearted' interchanges between men and women as sexual or as servicing. However, feminists have repeatedly pointed to the differences in men's and women's experiences, the power dimension involved and the no-win situation women find themselves in when men choose to involve them in a sexualized discourse (see eg Walkerdine, 1981; Mahony 1985).

2 For full details of the study see Adkins (1992).

3 Following Beechey (1978, 1982) and Bruegel (1982).

4 A variety of qualitative research techniques were used in these studies. These included the extensive use of in-depth interviews (with men and women throughout the occupational hierarchies), the use of documentary sources (eg 'in house' publications and employee records) and non-participant observation (eg of everyday working practices and staff training sessions).

5 Whilst the use of the concept 'sexual work' is fairly unusual, it is the only one

226

which adequately represents the work situation of the women in the workplaces studied – ie where to have access to employment, women had to exchange sexual labour, where they had to provide various forms of sexual servicing for men as a condition of their employment. Whilst I am not aware of the use of the concept in relation to employment, similar concepts have been used in other analyses. Delphy and Leonard (1992), for example use the concept of sexual work to refer to part of the unpaid work that wives do in marriage, and Tabet (1987) uses the notion of 'sexual economic exchange' to understand various forms of quasi-prostitution (ie, 'sex exchanged for something other than sex') relations cross-culturally.

6 This prior condition for women's employment is, of course, an element so far missing from feminist debates around the social construction of workplace politics and 'skills'.

7 See Adkins (1992), chapters 2 and 4, for a full account of this differentiation.

8 The ideological separation of sexuality and work has meant there has been minimal research on the significance of sexual relations for the gendering of work. The overlap between 'women's work' and service work, however, suggests that far from being untypical, it may be the norm for sexual relations to operate in women's work.

9 cf Hartmann (1979) and Walby (1986, 1988). See Adkins (1992) for the ways in which recognizing production as gendered problematizes this view.

References

Adkins, L., (1992), *Sexual Work and Family Production: A Study of the Gender Division of Labour in the Contemporary British Tourist Industry*, University of Lancaster, unpublished PhD thesis.

Barrett, M. and McIntosh, M., (1982), *The Anti-Social Family*, London: Verso.

Beechey, V., (1978), 'Women and Production: A Critical Analysis of Some Sociological Theories of Women's Work', in Kuhn, A. and Wolpe, A-M. (eds), *Feminism and Materialism: Women and Modes of Production*, London: Routledge and Kegan Paul.

Beechey, V., (1982), 'Some Notes on Female Wage Labour in Capitalist Production', in Evans, M. (ed.), (1982), *The Woman Question: Readings on the Subordination of Women*, Oxford: Oxford University Press.

Breugel, I., (1982), 'Women as a Reserve Army of Labour: A Note on the Recent British Experience', in Whitelegg, E. (ed.), *The Changing Experience of Women*, Oxford: Martin Robertson.

Cockburn, C., (1983), *Brothers: Male Dominance and Technological Change*, London: Pluto.

Cockburn, C., (1985), *Machinery of Dominance: Women, Men and Technical Know-How*, London: Pluto.

Cockburn, C., (1991), *In the Way of Women: Men's Resistance to Sex Equality in Organizations*, London: Macmillan.

Delphy, C., (1984), *Close to Home: A Materialist Analysis of Women's Oppression*, London: Hutchinson.

Delphy, C. and Leonard, D. (1992), *Familiar Exploitation: A New Analysis of Marriage in Contemporary Western Society*, Oxford: Polity.

Freidan, B. (1965), *The Feminine Mystique*, Harmondsworth: Penguin.

Hanmer, J. and Maynard, M. (eds), (1987), *Women, Violence and Social Control*, London: Macmillan.

Hartmann, H., (1979), 'Capitalism, Patriarchy and Job Segregation by Sex', in Eisenstein, Z.R. (ed.), (1979), *Capitalist Patriarchy and the Case for Socialist Feminism*, New York: Monthly Review Press.

Hearn, J. and Parkin, W., (1987), *'Sex' at 'Work': The Power and Paradox of Organisation Sexuality*, Brighton: Wheatsheaf.

Kelly, L., (1988), *Surviving Sexual Violence*, Oxford: Polity.

MacKinnon, C., (1979), *Sexual Harassment of Working Women*, New Haven: Yale.

MacKinnon, C., (1987), *Feminism Unmodified: Discourses on Life and Law*, Cambridge: Harvard.

MacKinnon, C., (1989), *Towards a Feminist Theory of the State*, Cambridge: Harvard.

Mahony, P., (1985), *Schools for the Boys? Co-Education Reassessed*, London: Hutchinson.

Pollert, A., (1981), *Girls, Wives, Factory Lives*, London: Macmillan.

Pringle, R., (1988), *Secretaries Talk: Sexuality, Power and Work*, London: Verso.

Rich, A., (1983), *Compulsory Heterosexuality and Lesbian Existence*, London: Onlywomen Press.

Russell, D., (1984), *Sexual Exploitation: Rape, Child Sexual Abuse and Workplace Harassment*, London: Sage.

Stanko, E., (1985), *Intimate Intrusions: Women's Experience of Male Violence*, London: Routledge and Kegan Paul.

Stanko, E., (1988), 'Keeping Women In and Out of Line: Sexual Harassment and Occupational Segregation', in Walby, S. (ed.), (1988), *Gender Segregation at Work*, Milton Keynes: Open University Press.

Summerfield, P., (1984), *Women Workers in the Second World War*, London: Croom Helm.

Tabet, P., (1987), Du don au tarif: les relations sexuelles impliquant une compensation' in *Les Temps Modernes*, No. 490, May.

Walby, S., (1986), *Patriarchy at Work*, London: Polity.

Walby, S., (ed.) (1988), *Gender Segregation at Work*, Milton Keynes: Open University Press.

Walkerdine, V., (1981), 'Sex, Power and Pedagogy', in *Screen Education*, 38, 1981.

Westwood, S., (1984), *All Day, Every Day: Factory and Family in the Making of Women's Lives*, London: Pluto.

Wittig, M., (1982), 'The Category of Sex', in *Feminist Issues*, 2:2, pp. 63–68.

Wittig, M., (1989), 'On the Social Contract', in van Kooten Niekerk, A. and van der Meer, T. (eds), (1989), *Homosexuality Which Homosexuality?: Essays from the International Scientific Conference on Lesbian and Gay Studies*, London: GMP.

Gender, history and management style in nursing: towards a theoretical synthesis

Celia Davies

A great deal of 'gender talk' occurs in and around contemporary nursing. There is the suggestion that nurses, because they are women, are highly committed to the activity of direct care and indeed that it is their 'womanly' commitment as much as their technical skill that is needed in the NHS. There is the further suggestion, in practice often linked with this, that nurses are not educated enough, or skilled enough to do managerial work properly and yet are too defensive to give it to others. There are claims (and here some anger comes in) that the men – approximately 10 per cent of the profession but 30 per cent and more of the senior grades – have never been really interested in nursing as such and are concerned only to gain the status and rewards that a managerial hierarchy can offer. There are suggestions (calling forth another kind of anger) that the senior women who are single resent their married staff and do not organize the work in a sympathetic way; there are claims too that nurses as women are hierarchical, passive, isolationist, and even 'bitchy' in their behaviour in relation to their colleagues. Gender talk such as this would be good grounds alone for sociological enquiry, but the fact that some of this gender talk is emerging in academic work, and the fact too that it so clearly devalues women, is, as the following section will show, an important impetus for this chapter.

A further starting point stems from personal experience of the contradictions of applying equal opportunities thinking to nursing. Whereas it can be a clearly illuminating exercise to study the administrative and clerical hierarchy in the NHS for the structural and attitudinal barriers that it presents for women's advancement, the same approach presents severe problems when applied to an occupation such as nursing (Davies and Rosser, 1986a, 1986b, 1987; Rosser and Davies, 1987). If women are in an overwhelming numerical majority, can one talk of their opportunities as unequal? If women want to do bedside care and chose to do it, is there really a hierarchy? If men, as one is often told, have to go for promotion because they are breadwinners, is there any more to say? In retrospect, it seems that much equal opportunities work that has been carried out in large, bureaucratized employment settings, particularly work of the applied, action research variety, has been about understanding and combatting gendered processes of exclusion. Yet there are gendered processes of inclusion that need to be tackled as well. The world of paid work, like the world of public participation, is a men's world both in the sense that it has excluded some women and in the sense that it has included others and included them on strictly male terms. As Carole Pateman has observed, if it were just a matter of exclusion it would be easy. What is not so easy, what is indeed deeply contradictory, is to ask for inclusion in a world that is already gendered (Pateman, 1988).

This chapter is based on a belief that we must look again at gender and the organization of paid work and try to build a new theoretical synthesis. Such a synthesis needs to transcend the uneasy 'gender talk' that surrounds nursing and needs to examine gendered processes of inclusion much more directly. My starting points are two-fold. First, I believe that we must start from the premise that social life in all its forms is deeply gendered and that this gendering operates at different levels and in different ways. Much work to date (especially that concerned with practical equal opportunity initiatives), rests on a quite different assumption, namely that gendered attitudes and gendered behaviour are a form of 'unwanted import', essentially foreign to and in contrast to the formal and rational world of objectively defined rules, roles and responsibilities. I am convinced that we must stop regarding gender in this way as something that the 'equal opportunities police' will eradicate and instead both acknowledge that it is built in to the very design and functioning of organizations, and demonstrate in concrete terms what this actually means. Secondly, we must abandon the concept of gender attributes (which fits with the gender-as-import model), and talk instead about gender relations, as enacted through daily organizational practice and as about power. Again the need is for specific demonstrations of what a gender relations approach entails. Acker (1989) has argued that the project of 'making gender visible' and uncovering the multiple and contradictory forms and levels of gender relations as they take place in organizations is something that has barely begun and more recently has spelled out what some of the levels of analysis might need to be (Acker, 1990; cf Scott, 1986). This paper builds on such work, arguing also that the new gender history, particularly of the health professions, is a key factor in allowing us to render gender visible in a more satisfactory way, and to tease out an approach that relies on (enacted) gender relations, not (imported) gender attributes.[1]

The paper begins with a review of three recent texts which, in different ways, offer insights into the theme of gender in contemporary British nursing. It then seeks to recast these in the light of a more resolute attention to gender as relations. It focuses on the topic of nursing management as a case study of how a rather different analysis could proceed and demonstrates the multiple levels at which gender might enter such an analysis.

Three approaches to the 'gender question' in nursing

Nursing accounts for nearly one quarter of the total expenditure of the NHS and over half of the total labour force. These are the starting points for a review of prospects for nursing in the 1990s (Beardshaw and Robinson, 1990). The authors draw a picture of neglect of nursing within the senior ranks of the NHS and point to an array of management problems that urgently need to be faced. Much of the text is taken up with a review of policy options in the context of demographic changes, of changing patterns of women's employment and of new aspirations within the profession itself. It is seen as important, for example, to create more 'woman-friendly' employment practices for a profession which is 90 per cent female and where one third are working on part-time contracts (cf Waite *et al*, 1989; Davies, 1990). It is seen as important to explore more rigorously the effectiveness of different nursing practices and as a consequence to reassess the traditional skill mix with which nursing care is delivered. It is seen as important also to find new approaches to nursing in the community.

Why is it that issues of such fundamental importance remain to be addressed in nursing? Why is it that the NHS, one of the largest bureaucratic organizations in the world, and one subject to repeated organizational scrutiny in recent years, has apparently ignored issues to do with nursing? The authors do not tackle these questions directly, although they confirm that the NHS has neglected nursing issues and argue that to some extent the Service has shielded health workers of all kinds from scrutiny. They also, however, look to nurses themselves for an explanation, and this is where gender begins to figure.

Beardshaw and Robinson note that nursing displays the classic characteristics of women's work – low pay and inferior terms and conditions. Drawing on the work of Carpenter (1977), they emphasize that it was established within a framework of 19th century ideas about gender which stressed discipline and dedication and portrayed the work as a wide ranging set of tasks set within a hierarchy that replicated the Victorian household – nurse subordinated to doctor as wife to husband, senior nurse controlling junior nurse as mistress to servant (Beardshaw and Robinson, 1990:11). Much of the ensuing routinization of work, and the role of nurse as handmaid to the doctor, they suggest, have simply remained, so that nursing was developed 'in parallel with the partial emancipation of women' (*ibid*:12). These remarks are not elaborated further. There is nothing to suggest what factors might serve to fix such relations, or to transform them. What on the face of it is sympathetic academic gender talk redounds in the end to the discredit of nurses. The implicit message for the reader is that nurses are a group of women who are oldfashioned, rigid in their thinking, hierarchical and ultimately passive in their subordination. Nurses, in a phrase often on the lips of nurses and those who work closely with them, are 'their own worst enemies.'

Strong and Robinson (1990), drawing on the findings of an ethnographic study of recent rounds of reorganization in the NHS, provide a second recent approach to gender issues in the management of nursing work and to handling the negative comments and assessments which surround it. Although the main theme of their study is general management, and their aim to 'capture a culture in the making', they too insist on the neglect of nursing and are particularly emphatic in their wish to remedy this.

Gender provides them with a starting point in explaining the changing social relations of health care delivery. They explain that for its first forty years:

> The NHS was a pyramid. Perched high on its apex stood the
> thirty thousand doctors – consultants a little above the general
> practitioners. Each had to cope with the grave responsibility of
> managing disease but each had also been trained in the best of
> modern scientific medicine. Below them, stretching out in ever

vaster numbers towards the base of the pyramid, came the support staff; those who nurtured, and aided the work of each doctor – around a million in total. On one side, stood the subordinate men: engineers, porters, administrators, ambulancemen, groundsmen, accountants, electricians, psychiatric nurses and scientists without medical degrees. On the other side, were the subordinate women: general nurses, cleaners, clerks, social workers, health visitors, midwives, laboratory technicians, the 'professions allied to medicine'. But although the jobs and genders might differ, they were handmaidens all: serving medicine as medicine, in turn served each patient – or so the old theory went. (Strong and Robinson, pp. 4–5)

Observation and interview data enable them to compare and contrast the styles of behaviour among the powerful men of medicine and the powerless women of nursing. Doctors, they observe, act individually, they bypass hierarchies, they negotiate directly for resources, they show strong group loyalty but refuse directly to speak for or commit colleagues. Nurses, by contrast, work in a quasi-military hierarchy. They are rigid and passive, they are 'defensive, sectarian, isolationist and Luddite'. Very importantly, however, and unlike Beardshaw and Robinson, these authors suggest that the conduct of nursing in this way is not a throwback to the past, but a direct response to powerlessness. The organization of nursing and medicine, they suggest, are intimately linked. The two should not be seen in isolation, rather the one should be seen as the mirror image of the other.

From the point of view of developing a gender relations analysis of nursing, this is more promising. Two difficulties emerge, however. First, although a structure of domination is clearly proposed and gender is clearly implicated, the positioning of gender in these relations of domination remains underdeveloped. Second, the insight about relations of domination is not explored in a sustained way. The idea that there is a structure of domination jostles, especially in the summary sections, with the notion once again that nurses are deficient or culpable in some way – that they lack expertise, that they do not know how to manage, that in a sense it is their own failings that are the source of their discontent. The two occupations of nursing and medicine are repeatedly juxtaposed in ways that invite invidious comparison and call attention to apparent deficiencies of nurses. They are described at one point as in a 'bizarre symmetry'. What has begun as a gender relations analysis begins to fold back into a gender attributes one.

This tension between gender as attributes and gender as relations is much more overt in the third work to be considered here, that of Lesley Mackay (1989). This, unlike the other two which have taken on the topics of nursing and of gender alongside other themes, is a direct study of the nursing profession itself, based on a questionnaire and interview study of more than 700 nurses in one health authority in England in the mid 1980s. Mackay's stated aim was put as much as possible in the words of the nurses themselves. Gender, she acknowledges, was not at the forefront of her own mind at the outset of the study. In coming to write it, however, she described gender as the recurrent theme of the work, something that 'fundamentally affects the way that nurses are seen and see themselves'.

A firm separation is made between the features of nurses themselves, and the features of the system within which they operate. 'The fault, if there is one,' she insists, 'lies with the nurses as much as with the system'. Like Beardshaw and Robinson, she looks back, arguing that nurses 'continue to be dominated by the class and gender antagonisms of a distant age' (Mackay, 1989:3, cf 71). By the end of the book she is more emphatic. Her analysis of gender is still two-fold. Gender is influential from the point of view of the managers who see women as 'somehow only playing, and temporarily, at a job'. Gender is also influential, 'perhaps even more so, in the perspectives of nurses themselves.' She goes on:

> In some respects, nurses are *their own worst enemies*. Many nurses seem to collude in maintaining the traditional subservient attitude towards the medical profession. . .On analysis it emerges that nurses do not appear to sufficiently value the work and the skills of their nursing colleagues. Nurses are unsympathetic to their colleagues. . . (*ibid*:180–1)

Mackay wonders at this point whether doctors' lack of respect for nurses and nurses' own lack of respect for each other can be accounted for by the form of training that nurses undertake. She draws a marked contrast of all this with the positive evaluations patients have of nurses.

Yet it is also very clear at some points in this study that 'the system' has at least as much to do with sustaining if not actually

234

generating these negative evaluations as does some kind of historically unchanging personality structure, reinforced perhaps by training. Two aspects stand out, both closely related and closely related to gender. One is the reliance on student labour to accomplish much of the day-to-day work of nursing and the constant replacement of cohorts of students as the normal way to provide staffing cover. The other is the failure to provide the kind of facilities that would allow women to combine motherhood and care of other dependents with responsible work and clear career possibilities as nurses in the NHS. Both of these, Mackay argues, result in a process whereby both nursing and nurses are trivialized. In a particularly important passage she explains:

> the disposable ethos – use-once-and-throw-away – is demeaning to the women who choose to take up nursing as a career. It also serves to reduce the prestige and status of nurses, nursing and women. Thus nursing can easily be seen as a job at which women are only playing. At the same time, the work of nurses can be trivialized if it can be done by a perpetual stream of young learners. How, then, can nursing be viewed as having a real contribution to make to the improvement of the health of patients? The past ease of replacement has meant that attempts to develop the skills and potential of the workforce are not made. What a waste!

Neither the student labour system, nor the perpetuation of a set of terms and conditions that favour men rather than women are new observations, yet it is new to point to the way in which they make it impossible for nurses, as women, specifically to demonstrate and enhance the value of their work.

Insights such as these, described as part of 'the system' or as part of a perspective on the part of managers that fails to take nurses seriously, are not taken any further. They coexist, as we have already seen, with the demeaning assignment of gender attributes to nurses themselves. A chapter entitled 'Bitchiness' shows the problem particularly acutely. Mackay advances gender as a 'powerful explanatory factor for the criticisms and complaints against each other that interviewees agree is a feature of nursing life', but in practice it is not at all clear what this means. Some quotations suggest that such behaviour comes from constant work overload and stress; others propose that it results from compassion being 'spent' on patients, and others say that 'women are the same everywhere'. Mackay in the end seems to favour lack of management skills and a learned subservience as key factors, though at one point she also advances an argument about the mysogny of doctors and the ensuing lack of self-esteem among nurses and at a final stage alludes to powerlessness of sisters. Either of these last two arguments might have enabled her to challenge the definition of 'bitching' and to place it in a wider set of social relations; nowhere is there a clear link to the structural features denigrating nursing work which she has earlier so cogently outlined. Ultimately the reader is left with the feeling, once again, that a gender analysis means in large measure that the women are themselves to blame. Elements of an analysis that would deal with gendering at the level of the organization do begin to be uncovered in this account, but in the end the interpretation comes rather closer to the reproduction of 'gender talk' rather than to the sociological analysis of it.

The overall picture of contemporary nursing that emerges from these writings and indeed from other sources[2] is both bleak and dismal. Individual nurses are portrayed as possessing many of the classic features that appear in the lists of feminine gender attributes as these have been set out in the research on gender stereotyping. The same mix that appears there, of care, commitment and self-sacrifice on the one hand, and irrationality, indecisiveness and passivity on the other, is apparent.[3] It is often acknowledged that nursing work, because of its parallels with unpaid care of dependents in the family and the community, because of the array of trained and untrained who carry it out, because of its lack of clear boundaries and demarcations, is easily devalued. And yet it is nurses' behaviour, rather than either of these which comes to the forefront of these authors' and lay accounts. Evaluations of nurses' behaviour seem to be resolutely negative. Nurses are said to be bitchy in their dealings with each other; they are assumed to be lacking in the skills to manage, to be defensive, isolationist (and because of this, 'hard to help').

It is worth noting that the collective strategies of nursing as a profession are called into question too. The profession has put a strong emphasis on breaking the link between education and service, on improving the quality of basic education and on developing postbasic educational facilities. With the implementation of Project 2000, it has had some partial success in this. But both outside and inside nursing, there are doubts as to whether this is simply self aggrandisement and a matter of nurses looking with envy to the status of doctors. New-style general management in the NHS is raising further awkward questions. Why is it that we know so little about the apparently high wastage and turnover of nurses? How can it be that there is no clear rationale for the skill mix in delivery of different types of nursing care? Again there is a focus on nurses' own deficiencies, in the shape at present of a call for better leadership which is endorsed both inside and outside the profession.[4] Only in their direct dealings with patients, in their daily delivery of nursing care on a one-to-one basis, are nurses seen in a positive light.

The material reviewed in this section both challenges this kind of thinking and tends to reproduce it. The authors discussed quite correctly point to the importance of bringing gender more directly into the analysis, but they also demonstrate just how difficult it is to do this in a way that does not simply reproduce and confirm negative gender stereotypes about women. In the next section I will draw on the valuable insights that these authors offer to suggest how we might provide a fuller and more satisfactory gender analysis, one which makes gender visible in its ideological aspects, and one which also allows us to begin to approach the partial and covert 'gender talk' which plays a role too in masking the nature of the social relations involved. Work at all these levels is necessary if we are to put in place the 'missing feminist revolution' in sociology (Stacey and Thorne, 1985).

From gender attributes to gender relations – the case of nursing management

The analysis which follows suggests two steps in providing an explanation of the negative evaluation of nursing that has been described. The first step is to provide an account of the style and process of management which is altogether less emotive than those at present on offer. It is not enough, in other words, to respond to the question 'how do nurses manage?' with the answer 'badly'! In what follows, therefore, I will seek to replace some of the more emotive terms with descriptive ones, and in doing so, will also attempt to set nurse management more firmly in the wider structure of which it is part. The second step is to begin to suggest how gender is implicated in the style of management which has been described. The analysis at this second point will suggest that there is at the very least a cultural/historical route and a route through what Acker (1990) would call 'organizational logic' that can be traced. Some of the ways that these might be inter-related are then examined.

Much of what has been described in the earlier part of this chapter can be understood by reference to a style of management of nursing work which might be called 'coping management'. The main focus of coping management is on the immediate work to be done and on the means by which it can be accomplished within existing resources. Coping management is a firefighting approach to management that is accompanied by a strong personal commitment to the task, a weak sense of status and position, and a willingness, sometimes quite literally on the part of the manager, to 'roll up the sleeves' and get on with whatever needs to be done. Coping managers both put a great deal of pressure on themselves, and also put a great deal of pressure on their staff, exhorting them to work harder, run faster, come in early at the start of the shift or to stay late at the end of it. This is because coping management looks inward, to the resources that are available; it means making all kinds of short term compromises to get results within those resources and – unlike Oliver Twist – it never asks for more. There are clear rewards for the manager who adopts the coping management style. These come in the shape of compliments, however, rather than of cash, and they involve praise for the individual rather than extra people to get the work done. But there are other consequences too.

Looking down the hierarchy, coping management is hard on subordinates. It trades on their goodwill and commitment and generates work overload and stress. It can also create a sense of confusion and guilt. The manager cannot easily be blamed, since she is clearly working just as hard as her subordinates. Ultimately there is likely to be low morale, burnout and high turnover. Looking up the hierarchy, issues of resource allocation, of organization and reorganization of work are not being addressed. As long as the coping manager copes, there is no incentive for others to enquire how the coping is achieved. And the coping manager herself, being so busy coping, is likely to resent and brush aside any overtures that may come from her seniors. This kind of dynamic creates a gulf between the coping management team and others, a gulf which can operate either with junior management against senior management within nursing, or between nursing as a whole and other health professions. Either way, the resort to idiosyncratic solutions together with the accusations that the other

Figure 1: *The internal dynamics of coping management*

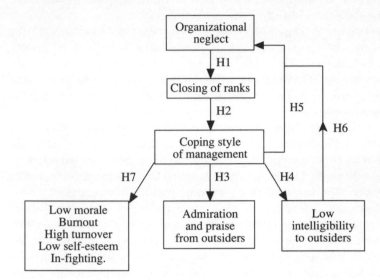

just does not understand serve to confirm and widen the gulf. The scene is thus set for an evaluation of the situation that focuses resolutely on the attributes of the individual coper, seeing by turns the exhausted heroine and the person who means well but cannot set priorities and manage time.

How does coping management come into play? I would not argue, as a gender attributes approach might, that it is in some sense particularly a women's management style, although as we will see later there may well be aspects of female socialisation which are conducive to it. Coping management seems better seen as a function of neglect by the powerful and of a subsequent closing of ranks. The longstanding neglect of nursing within the organization of the NHS, the failure to acknowledge and explore the issues that provision of a nursing service entails which the three sets of authors discussed in the previous section have described, would seem to lead very directly to a coping management style. Figure 1 draws the argument together at this stage, summarizing some of the processes that have been outlined and suggesting further that CM is both a response to organizational neglect and a strategy that in the end reinforces that neglect.[5] This can also be put more formally in a set of hypotheses as follows:

Hypothesis 1 The greater the organizational neglect of the issues faced by a group of employees, the more that group will close ranks against the rest of the organization.

Hypothesis 2 The more that a group opts to close ranks, the greater the likelihood that its behavioural style will be coping management.

Hypothesis 3 Coping management will give rise to praise and admiration from those outside and this in turn will reinforce the coping style.

Hypothesis 4 The more the resort to coping management, the greater the complexity of the internal arrangements for coping and the lower the intelligibility of those arrangements to outsiders.

Hypothesis 5 The more the resort to coping management, the greater the likelihood of continuing organizational neglect.

Hypothesis 6 The lower the intelligibility of the management arrangements, the greater the likelihood of organizational neglect.

Hypothesis 7 The more the resort to coping management, the greater the stress experienced by individuals within the group. This will result in low morale, burnout, low self-esteem and in-fighting.

Examined in this way, coping management can begin to accommodate a range of aspects of the gender talk in nursing with which this chapter began. Coping management does distance a group from others and can easily give that group the appearance of being 'isolationist' and 'sectarian'. The heavy demands that coping management makes on staff, while creating solidarity, run the risk of overstretching the capacity of those staff and creating an environment which is less than supportive and caring of individual members of the group. The process of coping also, while in one sense a very active one, can also be seen as 'passivity' in the sense of a failure to challenge the status quo and no effort to change the circumstances in which the work is done.

It is important to note at this stage, however, that the model suggests a dynamic that could in principle describe the behaviour of a number of occupational groups who occupy a relatively powerless[6] position in the division of labour. Having deleted gender as attribute, it remains to insert gender as relations. How can this be accomplished? There are, it will be suggested, a number of different ways in which gender relations might be conducive to the coping management style. To explore these, we need to take a further step in the analysis.

The discussion introduced below emphasizes two features of a gender relations analysis, namely, the gender division of labour in health care and the gender division of paid work. The term gender division of health care highlights the need to draw upon an historical understanding of struggles to establish the professions in health care and to acknowledge particular aspects of the male character of the 19th century professionalization project and their legacy for today. This is not to deny that there were a range of active female professionalization projects on health care (see Witz, 1990, 1992), but rather to emphasize the dilemmas and contradictions of such projects in cultural spaces colonized by men. The term gender division of paid work emphasizes the taken-for-granted organizational arrangements of the current delivery of health care. It is only by taking these together, it is claimed, that the trivialization of nursing work and the simultaneous devaluation of nurses, both as members of their occupational group and as women, can be understood and can be linked to coping management. These two key concepts are thus discussed briefly and in turn below. Figure 2 then summarizes some of the relationships to which they give rise.

Much detailed empirical work on 19th century struggles of occupations in health care has become available in the recent period. Drawing from contributions to critical theories of professions (Johnson, 1972; Larson, 1977; Saks, 1983), it has concentrated particularly on the dominance of the medical profesion (eg Freidson, 1970, 1986; Rueschemeyer, 1986) and, particularly in Britain, attention has focussed on occupations surrounding medicine (Larkin, 1983). Witz has recently drawn attention to inadequacies in the treatment of women in this literature and has pioneered a new approach integrating gender into theorizing about occupational closure (Witz, 1990, 1992). This work makes clear that in a gender-divided society, men's socially legitimated preferential access to economic and political resources gave them a head start in controlling the occupational division of labour and gaining status and economic rewards. Historically, women were excluded from the educational and training institutions and hence from the knowledge base which has given entry to prestigious areas of employment. Where women have been included, they have been offered or have won for themselves places that are clearly subordinate in terms of pay and status in the world of paid work.

Nowhere is this more clear than in the division of labour in

Figure 2; *The gender relations of coping management*

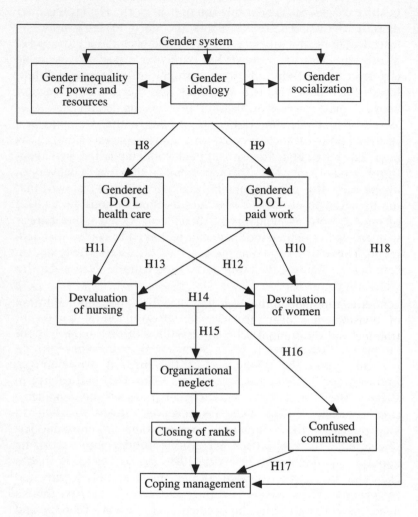

health care. Health work (as the earlier quotation from Strong and Robinson so vividly showed) is strongly imbued with gender divisions; it has been partitioned in such a way as to accord unambiguous status and respect to what is labelled medical and what until very recently has been overwhelmingly the preserve of men. Work that could be subdivided and routinized has been progressively handed over to others, work that involved dealing with sentiments and emotions was largely excluded from the male preserve, by being denied altogether as any part of the work project or by being handed over, explicitly or implicitly, to women.

The struggle for professional autonomy and status which these authors have described is also, however, a discursive struggle in which gender is used, by men and by women as a resource to give meaning to and conceptualize the work to be done and the relations of its delivery.[7] Gamarnikow (1978) provided an early account of the explicitly gendered imagery through which turn of the century medicine and nursing and the relations between them were discussed (cf Carpenter, 1977)[8]. Elston (1986) draws attention to the gender terms in which debates about women's admission to medical schools and to medical specialties was conducted. And there was an energetic debate, strongly saturated with gender imagery, around the creation of health visiting as work for women in public health as opposed to sanitary inspection as work for men (Davies, 1988).

Two changes obscure these gendered origins of the division of labour in health care. First, it is no longer feasible to appeal to gender as rationale in the same way; secondly, institutionalization of divisions has been accompanied by differential lengths of training and differential access to resources for research and for autonomous practice. The active role of gender ideology in creating and sustaining occupational divisions of labour has been replaced, at an overt level at least, by appeals to science and to bases in knowledge and in apparently incontrovertible merit. The sense in which gender is written in to the division of labour in health care is thus obscured, surfacing today perhaps in the repeated debates which can be observed about how nursing can be defined and in the proposition, for example, that nursing might be seen as a 'caring profession'.

The second key concept, that of the gender division of paid work, is used to draw attention to gender as a fundamental structuring principle by which not health work in particular but work in general is constituted. Joan Acker captures the essence of this idea when she argues that gender is a basic element in 'organizational logic', that is, in the underlying assumptions and practices that construct most contemporary work organizations. She goes on to locate the material forms of organizational logic in the written work rules, contracts, managerial directives and other documentary tools for running large organizations. She explains:

In organizational logic, both jobs and hierarchies are abstract categories that have no occupants, no bodies, no gender. . . .(F)illing the abstract job is a disembodied worker who exists only for the work. . .The closest the disembodied worker doing the abstract job comes to a real worker is the male worker whose life centers on his fulltime, life-long job, while his wife or another woman takes care of his personal needs and his children. . . .The concept 'a job' is thus implicitly a gendered concept, even though organizational logic presents it as gender neutral. 'A job' already contains the gender-based division of labour and the separation between the public and the private sphere. The concept of 'a job' assumes a particular gendered organization of domestic life and social production. (Acker, 1990:149)

Hierarchies, Acker argues, are similarly gendered because those who are committed to paid employment are deemed more suited to responsibility and authority, while those with additional commitments remain in the lower ranks.

This theoretically-driven approach dovetails well with themes emerging from more empirically-based equal opportunity research. The 'golden pathway' to senior management in the NHS (a barely articulated route by which a young manager makes a rapid series of geographical moves, studies at night to pass professional examinations and does both of these before the age of thirty) is, for example, clearly not a gender neutral way of arranging patterns of promotion, and, in the context of new target-setting for increasing the proportions of women in management has become the focus of new thinking about more flexible patterns of management development.[9] Acker's questioning of hierarchies and jobs also has its counterpart in practical demands from the equal opportunity lobby for career breaks and re-entry schemes, for rights and career prospects for those who work part time and for measures for the state, for employers or for both to provide childcare facilities.[10] As the quotation above makes clear, the gendering under discussion here is actually more than a matter of internal logic of organizations, and is predicated on the split between public and private, paid and unpaid work. Since it is not only jobs, but the very terms and conditions of paid work itself that render participation convenient for men and problematic for women, it seems preferable to refer to this phenomenon as the gender division of paid work.

Both aspects of the gender division of labour described above aid in understanding the uneasy status that nursing holds. As paid work done by women, nursing simply cannot be managed on the conventional, full-time, life-time pattern but must adjust to that pattern. It does so in a myriad of ways, all of which redound to its disadvantage as a 'serious profession'. Reliance on student labour, the use of part-timers, the close supervision of a transient workforce which includes both of these as well as nurses working for a nurse bank, all mean a constant juggle to achieve cover and a real need for close supervision of an unfamiliar work team. These features present themselves at best as a managerial headache, and at worst as the outcome of an apparently uncommitted workforce. In reality, they are all necessary adjustments to the impossibility of delivery of work on the male pattern. We are beginning to see here, set in a wider theoretical model, the processes of trivialization of work and devaluation of women that Mackay identified. The 'solutions' on offer are deeply problematic. They reinforce the unimportance of the work and the workers. They trivialize.

The questions of how, and in what way work might in principle be redesigned to break out of this dilemma are formidable ones. An examination of what would be involved in one specific area, in devising a policy for continuing education for members of a profession who regularly work part time, who routinely exit from and re-enter the labour force has recently been conducted. The shifts of basic values, the rethinking of financial incentives, the reframing of routine practices that would be required represent nothing short of a fundamental transformation of current nursing practice (Davies, 1990).

But there is also the matter, arising from the historical processes described above which have gendered the division of labour in health care, of the work itself as a female-gendered and devalued activity. One consequence of this is that support for the growth and development of nursing, through elaborating a knowledge base, is not granted in anything like the way it is for medicine; support for the shedding of routine work is at best erratic, since the work in many eyes is routine anyway. Nursing comes to be seen, from the outside at least, as a fairly homogeneous activity which requires pairs of hands, and qualities such as dedication, sympathy and altruism. We can return again here to the superimposition of ideologies of science, rationality and meritocracy on a division of labour that has been constructed and is still being sustained by gender. When, in a gendered division of labour that is widely regarded as 'rational', nurses claim development of their own knowledge base and improvements of their education, they are accused of engaging in battles for status and power. Fighting one's way out of a gendered division of labour is particularly fraught in this respect.

Figure 2 attempts to suggest how these twin aspects of the division of labour, embedded in wider gender inequalities,[11] tend in a mutually reinforcing way, to the devaluation both of nursing and of women and hence enable nursing to be neglected by those who have overall responsibility for health policy. Thus the chain of processes arising from neglect and identified earlier come into play. Two additional ideas are introduced. First, the devaluation which arises from the gender division of labour is not altogether negative; while nursing is devalued as a form of work and women are devalued as a species of worker, nurses are valued as women for the caring work they do. Historically and in contemporary settings women often face simultaneous valuation and devaluation and much of the 'confused commitment', anxiety, frustration and yet continued loyalty to nursing can be understood in terms of these three.[12]

Secondly, there is the question of gender socialization and its bearing on all the aspects so far considered. The model suggests that gender socialization, by underlining and endorsing a separation of spheres for male and female, reflects and reinforces gender ideology and hence supports the unequal distribution of resources and the gendered division of labour in both of the aspects previously discussed. It also suggests that gender socialization, both directly and through the gender division of labour, devalues women. This devaluation reinforces and is itself reinforced by the devaluation of nursing work. Further, to the extent that gender socialization is successful, it produces an inner psychic identity that has the same effect. There is now a considerable volume of research that points to female gender stereotypes as emphasizing service to others and personal self-sacrifice rather than individual autonomy, freedom and achievement, and that de-emphasizes organizational status, stressing shared goals, connection and communication rather than command and control.[13] To the extent that nurse managers bring such 'feminine' perspectives and values to the conduct of their work, this will point towards the use of coping management as earlier described, rather than towards a more confrontational strategy.

Putting all this rather more formally yields a second set of hypotheses as follows:

Hypothesis 8 The stronger the system of gender inequality, the more it is likely to shape the division of labour in an occupational area in a way that disadvantages women.

Hypothesis 9 The stronger the system of gender inequality, the more difficult it will be to alter the gender division of paid work.

Hypothesis 10 The stronger the gendered division of paid work, the more likely it will be that women as workers will be devalued.

Hypothesis 11 The stronger the gendering of the health care division of labour, the more likely it will be that the paid work that women do – in this case nursing work – will be devalued.

Hypothesis 12 The stronger the gendered division of labour in health care, the greater the devaluation of women as workers.

Hypothesis 13 The stronger the gendered division of labour in paid work, the greater the devaluation of the work of nursing.

Hypothesis 14 The devaluation of nursing will reinforce and be reinforced by the devaluation of women as workers.

Hypothesis 15 The devaluation of nursing work and of women will legitimize the organizational neglect of nursing.

Hypothesis 16 The devaluation of nursing work and of women will confuse but not lower commitment to nursing.

Hypothesis 17 Confused commitment will conduce to a coping management style.

Hypothesis 18 Gender socialization will tend to create gender identities which are consonant with the practice of coping management.

Concluding discussion

It has been the aim of this chapter to explore the notion of a gender relations analysis and to show what this might be able to offer by way of a new and more fruitful approach to some of the gender talk, both lay and academic, which surrounds the issue of nursing, and especially the management of nursing in the NHS at the present time. By taking as its topic the inclusion of women as nurses in the organization of health care, it has tried to identify some of the processes which confine nurses to a subordinate status and disadvantage them, despite their numerically major presence in the health care system.

Two factors have been suggested as central to this. The gender division of paid work, a concept invoked in rather different terms by many of the contributors to this volume, is a structuring principle that underpins the basic logic of bureaucratic organization and that redounds to the disadvantage of all women unless they can forge a strong separation between home and work, can prioritize work and rely on servicing in the domestic sphere to achieve this. The gender division of health care, on the other hand, draws attention to the more specific route whereby women as nurses have been disadvantaged. It is not only that professionalization was not open to women in the same way as to men, it is also that the professionalizing project of the men – in this case doctors – in elevating the status of their own work, simultaneously downgraded that of the nurses. These concepts, it is claimed, can help to uncover the gendered foundations of the contemporary organization of health care and demonstrate how apparently gender-neutral organizational arrangements inscribe power and rest on and in turn reproduce certain forms of gender relations (see introduction to this volume).

The analysis has involved successive stages of reformulating the gender question, first in shifting away from perjorative reference to nurses as poor managers in favour of a more neutral formulation of coping management, and then in regarding coping management not as an individual strategy favoured by women, but as a consequence of operating as women in a regime that is already gendered.

Nursing provides a particularly crucial testbed for understanding contemporary gender relations. High public esteem for nursing work is accompanied by a challenge to nurses' commitment as individuals and to their competence as a professional group in a male-gendered organization setting. Nursing does 'reflect the gender relations of a Victorian age', not because nurses themselves live in some special women's time-warp, but because the gender relations of that age are written in the organizational forms of today. An adequate theoretical understanding of this is important if we are to envision alternative forms of organizations and ones that respect women's worth and women's work.

Acknowledgement

Previous versions of this paper were presented at the Women's Studies Forum, Queen's University, Belfast, November 1991 and at a conference 'Professionalization and Gender', at the Centre for Women's Research, University of Trondheim, December 1991. I am grateful to colleagues at both venues for their comments and their support.

Notes

1 An insistence on gender relations is an attack not only on individualism but also, of course, on biologism and, more particularly in the context of this chapter, on those arguments which abound concerning women's management styles and natural differences in ways of working. The intensity of the reaction, both popular and academic to the contemporary 'difference authors' (see eg Gilligan, 1982; Tannen, 1991), suggests to me that the issue is not whether there are or are not innate differences, but how to shift from the description of differences to an adequate theorization of their production and change. For a good recent example in the area of management style, see Rosener (1990–1) and the confused debate published in the subsequent issue of the journal.

2 A survey of more than 7,000 nurses in 1987 showed that nurses felt undervalued and suffered from work overload and stress. Two out of three described nursing management as inflexible, 60 per cent said they do not get the right training to further their careers, over half said they were not told about decisions affecting them and did not have opportunities to discuss their concerns openly with managers (Price Waterhouse, 1988a,b).

3 For an account covering much recent research, see Powell (1988).

4 Work on leadership in nursing is currently being sponsored by the King's Fund, see Rafferty (1991). For a comment typical of much current thinking from the Chief Executive of the NHS see *The Guardian* 13 Sept. 1990. For a very interesting American discussion of the split between leadership and management and how it diminishes and trivializes the profound changes needed in the institutions of nursing see Krantz and Gilmore (1990).

5 The decision to neglect or the practice of neglecting is just as much an exercise of power as the decision to control or command, although it is much less usual for it to be given attention as such. The next section will suggest that neglect can only come into play if the commitment of the group can be assured and that there is a specifically gendered form of power at work here.

6 See note 5.

7 For a comment on the need to develop further the analysis of discursive strategies in the history of the professions see Witz (1992:7). For a further analysis of 'discursive politics', defined as the politics of meaning-making and discussed with reference to the possibilities of feminist transformations of institutions see Katzenstein (forthcoming).

8 This approach underlies the work of a number of historical researchers at the University of Trondheim in Norway. For an analysis of the case of Norwegian nurses and teachers, see Melby (1991).

9 The 'golden pathway' is further described in Davies and Rosser, (1986a:26–8). Following recent moves to redesign management development in the NHS and the decision of the Service to join the Opportunity 2000 Campaign and set targets for greater proportions of women in management, policy guidance has

been issued which draws attention to the dangers of the 'golden pathway' and highlights more flexible approaches to facilitate a wider range of disadvantaged groups (Davies and Parkyn, 1992).

10 For discussions of the extent to which equal opportunity demands are or can be transformative, see, for example, Jewson and Mason (1986), Davies (1989) and especially Cockburn (1991).

11 For more on the use of the term 'gender system' in this way, specifically comprising the three aspects shown in figure two, see Chavetz (1990).

12 For a more detailed discussion of the kind of dilemmas which arise in the context of health visiting see Davies (1988).

13 See Powell (1988) and also in particular the 'difference authors', Note 1.

References

Acker, J., (1989), 'Making Gender Visible', *in* R. Wallace (ed.), *Feminism and Sociological Theory*, London: Sage.

Acker, J., (1990), 'Hierarchies, Jobs, Bodies: a theory of gendered organisations', *Gender and Society*, 4 (2).

Beardshaw, V. and Robinson, R., (1990), *New for Old? Prospects for Nursing in the 1990s*, London: King's Fund Institute.

Carpenter, M., (1977), 'The New Managerialism and Professionalism in Nursing', *in* M. Stacey *et al* (eds), *Health and the Division of Labour*, London: Croom Helm.

Chavetz, J.S., (1990), *Gender Equity: an integrated theory of stability and change*, London: Sage.

Cockburn, C., (1991), *In the Way of Women: men's resistance to sex equality in organisations*, London: Macmillan.

Davies, C., (1988), 'The Health Visitor as Mother's Friend: A Woman's Place in Public Health, 1900–1914', *Social History of Medicine*, 1, pp. 38–57.

Davies, C., (1989), 'Workplace Action Programmes for Equality for Women: an orthodoxy examined', *in* C. Hussey *et al* (eds), *Equal Opportunities for Men and Women in Higher Education, Proceedings of a Conference, UCD, September 1988*, Dublin, UCD, 1989.

Davies, C., (1990), *The Collapse of the Conventional Career*, London: ENB.

Davies, C. and Parkyn, A., (1992), *Realising Potential – a practical guide to equality of opportunity in management development*, Bristol: NHSTD.

Davies, C. and Rosser, J., (1986a), *Processes of Discrimination*, London: DHSS.

Davies, C. and Rosser, J., (1986b), 'Gendered Jobs in the NHS', *in* D. Knights and H. Willmott (eds), *Gender and the Labour Process*, Aldershot: Gower.

Davies, C. and Rosser, J. (1987), 'A Male Pathway Unwilling to Bend?', *The Health Service Journal*, 5 February.

Elston, M.A., (1986), 'Women Doctors in the British Health Services: a sociological study of their careers and opportunities', Ph.D. Thesis, University of Leeds.

Friedson, E., (1970), *Professional Dominance: The Social Structure of Medical Care*, New York: Harper and Row.

Friedson, E., (1986), *Professional Powers: A Study of the Institutionalisation of Formal Knowledge*, Chicago and London: University of Chicago Press.

Gamarnikow, E., (1978), 'Sexual Division of Labour: The Case of Nursing', *in* A. Kuhn and A.M. Wolpe (eds), *Feminism and Materialism*, London: Routledge and Kegan Paul.

Gilligan, C., (1982), *In a Different Voice: Psychological Theory and Women's Development*, Cambridge (Mass): Harvard University Press.

Jewson, N. and Mason, D., (1986), 'The Theory and Practice of Equal Opportunities Policies – Liberal and Radical Approaches', *Sociological Review*, 34.

Johnson, T.J., (1972), *Professions and Power*, London: Macmillan.

Katzenstein, M.F., (forthcoming), 'Liberating the Mainstream: Feminism, Unobtrusive Mobilisation and Institutional Change'.

Krantz, J. and Gilmore, T.N., (1990), 'The Splitting of Leadership and Management as a Social Defense', *Human Relations*, 43(2).

Larkin, G., (1983), *Occupational Monopoly and Modern Medicine*, London: Tavistock.

Larson, M.S., (1977), *The Rise of Professionalism: A Sociological Analysis*, California: University of California Press.

Mackay, L., (1989), *Nursing a Problem*, Milton Keynes: Open University Press.

Melby, K., (1991), 'Women's Ideology: Difference Equality or a New Femininity: Women Teachers and Nurses in Norway 1912–1940', *in* T. Andreasen *et al* (eds), *Moving On: New Perspectives on the Women's Movement*, Aarhus: Aarhus University Press.

Pateman, C., (1988), *The Sexual Contract*, Cambridge: Polity Press.

Powell, G.N., (1988), *Women and Men in Management*, London: Sage.

Price Waterhouse (1988a), *Nurse Retention and Recruitment: Report on the factors affecting the retention and recruitment of nurses, midwives and health visitors in the NHS*, Bristol: Price Waterhouse.

Price Waterhouse (1988b), *Nurse Retention and Recruitment: A matter of priority*, (Summary Report) Bristol: Price Waterhouse.

Rafferty, A-M., (1991), 'Developing Nurse Leaders', unpublished paper, London: King's Fund.

Rosser, J. and Davies, C., (1987), 'What Would We Do Without Her?': Invisible Women in NHS Administration', in A. Spencer and D. Podmore (eds), *In a Man's World's World: Essays on Women in Male-Dominated Professions*, London: Tavistock.

Rosener, J.B., (1990), 'Ways Women Lead', *Harvard Business Review*, 68(6).

Rueschemeyer, D., (1983), 'Professional Autonomy and the Social Control of Expertise', in R. Dingwall and P. Lewis (eds), *The Sociology of the Professions*, London: Macmillan.

Saks, M., (1983), 'Removing the Blinkers? A Critique of Recent Contributions to the Sociology of Professions', *Sociological Review*, 31(1).

Scott, J.W., (1986), 'Gender: a useful category of historical analysis', *American Historical Review*, 91.

Stacey, J. and Thorne, B., (1985), 'The Missing Feminist Revolution in Sociology', *Social Problems*, 32, (4).

Strong, P. and Robinson, J., (1990), *The NHS – Under New Management*, Milton Keynes: Open University Press.

Tannen, D., (1991), *You Just Don't Understand: women and men in conversation*, London: Virago.

Waite, R., Buchan, J. and Thomas, J., (1989), *Nurses in and out of Work*, Brighton: IMS Report 170, Sussex University.

Witz, A., (1990), 'Patriarchy and Professions: the gendered politics of occupational closure', *Sociology*, 24(4).

Witz, A., (1992), *Professions and Patriarchy*, London: Routledge.

Gender, bureaucracy and organizational culture

Karen Ramsay and Martin Parker

Introduction

> Bureaucratic and patriarchal structures are antagonistic in many
> ways, yet they have in common a most important peculiarity:
> permanence. In this respect they are both institutions of daily
> routine. (. . .) The patriarch is the 'natural leader' of the daily
> routine. And in this respect, the bureaucratic structure is only
> the counter-image of patriarchalism transposed into rationality.
> (Weber in Gerth and Mills, 1948:245)

In that quote Weber captured much of what we wish to argue in
this chapter. Though we understand 'patriarchalism' in a far more
critical sense than he presumably intended at the time (op cit:
296), the idea that bureaucracy is a form of rationalised patriarchy
is clearly there. So too is the idea that these structures are based on
'daily routine' – the practices of actors in organized contexts.
However, against Weber's pessimism about the 'iron cage' this will
be a paper which assumes that it is not enough to theorize the
relationship between gender and bureaucracy. What is important
is to offer ways of changing it. This is also a paper that is written
with the caveat that we acknowledge other oppressions than
bureaucratic and patriarchal ones within organizations. Ethnicity,
(dis)ability, age and so on are also social divisions that shape the
texture of organizations and that we wish to see theorized and
addressed, but do not focus on in this paper, though we would
hope that some of the broader implications of this analysis can also
be applied to them.

This chapter proceeds in six sections. The first two outline our
understanding of the relationship between the terms bureaucracy,
gender and organizational culture. In it we suggest that the

dominant modes of operationalization of the bureaucratic ideal type are intimately related to patriarchal and capitalist assumptions about the nature of work in organizations. These structural pressures are then interpreted in each organization by and through the specific cultures of that organization. We suggest that this is an important step because it relates general structural pressures to the actions of specific groups of agents in reproducing these pressures. The third and fourth sections contain reviews of the literature on first, structural, and second, the cultural influences on the reproduction of patriarchy within organizations in an attempt to illustrate the importance of the theoretical argument presented in the first two sections.

The fifth section offers some suggestions as to how the preceding argument might be used to understand how organizations might be changed in an enduring way. We propose two more ideal types, the anti-bureaucracy and the neo-bureaucracy, in an attempt to show that organizations can be different whilst still recognizing the strength of the Weberian problematic. We conclude the discussion by suggesting that, whilst all organizations need to attend to the functional needs that Weber identified, they can develop cultures that might be able to work against the dominance of patriarchal and capitalistic assumptions. This might enable organizations to be formed that are efficient at performing their primary task but do not oppress their members in so doing.

1 Why Weber?

In order to understand the development of modern bureaucratic models of organization we need to read Weber's writings on bureaucracy in two different ways. These can provide us with an opening for organizations to be different, to be other than they are at present whilst still attending to the functional needs that Weber so clearly identified (Gerth and Mills, 1948:329–41, Weber, 1947:196–244). Whether Weber would have recognized either of the versions of his texts that we appropriate is unimportant for us; any commentator is always engaged in hermeneutics whether they acknowledge it or not. Indeed Weber may well have approved since, despite being 'a model of the self-conscious masculinity of Imperial Germany', he was apparently supportive of the women's emancipation movement in the early 20th century (Gerth and Mills, 1948:26).

The first interpretation of his writing, and the one that has been dominant in organizational and managerial thought throughout most of this century, is as a model to solve the problems of organizing. Thus the 'ideal' in 'ideal type' becomes a prescription for organizational excellence and the 'one best way' to construct an organization. For many authors throughout the century it seems that Weber, Taylor, Urwick and Gantt were all arguing different versions of the same prescriptive thesis and most American textbooks on organizational behaviour still adopt this framework (Bowditch and Buono, 1990:10–12, Hunsaker and Cook, 1986:16–19, Schermerhorn, Hunt and Osborne, 1991:317–8). This is a prescription that specifies a rigid hierarchy, top-down communication, specific role definition, the separation of public and private and so on. We argue that this is a particular solution to the Weberian problematic that reflects both capitalist and patriarchal assumptions about control, skill and rationality.

However, it is clearly a solution that differs from organization to organization. Bureaucracy is a model that many organizations aim for and is achieved with varying degrees of success. Authors such as Gouldner (1954) and Pugh and Hickson (1973) have identified that organizations may, in practice, be more or less bureaucratized. In Gouldner's case he distinguished between 'mock', 'punishment centred' and 'representative' bureaucracies, for Pugh and Hickson the terms 'full', 'workflow' and 'personnel' were favoured. We would argue that this indicates that there may be other solutions that are broadly within the framework of Weber's writing but have quite different consequences for the members of the organization themselves.

Yet, as has been pointed out many times, to see Weber's writings as a prescriptive solution is a crude interpretation of the 'ideal type' concept. Hence we propose a second interpretation of Weber as a formulation of problems that *all* complex organizations need to negotiate. Thus there need to be some rules, some internal differentiation, some way of making decisions and so on. This clearly echoes Parson's (1951) interpretation of the notion of 'functional prerequisites' for social systems and Miller and Rice's notion of organizations having to fulfil certain 'primary tasks' in order to survive (1967). For Parson's all systems must be adaptive, goal attaining, integrated and maintain cultural patterns. Throughout this paper we argue that this is an invaluable guide to the functional requirements of complex organizing and that any organization in whatever kind of social environment needs to find

255

some way of negotiating them. Bureaucracy is an 'ideal type' in the sense that it is a model of what all organizations need to do in order to be enduring and moderately successful in achieving their central tasks. However, the practical way that these problems are negotiated is contingent on various circumstances and choices. These are *problems* that any organizer needs to address and not ready made *solutions* that the organization can adopt. There are alternatives but they are alternatives within limits of possibility.

One way of illustrating this is to argue that Weber has pointed to the importance of any organization having some kind of co-ordination mechanism. For any complex organization to function it requires that one part of the organization ensures that the other parts are functioning in a way that is mutually supportive and meets the explicit goals of the organization. However, the usual resolution of this problem is the formulation of a hierarchy with the co-ordination mechanism at the apex. We would argue that this is a way to solve the problem that reflects patriarchal and capitalist assumptions. As Marglin argues:

> The social function of hierarchical work organisation is not technical efficiency, but accumulation. (in Thompson and McHugh 1990:49)

There is no logical reason why the co-ordinators should be given a higher status and reward position within the organization. Indeed they could simply be seen as another part of the organization, no more or less functional or central than other parts (see for example the debate on the functions of social stratification, Davis and Moore, Tumin in Bendix and Lipset, 1967).

In response, those who believe in the inevitability of stratification may assert that the term co-ordination actually hides the fact that many organizational members may need to be coerced into performing their tasks. The status of the manager thus reflects the necessity of formalizing authority. This is certainly true within the contexts that we currently construct organizations. Because of the likelihood of resistance within a society divided by class, gender and so on then organizations become structured to cope with these assumptions. However, what we are proposing is that this is a result of the specific pressures on bureaucracies within a particular social context. It is not a functional requirement of organizing. If the pressures of patriarchy and capitalism were actively resisted, or hypothetically were not there, then hierarchical organizations would no longer be an 'obvious' solution because conflict, and thus resistance, would no longer be structurally determined.

The same argument can be used for other parts of the bureaucratic model. Specialization is undoubtedly a functional result of complexity, if an organization did not have specialized roles it would not be able to perform complex tasks. Yet the permanent association of particular persons to particular roles is not a logical consequence of this and neither is the assumption that some specialisms are more important than others. In addition the assumptions that particular roles have to be carried out by one person, rather than a group, and that such roles are fixed, and not negotiable, may also be unjustified. With regard to rules it is again taken as read that organizations need rules in order that they be constituted as 'organized'. Yet it is not a consequence of this that the rules are not re-negotiable and contingent on the organization members' perceptions of the organizations central task (Mills and Murgatroyd, 1991). As Wittgenstein (1968) argues, rules are necessary to play a game, but the object of the game and the characteristics of the rules are constructed by the participants.

One further way of illustrating what we mean is articulated in the difference between formal (*zweckrational*) and substantive (*wertrational*) forms of rationality (Weber, 1947:184–86). The hypothetical conditions for formal instrumental rationality are certainly delimited within the bureaucratic model. If an organization wishes to achieve a given end it must establish the organizational conditions for its achievement and these can be understood as functional conditions for organization. However, decisions about the actual means and ends themselves are value rational. It is possible to achieve a given goal through a number of means and to debate the value of the ends. The structural conditions for organization do not determine the actions of actors within those organizations. A metaphor might help to illustrate the point. A durable building of any kind must have foundations, walls, roof and so on. Were it not to possess these features it would be substantively irrational – it would not be fit for the purpose it was intended. Yet these limitations do not prevent architects elaborating the structure according to their conceptions of aesthetic rationality or the building being used by many different people for many different things. The shell is necessary, just as the formal organization is necessary, but the use to which it is put and the arrangement of the internal partitions can be largely up to the inhabitants.

2 Organizational structure and organizational culture

Hence we start from the assumption that most current bureaucratic solutions arise from the twin imperatives of patriarchy and capitalism. Bureaucracy as a prescription, our first interpretation of the term, reflects the rationality of capital accumulation as well as the rationality of patriarchal domination. In that sense then, all bureaucratic organizations are the same because they respond to conditions that are generalizable. Despite this, each enduring organization develops an unique way of mediating these two pressures, its own value rationality. The particular discourses and practices that achieve this we will refer to as the organization's culture. The culture of a given organization embodies accepted assumptions about the 'correct' way that a particular organization should operate. In a second sense then, all organizations are different because they mediate structural pressures in different ways. This has been long recognized by writers on organizations, particularly those who were concerned to stress that organizations did not in fact function in the way that the Weberian solution suggested they did (Merton 1968, Gouldner 1954, Blau 1963). Once again, this can be taken to suggest that there are alternative solutions to the functional requirements of complex organizing.

On an analytical level we therefore separate structural conditions for organizations and the practices of actors within those organizations. Yet, in the most obvious sense, these two categories are inseparable since just as organized structures make people so do people make organized structures. As Giddens (1979) notes, language is a structure that stands outside and before individuals but it is also a structure that is continually reproduced by individuals and consequently undergoes change. Hence, one of the sites for the reproduction of patriarchal and capitalistic structures is bureaucratic organizations and from a distance they may appear solid and unchanging. Yet, if we look at organizations as cultures, they begin to appear as webs of meaning that are constructed through the everyday practices of actors. Dress, language, symbolism and so on become the unrecognized material out of which the organization is built. Attending more closely to the process, rather than the organization chart, might begin to reveal how organizational practices are related to ideas about their proper purpose and their rationality.

There has been a great deal of writing on organizational/ corporate culture in the last ten years, both academic and popular (Pettigrew, 1979; Peters and Waterman, 1982; Frost, 1985; Deal and Kennedy, 1988; Turner, 1989). Much of the popular literature has been highly functionalist and managerialist in tone, yet the term itself appears to us to hold much promise for a sociology of organizations. For our purposes we wish to use the term to indicate an interpretive approach to organization as a process involving agency. Organizations have many alliances and divides that are related to wider structural factors, but each crystallization of these pressures is unique to any and every organization. Again, this would seem to correspond broadly with Weber's insistence on *verstehen* (Weber, 1947:88), a sociology that takes the subjective constitution of meaning as its starting point but does not disavow the possibility of comparison. In that sense, organizations are constructed with the interpretive resources that any culture provides but this does not mean that every organization is the same. Gender oppression is common to most, if not all, organizations but it takes unique forms within each organization according to their local histories, symbolic languages and senses of commitment or opposition. The next section of the paper will substantiate some of the argument above by looking at the wider pressures that tend to push organizations to the bureaucratic solution.

3 Bureaucracy and the structure of gender oppression

In this section we argue that the intersection of patriarchy and formal rational authority has resulted in the modern bureaucratic organization and the discourse of the bureaucratic solution. Within the organization all members are subject to controls over their behaviour through the structure and discourse of bureaucracy, just as they continually erect these structures themselves. Within organizations women experience a double oppression. As subordinates they are subject to bureaucratic regulation of their behaviour, and as women they are excluded as equal organizational participants by patriarchal structures and processes.

In empirical terms, research which has as its focus the position of women in employment (although not necessarily dealing directly with organizational issues) has shown that women are horizontally and vertically segregated into certain occupations and into lower status positions within these occupational areas (Hakim, 1979; Walby, 1986; Crompton and Sanderson, 1990). Women are placed differently in the organizational hierarchy, their orientation to careers differs and women commonly perform different tasks to those performed by men.

This sexual division of labour and authority is rooted in the development of capitalist organizations and the patriarchal character of management. The history of organizations and administration clearly indicates that men, and not women, were the key actors in the shaping of organizational structures. As Meredith Gould (1979) argues, the structure of hierarchical organizations and the patriarchal division of labour were founded on the patriarchal family. As a group men retained power and authority in the new organizations partly through legitimizing hierarchical organization structures. The logic of capitalism generated economic rational decision making theories which supported patriarchal power over women's labour and created what Rosabeth Moss Kanter (1977) describes as the 'masculine ethos' of managerialism.

Women, as visible organizational participants, entered the administrative function as 'control adjuncts' (Tancred-Sheriff in Hearn *et al*, 1989). The growth of capitalism required clerical labour, and patriarchal processes at work excluded women from high status positions. In addition women were continually being defined through the emotional labour of the domestic sphere which was accorded lower status according to the value rationality of capitalism. The separation of the public and private spheres, the association of women with the latter and the higher status accorded to what men do in the public sphere has left its legacy in the association of masculinity with prestige and status. Karen Legge (1987) has shown, using the personnel function as a case study, that as an occupation or function formally performed by women becomes visible and achieves greater importance to the managerial function, it is accorded higher status and is appropriated by men. The same process is illustrated by Ann Phillips and Barbara Taylor (1980) in relation to skilled manual work. In much research too, women's role as processors of administrative decisions has been viewed as unimportant because of the conceptions of formal organization held by many researchers.

On a structural level Sylvia Walby (1986) firmly locates the cause of women's oppression and subordination within the economic sphere. Women are exploited in the family because they are segregated into lower status and lower waged positions within organizations. Drawing on Heidi Hartmann (1979), she identifies a cycle of oppression which is rooted in the organization of paid employment. Although sensitive to the conflict inherent in the appropriation of women's labour by capitalist and patriarchal systems, she notes that women's segregated labour benefits both systems: men retain their domestic labourers while capital benefits (especially in the case of part-time workers) from a cheap and flexible work force. Whilst on one level we are persuaded by this argument, it runs the danger of underplaying the role that actors in organizations have in reproducing patriarchy and capitalism. Economics and ideology undoubtedly provide the backdrop to any explanation of gender oppression but, as we have argued above, these structures are continually recreated by actors, both male and female, who assume the inevitability of the bureaucratic solution.

One way of illustrating the recreation of the bureaucratic solution by actors in organizations is with reference to the concept of leadership and culture as the 'management of meaning'. As Gareth Morgan and Linda Smircich (1982) note, entry to an organization requires some submission of the self to the needs of the organization; the newcomer has to allow her/his understanding of the world, of the organization and of their goals to be framed by others. If this does not occur the newcomer remains an outsider, with her/his needs for belonging unmet and as a worker, of marginal use to the organization. The act of leadership, Morgan and Smircich argue, is essentially the ability to shape the meanings other people give to the world and the organization. The meaning given to action in organizations is frequently defined with reference to goals, roles and rules, a particular bureaucratic solution. Understandings of responsibility and authority within organizations are not given by structures but built through practice and experience – the distinct culture of the organization. We will expand upon this in the next section.

4 Bureaucracy and the culture of gender oppression

It is characteristic of patriarchal and of patrimonial authority, which represents a variety of the former, that the system of inviolable norms is considered sacred; an infraction of them would result in magical or religious evils. (Weber in Gerth and Mills, 1948:296)

Various features of day-to-day work organizations have been identified as critical to an understanding of the culture of gender inequality at work. This section will review some of these taken for granted features of organization. These include the rationality of meritocracy and gendered understandings of rationality, individual ownership of achievement, the reproduction of organizations and the symbolic environment which patriarchal organizations construct. These are defined, not only in terms of gender, but also in terms of sexuality. As Lisa Adkins, in this volume, clearly indicates, women are not asexual organizational actors, and the work women do is fundamentally constructed around heterosexual understandings of women as sexualized actors. We would argue that although these features should not be seen simply as the *cause* of gender inequality in organizations, they are fundamental to the daily reproduction of structural inequalities and to continuing assumptions about the inevitability of the bureaucratic solution. We will begin with the ideology of meritocracy.

It has been argued that the barriers to women's equality rest with the criteria used to recruit and promote within organizations. Jewson and Mason (1986) argue that not only should these processes be formalized and monitored, the criteria used to select personnel should be scrutinized to ensure neither direct or indirect discrimination takes place. Their argument rests on the assumption that formal organizational rules determine and constrain the behaviour of its members. In our view, such an approach overlooks the negotiated and culturally mediated character of rule use. The recommendations discussed by Jewson and Mason or Gutek (in Hearn *et al* 1989) assume that the bureaucratic process is impersonal and meritocratic and that bureaucratic structures can be used to solve the problems they play a part in creating. Against this we would argue that it is not the formal rules as such that are the problem but assumptions about their efficacy combined with assumptions about the forms of rationality appropriate to bureaucratic organizations.

In support of this view it is worth noting that an emphasis on formal qualifications for entry to an occupation or profession can also convey an impression of meritocratic values which mask the hidden and covert assumptions concerning suitability. Sara Delamont (1989) uses the concept of the 'Saturn's Rings' phenomena. The dust of an organization's formal rationality hides the gendered values and taken for granted assumpions, leaving only the technical rules or components visible. Hence the structure appears to be the component which determines women's careers and the culture is left, often unacknowledged, in the background.

For example, research conducted in highly bureaucratised organizations such as the Civil Service (Walters, 1987) and the finance industry (Crompton and Sanderson 1990) illustrates the patriarchal character of the criteria used to recruit and promote members. The justification for not recruiting women sales representatives discussed by Knights and Morgan (1990) rested on arguments about women not being able to 'take the pressure' of a highly competitive occupation. Similarly, in terms of recruitment to management the justification has been the 'rational' element in decision-making. Since women are defined as the bearers of emotion they are seen as too emotional to make abstract strategic decisions.

Along these lines Sonia Liff and Jennette Webb (1988) point out that the bureaucratic solution to gender oppression does not address the male-defined structure and character of work roles and the subsequent criteria used to assess the suitability of applicants. They recommend a restructuring of work tasks to make them accessible to all people, rather than only those who have no domestic responsibilities. The restructuring approach may encourage more women to apply for senior positions and may, by breaking down the perception of managerial positions as an element in a linear career, begin to deconstruct masculine definitions of management. We will expand upon this possibility later in the paper.

Another feature often commented on in the literature is the importance of gender in interpretations of rationality. Jean Grimshaw (1986) makes a distinction between male and female types of social action. These do not necessarily relate to men and women as particular individuals but to gendered Weberian 'ideal types'. The male, abstract principle is primarily concerned with the adherence to a value or belief, irrespective of the consequences. There are shades of this principle in decision-making theory and Tayloristic 'one best way' methods of labour motivation and control. The female ideal type values emotional connection and human interaction above a single goal or ideal. Both are substantively rational, in that there is a means-end relationship, however the former has as a value the achievement of a goal or task while the latter stresses the process as being as valuable as the final outcome. In Grimshaw's terms, for men the end of bureaucracy is its strength, for women the bureaucratic solution may prevent debate over the appropriatenes of the means to be used.

This dual understanding of rationality crops up in other forms in the literature on gender and bureaucracy. Alison Baines (1988) uses the terms 'success' or 'satisfaction'; Rosalyn Bologh (1990) 'greatness' or 'love'. Judi Marshell (1984) reported from her study of women managers that on the whole the women were concerned with promotion (the organizational definition of success) only when they became dissatisfied with their current situation. Promotion, and hence individual success, appears not to be an end in itself for many women, but instead a way of escaping from organizational situations which they found to be unacceptable. However, it is worth noting the conclusions drawn by Mike Savage in this volume. He observes that while women in middle class occupations have a considerable degree of autonomy to exercise their expertise, they do not have equal access to the promotional career paths. In the light of these findings it could be argued then that women perceive their limited chances and so focus on personal rather than organizational reward.

Developing this analysis further, the promotional system itself is founded on a concept of the individual ownership of achievement (Baines, 1988) which again corresponds to ideas about the male manager-hero figure. The individual who climbs the hierarchy on their own merits to a position near the apex of the organization is a powerful symbol of impartial reward. However, as Jane Skinner (1988) argues, this individualism conceals the labour of the team which enabled the promoted individual to succeed in the first place. It is also expressive of values which have come to be associated with masculinity and the public world of work – the promotion of the self over others. Team work requires an awareness of interdependence between members and interpersonal processes. That this 'emotional labour' (Hochschild, 1983) is frequently unacknowledged and goes unrewarded in organizations reflects the greater value given to rational, task-orientated behaviour. It also reflects the hidden work in the domestic sphere which enables the manager to function in the public sphere of paid work.

In the previous section we noted how clerical and managerial work became gendered categories. The technical and indeterminate

components of the functions became sex-typed and the reproduction of sexuality in the workplace meant that women and men
became associated with the tasks they carried out. By referring to
Walby (1986) and Hartmann (1979) it is possible to understand
why this situation occurred and the tensions created in the male
work force when attempting to alter occupational segregation
through organizational restructuring. However, on a more 'cultural'
level Kanter (1977) provides an insight into why it may be difficult
to alter the situation without focusing on the organizational need
for predictability and the way in which this focus on predictability
is perpetuated through the discourse of the bureaucratic solution.

Moss Kanter's description of Indsco is interesting and useful as
it points to the issue of uncertainty in determining the reproduction
of gendered organizational structures. Strategic management
requires that the internal activities are self-regulating in order that
critical energy and attention can be focused on longterm activities
and boundary control. Individual self discipline and a sense of self
constructed in relation to others in a work environment serves as
an internal control function. Authors such as Toffler (1980) view
this self control as part of the 'Third Wave' and as a movement
which is replacing bureaucratic and Tayloristic techniques but it
can be traced further back to the activities of Henry Ford's
'Sociological Department' and the early human relations movement (Thompson and McHugh, 1990:75). In order to achieve the
bureaucratic solution, conformity is valued over innovation where
core organizational cultural values are concerned.

For Kanter, the search for certainty and predictability within
Indsco resulted in a preference for the inclusion of people who
overtly shared the 'ingroups' values and frame of reference. Given
the history of management in this company, these values revolved
around a concept of masculinity which was constructed in relation
to the perceived 'nature' of the work: rational, unemotional
decision making. Women, again as bearers of emotion, were seen
as potentially dangerous to the smooth functioning of the
company. The ideal organization member had to be minimally
different from others in the organization and hence able to
function within a rational/male role.

The research conducted by Kanter indicates that removing
formal barriers to women's organizational progression is not
sufficient to ensure their equal participation at senior level. The
need to control uncertainty and ensure the predictable behaviour
of employees, especially at senior levels where bureaucratic

methods of control are less applicable according to the needs for discretion in decision making, is a frame of reference which precludes the inclusion of previously unknown groups. To use Giddens' (1982) phrase, the desire for 'ontological security' amongst organizational members reflects the need for certainty and predictability amongst co-workers. For women to be included would require that the values of uncertainty and risk be incorporated into the taken for granted schema of the organization.

The desire for security and control can also be embodied in more concrete material codes within organizations which reinforce the taken-for-granted nature of the bureaucratic solution. Buildings themselves are powerful symbolic structures, the values of the organization man are all too obvious in the massivity of the office skyscraper with senior management in the penthouse suite. Yet the internal partitioning of space is often also symbolically suggestive – the secretary or switchboard operator as gatekeeper to the manager, the typing pool, the cleaners cupboard or the assembly shop foreman's view over the assembly floor. The privacy is often male and the surveilled are often female – the manager may walk into the secretaries' space unannounced but not vice versa (Burrell and Hearn in Hearn *et al* 1989). The segregated car park or dining area also reinforces assumptions about hierarchy and status which, as we have argued above, are difficult to separate from patriarchal assumptions about the way an organization is supposed to be structured.

Clothing has long been recognized as a major signal of culture, both within and between organizations. Moss Kanter was aware of this in noting that the men were similar in appearance and dress. Women, however, do not have an easy clothing model to adopt and several books have been published for women executives concerning impression management (Molloy, 1977; Scollard, 1983). The women managers Deborah Sheppard (in Hearn *et al* 1989) interviewed commented on the importance of dress, jewellery and make-up in conveying status. This status related both to their gender and to their position within the organization. As Gutek (in Hearn *et al*, 1989) notes this involves not being *too* feminine while fitting the 'other' role of manager. The balance of gender and role appropriate clothing expresses the tensions inherent in women as *man*agers in bureaucratic organizations yet for men too the wearing of earrings, beards or unconventional dress may be formally or informally prohibited. The symbolic expression of gender via clothing is clearly a highly problematic issue.

Common symbols also often reinforce the rationally masculine order. These may range from the sex for sale pinup on the factory floor to the stern wood panelling of the directors office. The images of the manager dictating to the secretary with head bent or the oily, muscled sweating craftsman are powerful metaphors for gender appropriate behaviour (Burrell and Hearn in Hearn *et al*, 1989). In addition the singularity of the male manager hero is a theme which has been common in mangerial (auto)biographies for some years (Rodgers, 1970; Kiam, 1986; Lacey, 1986). Rifkin and Harrar's (1988) biography of Ken Olson of DEC is interesting in this respect. Olson is presented as an everyday patriarch in check shirts and jeans who founded a company with its own philosophy, stories, culture and so on – 'The Ultimate Entrepreneur'. The tale of the manager under scrutiny is told as an epic fable which can illustrate their wisdom and the lessons to be learnt from their experience. They can become generalizable culture heroes in charge of their destiny, with a vision of a particular market, company or product to inspire others – 'John Wayne in pinstripes' (Thompson and McHugh, 1990:229). In addition ritualistic assumptions about the secretary watering the plants, bringing food and drink and accepting sexual flirtation or harrassment are all too common. Add to this assumptions about the formal bureaucracy being, of necessity, a child-free space and celebrations being alcoholic lunchtimes in the pub and the picture of a gendered culture becomes powerfully evident.

Finally, the language of business is also replete with gendered assumptions. Apart from the obvious manager, master copy, craftsman and so on the analogies of combat and sexual domination often articulate in the malestream. Opponents are 'screwed' or 'fucked', mountains are climbed and battles are won. Conquest and competition are the dominant metaphors to express what the organization is, and should be, doing with the marketplace described as the terrain upon which this struggle takes place. In addition colleagues, male or female, who do not conform to dominant values are the victim of speculation about their sexuality as a means of social control.

Given that all these cultural features of organization are gendered it is hardly surprising that the structural inequalities are so manifest. What is curious is that there has been so little attention to the relationship between the two. In part this may have something to do with Weber himself. Rosalyn Bologh (1990) clearly illustrates that Weber's discussion of the bureaucratic organization was shaped by his own patriarchal understandings of the world in which he lived. He saw the separation of the domestic and productive spheres, the association of women, emotionality and erotic love with the former and men, rationality and brotherly love with the latter as an unquestioned element in the modern social order. Yet the possibility of seeing any action as value rational opens a space for defining rationality as otherwise. If there are no absolute criteria for the meaningfulness of action then we become free to define ourselves and our organizations in alternative ways. Hence an organization might be rational and functional without corresponding to accepted cultural definitions of how this is achieved. In the next section we attempt to show how this might be done.

5 Towards a neo-bureaucracy

We propose that, since the culture of bureaucratic organizations is in some sense created by patriarchy and capitalism, then if either of those structural conditions change then so will organizations. However, like Weber, we have litle faith in the likelihood or outcome of revolution – particuarly a revolution based on overturning gender inequalities. That is why the foregrounding of agency is politically important because it opens a space for change at an organizational cultural level. Because organizations reproduce the structural conditions, changes in an organization's culture will begin to change patriarchy and capitalism. We believe this is an essential step for the argument since if it is not accepted we are all doomed to reproduce structural conditions without the possibility of any resistance or change. However, it should not be assumed that this necessarily gives us any easy grounds for optimism – simply the possibility that things could be other than they are at present.

Drawing on Foucault (1977), Kathy Ferguson (1984) argues that bureaucracy can be understood as a web of power, which controls even those who use it to serve their own purposes. The bureaucratic frame of reference creates limits to what can and can not be imagined. As a result, individuals are shaped by the assumptions which are built into hierarchical organizational structures. Whilst we agree with this assertion where the bureaucratic solution is concerned we believe that it is important to recognize organizations as webs of power that are also enabling.

Any organization must have a structure that allows it to be organized but that structure does not have to be visualized as an 'iron cage'. If we are implicated in making the cage we can also be responsible for unlocking it. If current understandings of the solution to the functional problems of organization are culturally and structurally mediated by patriarchy then, theoretically, there should be other ways of satisfying functional imperatives that move away from the patriarchal framework. With these theoretical assumptions in mind we suggest that there may be two other bureaucratic ideal types that are theoretically possible and that one of them is politically desirable.

Our second ideal type is the anti-bureaucracy which essentially constitutes an attempt to refuse the existence of the functional imperatives themselves. This would simply not be an organization as we understand the term since it would continually refuse any structure or internal differentiation. It would have no task specialization, no hierarchy (therefore no promotion) and no rules. Members would drift in and out according to their own interests and make no distinction between their selves in the organization and their selves outside it. We propose that, though this may be an appealing anarchy for some, this kind of theoretical construction reveals the importance of Weber's ideal type as a set of structural problems for any organization. The anti-organization seems to us not to be able to handle many of the complex tasks that we require organizations to perform – trains would not run on time if there were no way of ensuring that the driver knew that she should perform a particular set of duties at a particular time. If we desire a world that benefits from the products of organized labour the anti-organization is not adequate.

We therefore suggest a third ideal type which lies between bureaucracy and anti-bureaucracy. We term this the neo-bureaucracy. Neo-bureaucratic organizations would be continually attempting to refuse the fixity of patriarchal and capitalist imperatives whilst recognizing the power of organized labour to bring wider social benefits. They would recognize the functional imperatives of bureaucracy whilst refusing the definitions of the solution outlined above. Thus there would be limited task specialization that acknowledged areas of expertise but would not imply that only experts/professionals have power over particular areas of the organization's activity. Individual ownership of success would be replaced by an accent on teamwork and group achievement. Specified roles would be replaced by negotiated allocations of personnel to cope with particular problems or opportunities.

There would need to be a centre which was responsible for strategic decision-making and co-ordination but its power would be continually re-negotiated by the members of the organization. 'Promotion' would be replaced by an agreement that a particular individual or group had certain skills that required them to take a certain position within the organization for a determined period. The organization would also need to be continually refusing to reproduce itself by only appointing those who were like those in the centre. A neo-bureaucratic organization would be one that depended on certain rules, such as the circulation of decision makers, but never acted as if these rules were other than guides to action. In Weberian terms substantive rationality would be more important than formal rationality – there could be no final appeal to the 'rulebook'. It would be expected that debate over the organization's means would be just as important as debate over the organization's ends.

Finally, and most importantly, the neo-bureaucracy would be an organization which continually stressed its processual nature and the necessity to rework organizational rationality for the next task and priority. The members of this form of organization would not be forced to make any clear distinction between the formal/public and informal/private aspects of their selves. The organization would not require them to act without hatred and passion, it would be expected that their hatreds and passions could be negotiated in and through the organization. The individual member must feel that they have a chance to influence the organization in ways they felt were desirable. A continual encouragement of public debate about the nature of the organization would therefore be necessary to ensure that members felt committed to all or part of its activities.

The anti-bureaucracy would be an organization as a verb rather than a noun, one in which cultural assumptions about both means and ends were continually being renegotiated. One analogy for this form of bureaucracy we are attracted to is the 'Maoist' organization – one which undergoes continual revolution. The reason that this is necessary is to prevent the organization becoming too stable. The pressures of 'institutional isomorphism', of becoming like other organizations in the environment, are immense (DiMaggio and Powell, 1983). If they are to be successfully resisted it will require continual reflection on its relationships to other organizations, how it works and what it is doing.

In the light of Rosabeth Moss Kanter's work (Moss Kanter, 1977) it is clear that the neo-bureaucratic organization would need to stress the values of uncertainty, vagueness and instability as part of its culture. This would be necessary for two reasons. The first is, in order to change current structures and shared values, the organization would require that past information, previously used to make sense of the current situation, should no longer be taken for granted. The second is to prevent a fixing of any one group as dominant in the organization which would require that the needs, interests and perspectives of all groups be heard and responded to. While this is an issue which has fragmented feminist organizations (Gould, 1979; Liedner, 1991), we argue that it is possible, within the structured environment of the neo-bureaucracy, to accept diversity.

To summarise this section, neo-bureaucracies may enable patriarchal and capitalist pressures to be resisted and changed. An essential feature of our argument is that it is at the organizational cultural level that such change must be initiated. Specific and local organizational rationalities and practices must be revised if the organization is to develop features that correspond to this model. The neo-bureaucracy is based on the assumption that organizations need to do certain things in order to be organized but how it manages these things is a cultural matter that reflects the understandings of agents within the organization. The alternative is bureaucratic rules that often become, like equal opportunity policies, pieces of paper that do not reflect or influence the actual texture of life within the organization. Putting it another way, what we are proposing is that the neo-bureaucratic organization needs to capture the hearts and minds of its members in order to ensure its functioning. Since formal rules are largely absent, control must be exercised through consent and common purpose. If this were not the case the organization would cease to function or become, of necessity, more formally bureaucratic.

Discussion

The corporate goal must be constantly renewed. Any firm that wants to remain mentally alive must seek new goals, must, in a sense, wantonly engender stress. (. . .) Those most 'loyal', those

most identified with the status quo, will be the most reactionary
and the most confirmed in their rejection of the new. For the
status quo will be 'their' status quo and criticism thereof will be
taken personally. (Roger Holmes in Pym, 1968:370).

The neo-bureaucracy is clearly an ideal type in both senses of that
term. It is a model that we believe is theoretically possible but also
that we find politically attractive. In this we echo some other
writing within organizational analysis such as Thompson and
McHugh's 'minimal bureaucracy' (1990:367). Proposing it is not
necessarily to suggest that such organizations actually do exist but
that such organizations might be aimed for – the process will be as
worthwhile as the end. However, it might be argued that such
organizations do in fact exist, feminist and worker co-operatives
are a small but significant feature of contemporary industrial
capitalism (Turton, 1991:316–26; Leidner, 1991). However, in this
paper we are not primarily interested in identifying cases but in
opening a space for debate. The core of our argument is that a
bureaucratic solution to the problem of gender equality in
organizations will not work. A neo-bureaucratic solution which
acts on the terrain of organizational cultures has a much greater
chance of success, even if it may require the risk of greater failure.

This model clearly has many resonances in terms of the history
of organizational sociology. Ever since Taylor, Urwick, Gantt and
others proposed constructing organizations based on a structural
logic of external control, others have pointed to the possibility of a
logic of commitment. From Mayo's explorations at the Hawthorne
plant there emerged a strand of utopianism that has many facets in
humanist psychology, social futureology and new age managerialism.
The neo-bureaucracy hence has surface similarities with McGregor's
'Theory Y' (1960), Likert's 'System IV' (1961), Toffler's '3rd Wave'
and 'adaptive corporations' (1980, 1985). Ouchi's (and originally
Maslow's) 'Theory Z' (1981), Peters and Waterman's 'Excellence'
(1982), Mintzberg's 'adhocracy' (1985) to name but a few.
However, whilst clearly utopian, it is an attempt to integrate a
macro-sociological acknowledgement of the power of structures to
constrain with a micro-sociological insistence on the power of
actors to alter those constraints. It differs from any of the above
models in that it does not attempt to valorize the manager as hero
and is not intended simply to make capitalism more 'efficient'.
Instead it is intended to be read as a challenge to the contemporary
politics of organizing.

Because of this we would hesitate to argue that the current debates about flexibility, post-Fordism and postmodernity within organization studies indicate that the neo-bureaucracy is an emergent form (Piore and Sabel, 1984; Murray, 1989; Parker, 1992). Whilst there are clearly elements in these debates which echo our formulation most of the ideas are simply based on structural speculation and have little moral or political content. Similarly, the explosion of interest in organizational culture is mostly of an analytic or managerialist nature and does not say much about the possibility of questioning the very grounds of organization itself. Whilst all these debates are valuable in that they have sensitized us to new issues, we suggest that they are still taking far too much for granted. Whilst they claim to recognize an evolution in organizational forms we propose a revolution from below. The formulation of the neo-bureaucracy came out of an attempt to think beyond what organizations currently do. Whilst some of these things appear to us to be functionally necessary, others are only necessary insofar as they are 'given' cultural assumptions about gender, rationality and power. If these are created by people then they can be changed by people.

As cautious academics we are wary of any instant futurology or airport bookstall managerialism and would agree with Pahl (1988) that much careful analysis of the present and past needs to be done before we can begin making assertions about the future. However, we believe that there is a place for utopias for two reasons. One is that they make us aware of the shortcomings of our present. Some of the more distasteful features of organizations can be better appreciated if we imagine what life might be like without them. The second is that an utopia, if carefully constructed, can give us a model to aim for and provoke debate about the social order we wish to inhabit – an essential element of the enlightenment modernist ideal. If the argument of this paper is accepted then there are certain formally rational aspects of organizations that must be attended to but this does not mean that our assessment of value, 'efficiency', 'productiveness', 'service' and so on can not be the subjects of alternative definition. As Thompson and McHugh point out, a privately owned company and a workers co-operative could both be regarded as efficient – it depends on your criteria of value (1990:21).

Finally, it is important to temper our polemic by stressing that we do not believe that by changing one organization that the wider world will necessarily change that much. We do not share Weber's pessimism about 'the polar night of icy darkness' (in Gerth and Mills, 1948:28) but neither do we wish to be seen to be proposing a 'quick fix' to the problem of gender inequality. Changes to structural conditions would require that many more organizations, sites and practices became oppositional to patriarchy and conventional capital-labour assumptions. However, since it is through the microsocial that the macrosocial is reproduced we insist that small changes are an effective place to begin where organizations are concerned. The personal is undoubtedly the political. It is only by changing the culture of particular organizations that the members of other organizations will begin to perceive alternatives to current bureaucratic rationalities and practice. Consequently, if many organizations change in the way we have outlined then changes will take place in the structural conditions that act as pressures on all organizations.

References

Baines, A., (1988), *Success and Satisfaction*, London: Paladin.
Baker-Miller, J., (1978), *Towards a New Psychology of Woman*, Harmondsworth: Pelican.
Bendix, R. and Lipset, S., (1967), (eds), *Social Stratification*, Englewood Cliffs: Prentice-Hall.
Blau, P., (1963), *The Dynamics of Bureaucracy*, Chicago: University of Chicago Press.
Bologh, R., (1990), *Love or Greatness*, London: Unwin Hyman.
Bowditch, J. and Buono, A., (1990), *A Primer on Organisational Behaviour*, New York: John Wiley.
Crompton, R. and Sanderson, K., (1990), *Gendered Jobs and Social Change*, London: Unwin Hyman.
Deal, T. and Kennedy, A., (1988), *Corporate Cultures*, Harmondsworth: Penguin.
Delamont, S., (1989), *Knowledgeable Women*, London: Routledge.
Di Maggio, P. and Powell, W., (1983), 'The Iron Cage Revisited: Institutional Isomorphism and Collective Rationality in Organizational Fields', *American Sociological Review*, 48.
Ferguson, K., (1984), *The Feminist Case Against Bureaucracy*, Philadelphia: Temple UP.
Foucault, M., (1977), *Discipline and Punish*, London: Allen Lane.
Frost, P. *et al*, (1985), *Organisational Culture*, Beverley Hills: Sage.
Gerth, H. and Mills, C., (1948), *For Max Weber*, London: Routledge and Kegan Paul.
Giddens, A., (1979), *Central Problems in Social Theory*, London: Macmillan.
Giddens, A., (1982), *New Rules of Sociological Method*, London: Hutchinson.
Gould, M., (1979), 'When Women Create an Organisation: The Ideological Imperatives of Feminism', in D. Dunkerley and G. Salaman, *The International Yearbook of Organisation Studies*, London: RKP.

Gouldner, A., (1954), *Patterns of Industrial Bureaucracy*, Glencoe: Free Press.

Grimshaw, J., (1986), *Feminist Philosophers*, Brighton: Wheatsheaf.

Hakim, C., (1979), *Occupational Segregation*, Department of Employment Research Paper 9, London: HMSO.

Hartmann, H., (1979), 'Capitalism, Patriarchy and Job Segregation by Sex', in Z. Eisenstein (ed.), *Capitalist Patriarchy*, New York: Monthly Review Press.

Hearn, J., Sheppard, D., Tancred-Sherif, P. and Burrell, G., (1989), *The Sexuality of Organisation*, London: Sage.

Hochschild, A.R., (1983), *The Managed Heart: The Commercialization of Human Feeling*, London: University of California Press.

Hunsaker, P. and Cook, C., (1989), *Managing Organisational Behaviour*, Reading: Addison-Wesley.

Jewson, N. and Mason,D., (1986), 'Mores of Discrimination in the Recruitment Process: Formalisation, Fairness and Efficiency', *Sociology*, 20/1:43–63.

Kanter, R., (1977), *Men and Women of the Corporation*, London: Basic Books.

Kiam, V., (1986), *Going for It*, London: Collins.

Knights, D. and Morgan, G., (1990), 'Management and Control in Sales Forces: A Case Study from the Labour Process of Life Insurance', *Work, Employment and Society*, 4/3:369–89.

Lacey, R., (1986), *Ford*, New York: Ballantine.

Legge, K., (1987), 'Women in Personnel Management: Uphill Climb or Downhill Slide?', in A. Spencer and D. Podmore (eds), *In a Man's World*, London: Tavistock.

Liedner, R., (1991), 'Stretching the Boundaries of Liberalism: Democratic Organisation in a Feminist Organisation', *Signs*, 16/2:263–289.

Liff, S. and Webb, J., (1988), 'Play the White Man: The Social Construction of Fairness and Competition in Equal Opportunity Policies', *Sociological Review* 36/3:532–51.

Likert, R., (1961), *New Patterns of Management*, New York: McGraw-Hill.

Marshell, J., (1984), *Women Managers: Travellers in a Male World*, Chichester: Wiley.

McGregor, D., (1960), *The Human Side of Enterprise*, New York: McGraw-Hill.

Merton, R., (1968), *Social Theory and Social Structure*, New York: Free Press.

Miller, E. and Rice, A., (1967), *Systems of Organisation*, London: Tavistock.

Mills, A. and Murgatroyd, S., (1991), *Organisational Rules*, Buckingham: Open UP.

Mintzberg, H. and McHugh, A., (1985), 'Strategy Formation in an Adhocracy', *Administrative Science Quarterly*, 30.

Molloy, J., (1977), *The Woman's Dress for Success Book*, New York: Warner.

Morgan, G. and Smircich, L., (1982), 'Leadership: The Management of Meaning', *Journal of Applied Behavioural Science*, 18/3:257–73.

Murray, R., (1989), 'Fordism and Post-Fordism', in S. Hall and M. Jacques *New Times*, London: Lawrence and Wishart.

Ouchi, W., (1981), *Theory Z*, Reading: Addison-Wesley.

Pahl, R., (1988), (ed.), *On Work*, Oxford: Blackwell.

Parker, M., (1992), 'Post-modern Organisations or Postmodern Organisation Theory?', *Organisation Studies*, 13/1–17.

Parsons, T., (1951), *The Social System*, New York: Free Press.

Peters, T. and Waterman, R., (1982), *In Search of Excellence*, New York: Harper and Row.

Pettigrew, A., (1979), 'On Studying Organisational Cultures', *Administrative Science Quarterly*, 24, 570–81.

Phillips, A. and Taylor, B., (1980), 'Sex and Skill: Notes Towards a Feminist Economics', *Feminist Review*, 6.

Piore, M. and Sabel, C., (1984), *The Second Industrial Divide*, New York: Basic Books.

Pugh, D. and Hickson, D., (1973), 'The Comparative Study of Organisations', in G. Salaman and K. Thompson, (eds), *People and Organisations*, Harlow: Longman.

Pym, D., (1968) (ed.), *Industrial Society: Social Sciences in Management*, Harmondsworth: Penguin.

Rifkin, G. and Harrar, G., (1988), *The Ultimate Entrepreneur*, Chicago: Contemporary Books.

Rodgers, W., (1970), *Think*, London: Weidenfeld and Nicolson.

Schermerhorn, J., Hunt, G. and Osborn, R., (1991), *Managing Organisational Behaviour*, New York: John Wiley.

Scollard, J., (1983), *No-Nonsense Management Tips for Women*, New York: Pocket Books.

Skinner, J., (1986), 'Who's Changing Whom? Women, Management and Work Organisations', in A. Coyle and J. Skinner, *Women and Work: Positive Action for Change*, London: Macmillan.

Thompson, P. and McHugh, D., (1990), *Work Organisations*, London: Macmillan.

Toffler, A., (1980), *The Third Wave*, London: Collins.

Toffler, A., (1985), *The Adapative Corporation*, New York: McGraw-Hill.

Turner, B., (1989), *Organisational Symbolism*, Berlin: de Gruyter.

Turton, R., (1991), *Behaviour in a Business Context*, London: Chapman and Hall.

Walby, S., (1986), *Patriarchy at Work*, Oxford: Polity.

Weber, M., (1947), *The Theory of Social and Economic Organisation*, New York: Oxford University Press.

Wittgenstein, L., (1968), *Philosophical Investigations*, Oxford: Blackwell.

Notes on contributors

Lisa Adkins is a lecturer in Sociology at Bristol Polytechnic. She previously taught Sociology/Women's Studies at the University of Lancaster.

Rosemary Crompton has been Senior Lecturer at the University of Kent for the past three years, having previously worked at the University of East Anglia for over twenty years. She is the author of a number of books and articles on work and organizations, and social stratification. Her most recent book (with Kay Sanderson) is *Gendered Jobs and Social Change* (Unwin Hyman, 1990).

Celia Davies is Professor of Women's Studies at the University of Ulster and has carried out research on gender and professionalism.

Susan Halford is Lecturer in Sociology at Southampton University after having spent six years as Research Fellow in Urban Studies at the University of Sussex. She has carried out research on the implementation of equal opportunities initiatives in local authorities.

Nicola Le Feuvre has been Maitrise de Conference in the Sociology Dept at the University of Toulouse since 1991. She gained her first degree, and her Doctorate, from Aston University (Birmingham). Her thesis investigated the use of time in the work and family lives of French and British women. She has published articles on Franco-British comparative research and on the leisure experiences of French women.

Martin Parker is a lecturer in the Department of Sociology at Staffordshire Polytechnic in Stoke-on-Trent. He holds a BA in Anthropology from the University of Sussex and an MA in Sociology from Goldsmiths College, University of London. His research interests are in the sociology of culture, postmodernism and organization theory.

Karen Ramsay is undertaking doctoral research in Sociology at Staffordshire Polytechnic. Her PhD project explores how academic organizational cultures mediate and shape equality of opportunity for women academics. Her other interests include the sociology of emotions and feminist debates on methodology and epistemology.

Mike Savage is Lecturer in Sociology at the University of Keele. Amongst his recent publications are *Property, Culture and Bureaucracy: middle class formation in contemporary Britain*, (with James Barlow, Peter Dickens and Tony Fielding), and *Urban Sociology, Capitalism and Modernity* (with Alan Warde).

Anne Witz is Lecturer in Sociology at the University of Birmingham. Her most recent publication is *Patriarchy and Professions*.

Sophie Watson is Professor of Urban and Regional Planning at the University of Sydney and was formerly Reader in The Dept of Social Policy and Planning, University of Bristol. Her publications include, *Housing and Homelessness: a feminist perspective*.

Meta Zimmeck is based at the Institute of Historical Research and has published extensively on gender relations in the Civil Service.

Index

Index

Index